TOUCHING ON THE INFINITE
Explorations in Christian Hope

Tony Kelly

COLLINS DOVE
A Division of HarperCollins*Publishers*

Published by Collins Dove
A Division of HarperCollins*Publishers* (Australia) Pty Ltd
22–24 Joseph Street Blackburn Victoria 3130

© Copyright Tony Kelly 1991
All rights reserved. Except as provided by Australian copyright law, no part of this book may be reproduced without permission in writing from the publishers.

First published 1991
Designed by William Hung
Cover design by William Hung
Cover photograph by Bill Thomas

Typeset in New Century Schoolbook by Collins Dove Desktop
Printed in Australia by Griffin Press Pty Ltd

The National Library of Australia
Cataloguing-in-Publication Data:

Kelly, Anthony, 1938–
  Touching on the infinite.
  Bibliography.
  ISBN 0 85924 973 5.
  1. Hope — Religious aspects — Christianity.
  2. Spiritual life — Catholic authors. I. Title.
234.2

Acknowledgements

"The Scripture quotations in this publication are from the Revised Standard Version of the Bible, copyrighted 1971 and 1952 by the Division of Christian Education of the National Council of the Churches of Christ in the USA."

Our thanks go to those who have given us permission to reproduce copyright material in this book. Particular sources of print material are acknowledged in the text.
Every effort has been made to contact the copyright holders of text material. The editor and publisher apologise in those cases where this had proved impossible.

Contents

Preface		v
Chapter 1:	The World of Hope	1
Chapter 2:	The Language of Hope	12
Chapter 3:	The Ground of Hope	39
Chapter 4:	The Dead End	48
Chapter 5:	Meditation on Death	67
Chapter 6:	The Paschal Mystery: the Parable of Hope	80
Chapter 7:	The Eucharist: Sacrament of Hope	129
Chapter 8:	Purgatory: the Realism of Hope	154
Chapter 9:	Hell: the Limit of Hope?	178
Chapter 10:	Heaven: the Fulfilment of Hope	196
Chapter 11:	Conclusion: Hope in Action	229
Select Bibliography		236

Preface

This book belongs to the theological genre of eschatology, a study or exploration of 'the last things', *ta eschata*. These have been listed in various ways through the centuries, and I suppose the most stable list, so beloved of the dramatic mission preaching of a past era, is 'death, judgment, heaven and hell.' But especially now, as we come to the end of our own tragic and wonderful century, the fact is that such themes have appeared almost trivial compared with the drama of the last things we human beings have actually been facing. It is not comfortable to be living at the end of an era, and certainly no consolation for those of us who have grown up or grown old in the midst of so much change, collapse, decay, and confusion. No doubt, we of the ideological 'West', whatever our geographical location, were able to cosset our imaginations, for a decade or so during the fifties, with the conceit that we were somehow closer to heaven, just as the great *gulag* of the East was the infernal region, the domain of the evil one. We smile wryly now at such naivety; for the decades have rolled on and stripped us all of such handy simplicities. Where is the enemy now? Who is on the side of the angels?

All our ideologies have collapsed: the freedom of the individual, so prized in the capitalist West has ended in the doomed rootless individualism of the modern 'consumer society', while the once noble Marxist vision of collective humanity froze into grim totalitarian oppression, and collapsed before our very eyes. There was a time when capitalism and communism were each the 'latest thing' in human interest. What the world has seen is that neither was the last thing. In the meantime, unnoticed beneath our ideological posturing and power blocs, the very fate of our living planet was becoming problematical, the number of the poor was growing, and the old resources of hope of any kind were being spread very thin.

It is impossible to say what will emerge. The most we can honestly say is what we hope will emerge. That is where our century has left us, stripped of everything except hope—that strange human capacity to go beyond oneself, relying on something other, something more, to achieve what is indefinable, seemingly impossible, but what alone will make for life. After the martyr, only the artist knows what hope really means.

It is here that Christian faith can be splendidly and defiantly revitalised, precisely as the energy of hope. For, whatever the lists of last things that have been made, or might be made, whether they are desired or dreaded, in that Christian sense of hope, there is really only one 'last thing', one *eschaton*: the infinite love that has been shown us. It seems more and more clear that if we can allow ourselves to be released into *that*, as individuals, as communities, as a Church, and find in that limitless grace a future inclusive of everyone and everything, then a great new energy will be released, vibrant with the evident meaning of Gospel as 'good news'. If, ultimately, we belong together, there must be a time of healing now, a more truthful affirmation of one another which is both tender and just, a deeper cherishing of human works and of the earth itself, so that everyone and everything may be newly valued, enabling us to step more lightly into a welcoming future; and to contribute to its making in our lives, and even in our deaths.

Choosing a title for a book is always problematical.

In the end, the words of Thérèse of Lisieux, a young French woman who died at the end of the last century, consumed by the hope she heroically lived, won the day: 'My hopes touch on the infinite'. I must confess, however, that I was tempted to use the title of a poem by the celebrated Swedish poet, Tomas Tranströmer— 'The Half-Finished Heaven'. In either case, the spirit of his poem, and of this series of explorations in hope, is well expressed in two lines from the poem in question:

> Each man is a half-open door leading to a room for everyone.[1]

I like these lines in the present context because one of the difficulties in exploring the various themes of hope is that of holding together the individual and the communal, and even cosmic, nature of our hope. I have tended here, within the limits of this kind of book, to work from the point of view of individual destiny, but always with a sense of the 'half-open door', and the 'everyone and everything' of Paul's great vision (I Cor. 15:28).

While, in what follows, we deal eventually with the themes of death, purgatory, hell and heaven, the pith of what we have to say in terms of hope lies in the chapters devoted to the paschal mystery of Christ and the sacrament of the eucharist. Detached from the basic parable of Christian existence and the fundamental sacrament of Christian community, any attempt to explore the ultimate in human destiny can become very odd: necessarily figurative expressions can float off in a variety of fantastic ways and so discredit this kind of theological effort. So, while hoping that readers might profitably dip into any chapter, may they not overlook the larger 'interconnection of mysteries' on which Christian hope depends.

Finally, I would like to dedicate this book to my Redemptorist confrères who, in the vivid memory of many, were great 'hell-fire' preachers on the parish missions. I hope we will still preach with plenty of fire, but in a new era, especially at this ending of an age, may it be the flame of the living God.

One last word of thanks: I am especially grateful to Cathy Jenkins of Collins Dove for her editorial encouragement; and to my confrère and colleague, Michael Mason, CSSR, for his patience in resisting the chaotic proclivities of my computer; and to so many others—confrères, colleagues and friends—who, in their different ways, have supported the production of this work.

Tony Kelly, CSSR.

1 Tomas Tranströmer, 'The Half-Finished Heaven'. *Collected Poems*, tr. Robin Fulton. Bloodaxe Books, Newcastle Upon Tyne, 1987, p.65.

1 The World of Hope

We are living in a time of profound change, affecting every aspect of human life. One way or another, we all feel the force of the age-old questions: What on earth is happening? What is the world coming to? Where will it all end? What does it all mean?

In a conflict-ridden world, doom-laden reports and predictions about the ecology, the economy, the state of our society and our culture are the daily stuff of the media, and the path to any desirable human future seems to be almost unbearably hard.

Basic human experiences such as getting married and having children were once part of the sturdy framework of a confident world, but now carry within them an enormous sense of vulnerability. Many of those who enter the professions of medicine, science, business, law, the media and politics today will find that their ideals of serving society quickly come up against networks of influence so vast and often so menacing that the happy confidence of doing a good job is often undermined by the question, Who am I really working for? Then, again, any serene determination to grow old gracefully in grand-parental benevolence now has to deal with the isolation of the nursing home and years of frustrating enfeeblement, all but imposed by medically supported longevity.

As the dimensions of global problems emerge, anyone in their right mind will have to ask, what conceivable difference can my contribution make? As problems increase, solutions seem to become more and more elusive. The future resists any easy access. We commonly concede that no one has all the answers. On whom, then, do we rely? On all of us of working together? Surely. But how do we come together, even to want a common future? Planning for, or against, possible futures has become a fairly refined science, but no amount of planning can transform human beings. It can tell us what we need to do, but it cannot *do* much about what we need to *be*—more just, less addicted to material possession, less violent, more loving. Education might help, but where does the transforming inspiration arise? Planners and educators cannot reach into the human heart. The age-old conundrum remains: How might we really want what we should want?

To ask such questions is to begin reflecting on hope. Thomas Aquinas[1] spoke of hope as a fundamental human passion reaching out to a *bonum futurum, arduum et possibile*, a 'possible, future but difficult good'—some important thing, eminently desirable, but eluding one's grasp; out of our reach unless help in some form intervenes—sudden rescue, a happy inspiration, a surprising turn of events, unforeseen deliverance.[2]

For example, a poet can be expected to supply verses for an occasion, but he can only hope that the inspiration will come for a true poem. An artist might accept a commission to paint a portrait, but all parties concerned know that between a pleasing likeness and an inspired portrait there lies a great gulf. They can *expect* a technically good job; but they can only *hope* for the elusive and seemingly magical outcome that would make the artist exclaim, 'I've got it!', and viewers acclaim the work as an astonishing depiction of the real person. Hope always seems to be envisaging that indefinable something that is beyond us, but which, when it appears, is the reality we recognise and delight in as what we wanted all the time!

The Point of Hope

In contemporary experience, the field of hope has dramatically expanded.[3] The old order of things can no longer be taken for granted. As all the utopias of a century collapse, we live in a disappointed stage of history. Perhaps the worst disappointment of all is that of having lived in utopia as our ancestors might have imagined it, only to find that it has turned out to be such an unfulfilling experience. It is all very well for the Berlin Wall to come down, the Iron Curtain to go up, and the peoples of Eastern Europe to rejoice in the freedoms of the West. But we of that West know that the nameless something necessary for our humanness is not yet.[4]

It would seem that true hope only becomes possible at the point of disappointment. Matters are not so neatly under our control. Freedom is action, but it is also patience—rejecting false hopes, waiting for the one thing necessary, settling for nothing less: not more things, not more power, not this, not that, but what?

Here the great religions of the world are emerging once more as a fundamental resource in human culture. As the economist, J.W. Forester wrote:

> *If the moral system does not contain any single institutional component that maintains an open regard for the future, then all social systems are subject to the decay of values with regard to long term conceptions of value...Apart from religious organisations, there are no institutions for long term goal-projections that are not traditional and point to the future. It is on religions and religious communities that the responsibility rests of maintaining the long-term conceptions of value and preventing the destruction of values of this kind.*[5]

Where once exultant secular utopias dismissed religious faith as a pitiable search for security, or as the dead weight of the past blocking the path of progress, now the mood has changed. The promised futures of progress have arrived. They have delivered to the governments of rootless and disorientated peoples an enormous technological power. So much was promised; but *this* was all that was delivered.

Yet from the depths of such disappointment, the times are ripening for a far more profound exploration of the whole mystery of life. Our hitherto conflicting histories have been knotted together by common crisis: the threat of global war, ecological catastrophe and the planetary dimensions of poverty.

But with that sense of common crisis there is also present a global aspiration toward a new common good, however difficult to attain. The peoples of the earth are feeling the stirring of a great dream. Out of the disillusioned utopias of this century, a great vision is being born: a truly human future in which past enmities can fall away, where the millions of the forgotten poor can find their worth, where the planet itself, in all the marvels of its varied life will be treasured. We long for a more celebratory existence so that all can live in an ever-astonishing universe, as the cosmos, in all its vital energies, uncanny intricacies, delicate patterns and vast proportions, shapes itself in a consciousness liberated to rejoice in the wholeness of things.

How do we keep such hopes alive? How does such hope become the passion and energy of life? How can the future be more than an extension of a defeated present?

In a striking way, reality, for modern people, lies in the future. Vatican II's document *On the Church in the Modern World* notes a massive cultural change:

> *Ours is an age of history with critical and swift upheavals spreading gradually to all corners of the earth...The accelerated pace of history is such that one can scarcely keep abreast of it.*

The destiny of the human race is viewed as a complete whole...And so mankind substitutes a dynamic and more evolutionary concept of nature for a static one, and the result is an immense series of new problems calling for a new endeavour of analysis and synthesis.[6]

With the emergence of such new problems and with our efforts to address them, the presence of the future is being experienced in two ways: firstly, as a place of promise; secondly, as a place of threat.

When we envisage it as a place of promise, we plan for the future and welcome it. It will be utopia, a time and place of the fuller realisation of our humanity. It shines as the light at the end of the tunnel, inviting human freedom to break out of the constrictions and oppressions of the past into an open space. The modern era is uniquely one in which new capacities for self-determination have been discovered. These have been expressed in the many emancipation movements affecting the Western world which have rejected the dehumanising conditions of racism, colonialism, sexism and militarism. Oppressive, long-established forms of economic, political and cultural domination have been dramatically confronted. The most recent flowering of this great historical trend toward a more liberated humanity can be seen in the growing ecological awareness: nature itself must be freed from the mindless plundering of centuries.

Though it is no small challenge to make an exhaustive list of all these emancipatory movements, they do have one thing in common: a deliberate option for a future which in some way contradicts the present. This option, often bringing with it great social and economic tensions, is based on the hope that something better can emerge; that the only way to be human is to be in a state of becoming. To refuse to change is to resign oneself to stagnation. That would be a timid compliance with a truncated humanity. In such contexts,

J.H. Newman's words are often quoted, 'In a higher world it is otherwise; but here below, to live is to change, and to be perfect is to have changed often.'[7]

In contrast, there is that second way of imagining the future, not as a utopia, the native land of hope, but as a no-man's land, a place of threat and danger. For there is a kind of future that overtakes our familiar human ways to shock us with its strangeness, as Alvin Toffler's *Future Shock*[8] made clear. It is due in part to technocratic elites who have made decisions without any critical moral or political control. When the logic of 'what can be done, has to be done' triumphs, the world of human values limps behind the actual performance, occasionally protesting, sometimes justifying, but always after the fact, never quite able to catch up—let alone take the lead in determining what might really be the true human good. The examples that come to mind are genetic engineering, *in vitro* fertilisation, the still largely unrestricted production of armaments and nuclear weapons; and, of course, the decisions of international business and banking corporations which can cause, overnight, practical destitution for whole populations.

Add to such a vision of an un-valued future, the extreme acceleration of time made possible through the machine, the computer, the micro-chip and satellite communications systems, and you have an experience of the future which is not only not chosen by anything resembling a human consensus, but one which is occurring already equipped with enormous impersonal powers to manipulate reality and control the way we live. This is the sense in which no one really knows what is happening, what the world is coming to: it is a future that is taking the present by storm, imposing itself before anyone can fully realise the nature of the promise or the threat it offers.

Admittedly, the future as the direction of a hopeful choice and the future as a dread occurrence cannot be neatly distinguished. For, essentially, any future is always unknown and beyond experience: in some measure, both a promise (Life can only get better!), and a threat (Who really knows?). Then, there is another point, evident in today's pluralistic world. One group's chosen future is another group's dreaded imposition. One group emancipating itself to be the standard-bearer of civilisation necessarily leaves others behind, casualties to progress, presumably those who were not fit to survive, relics of a bygone era.

Yet, despite the unevenness and conflict in the ways we envisage or desire the future, there is some sense of shared experience: a radically new future is what we have in common. We can let it overwhelm us with its great strangeness, or we can choose to humanise it as much as possible. Therein lies our only hope of reconciliation. In the midst of such an emerging world, there is a particular way of hoping native to the Christian tradition.[9] Its particularity derives, of course, from its focus in Christ.[10] In his light, God, the universe, human existence and human history take on a new meaning, to become intrinsically hope-filled realities. In him, we believe something fundamentally hopeful has happened. An ultimate love has appeared in our history and, indeed, on our earth to open every moment to a divinely promised future. As the Marxist philosopher Ernst Bloch has remarked, 'Christianity...seems like a final emergence of what religion is—a total hope and an explosive one.'[11]

Whether we call this future the 'Kingdom of God' or 'eternal life' or any of the other biblical terms, it is a future with God. It has irreversibly broken into our history to make the present, in an absolute way, full of promise. In Christ's cross and resurrection, both the disappointment and hope of the world are embodied. Such a hope is essentially unlimited, since its fundamental origin, energy and ultimate goal is the limitless mystery of God himself. The future the Christian awaits is fundamentally *God*. For the essential reality, the inexhaustible power of life, is the divine mystery graciously giving itself to creation. This self-giving looks to a point of consummation when 'God will be everything to everyone' (I Cor. 15:28).

Yet the future of Christian faith is not such that, by stimulating hope in God, it lessens hope for ourselves or our world. Our humanity is not vaporised by the infinite flame of the divine. For the Word became flesh and dwelt among us. God is not only the ultimate ground of our past and present: he has personally given himself into our world, to make it, in Christ Jesus, his own. In Christ, our crucified humanity is already risen into its divine future. In that future Christian hope envisages God and the human being belonging together.

One of the most appealing ways of describing the mission of the Church in the present context is in terms of its providing a space of hope in human history.[12] When the Church understands itself as the community of hope that never loses hope for our world, and when it sees itself as that part of the world alive to an absolute future, its mission is most authentic.

Nonetheless, let us stress that Christian faith has not abolished hope, but liberated it. For Christian activity in the world cannot be reduced to watching a replay of 'resurrection highlights' once our team has won; since finally the team is everyone, and the game is not yet over! Christians are not spectators, once or twice removed from the great contest of history. As immersed in the human drama, we have still to confront the many faces of despair in ourselves and others—inexplicable suffering, inevitable death, humiliating failure, meaninglessness and fear in all its forms. For whatever Christian faith and hope and love are, they are not a controlling vision of things. What is given is an inexpressible assurance that we are moving with God into a God-given future. The rest is the drama and patience of our stumbling and often perverse human freedom. Hope has to be continually refashioned through faith 'as the assurance of things hoped for, the conviction of things not seen (Heb. 11:1).

Though it moves in darkness and knows its own struggle, hope is based in some experience of joy, often quite nameless, but bearing in itself a sense of reality demanding completion. Those who most hope are those who most love: the goodness they have perhaps only fitfully seen cannot but have a future. As Peter's first Letter has it:

> *Without having seen him, you love him; though you do not now see him you believe in him and rejoice with unutterable and exalted joy. As the outcome of your faith, you obtain the salvation of your souls.* (I Pet. 1:8–9)

Despite the obvious conviction of the New Testament that hope moves in its own darkness and mystery, Peter does not hesitate to urge Christians to 'always be prepared to make a defence to anyone who calls you to account for the hope that is in you' (I Pt. 3:15). Somehow words have to be found, to form an account of the meaning of what we hope for. This is where the challenge begins all over again, for every age in all the varied contexts of Christian life in the world.

These reflections are offered as a contribution to a contemporary account of Christian hope. In the next chapter, we shall examine some of the features of the traditional expression of the last things in order to grasp more clearly the reasons for our present sense of incompetence or hesitancy in hope's language. From there, we try to concentrate on what really is the *last* thing in hope's varied efforts to speak of the ultimate.

Then, in a sense, we come back to scratch. Unless our hope integrates a sense of the grief and tragedy inherent in our human condition, its language will be paper-thin. To preclude that possibility, chapters four and five are a kind of extended meditation on death. After that, we proceed to a rather lengthy meditation on the passion, death and resurrection of the Lord, to awaken a sense of the fundamental Christian *parable* of hope as it unsettles and illumines our existence. Then, to anchor our hope more deeply in the fundamental vitality of the Church's life, we consider the eucharist as hope's basic *sacramental* form.

After these introductory and fundamental sections, we treat some specific themes. Chapter eight reflects on the realism of hope in terms of the traditional Catholic doctrine of purgatory. The chapter following is somewhat paradoxical, since it asks how even the language of hell has a place in our overall account of hope. Then, more positively, we move on to the great theme of heaven as the fulfilment of hope. Finally, we bring together the themes of hope and conversion, in order to stress the ongoing, critical and very personal nature of the actual life of hope.

In such a play of light and darkness, my special concern is to bring the rather neglected traditional themes of the last things back into contact with the basic Christian mystery of God's love in Christ. There is an abundance of scholarly material to draw on, and attempting a more accessible type of eschatology does pose its problems. Some might think this approach is rather old-fashioned. Still, I think there are some deep questions that do not simply disappear in the emergence of a more contemporary and critical Christian world-view. Or, if they do, the realism and defiance of hope suffers. Whatever the case, it is part of hope to keep trying, even if one's efforts are likely to fail in any number of ways. All this is involved in the effort to give an account of the hope of which Peter speaks.

1. *Summa Theol.* I–II, q.40, a.8; II–II, q.17, a.1–8; q.18, a.1–4. For extensive commentary: *See* William Hill, *St Thomas Aquinas Summa Theologica, Volume 23: Hope,* Blackfriars in conjunction with Eyre and Spottiswoode, London, 1966.

2. For a good account of the phenomenon of hope: See John Macquarrie, *Christian Hope*, Mowbray, London, 1978, especially pp. 1–31.
3. The extent of the vast cultural changes affecting faith and thought is well documented in Diarmid Ó Murchú, *The God Who Becomes Redundant*, Mercier Press, Dublin, 1986.
4. Such books as those of Gabriel Marcel, *Homo Viator: Introduction to a Metaphysic of Hope*, tr. E. Crauford, Harper and Row, New York, 1962, and Ernst Bloch, *The Principle of Hope*, tr. N. Plaice, S. Plaice, P. Knight, MIT Press, Cambridge, Mass., 1986 have elevated hope from comparative obscurity to a major theme in modern philosophical and theological thought. For a crisp but comprehensive overview: See Josef Pieper, *Hope and History*, Burns and Oates, London, 1969. A seminal theological work has been Jürgen Moltmann, *Theology of Hope*, tr. J.W. Leitch, SCM, London, 1967.
5. Quoted in Walter Kasper, *Faith and the Future*, Crossroad, New York, 1982, p.5.
6. *Gaudium et Spes*, par.4–5.
7. John Henry Newman, *An Essay on the Development of Christian Doctrine*, Doubleday, New York, 1960, p.22.
8. Alvin Toffler, *Future Shock*, Bantam Books, New York, 1970.
9. Valuable resources here are Zachary Hayes, *Visions of a Future. A Study of Christian Eschatology*, Michael Glazier, Wilmington, Del. 1989—hereafter, Hayes, *Visions...*; Josef Ratzinger, *Eschatology: Death and Eternal Life*, tr. M. Walstein, The Catholic University of America Press, Washington, D.C., 1988—hereafter, Ratzinger, *Eschatology...*; Peter C. Phan, *Eternity in Time. A Study of Karl Rahner's Eschatology*, Susquehanna University Press, Selinsgrove, 1988—hereafter, Phan, *Eternity....*
10. *See* especially Gustave Martelet, *L'au-delà retrouvé: Christologie des fins dernières*, Desclée, Paris, 1975—Hereafter, Martelet, *L'au-delà...*
11. Quoted by J. Macquarrie, *Christian Hope*, on frontispiece.
12. *See* Carl Peter, 'The Last Things and *Lumen Gentium*', *Chicago Studies* 24/2, August, 1985, pp.225–237.

2 The Language of Hope

Let me open this chapter with a light but penetrating observation of one of the great patristic scholars of the age:

> *Various observers have suggested that the nervous laugh is the infallible key to the deepest anxieties of any society. By that index not merely death but all the major themes of eschatology...must be reckoned as unfinished business for many supposedly secularised moderns, for any public reference to them almost inevitably evokes a giggle. Modern Christians are no less embarrassed to be caught dealing seriously with eschatological questions.*[1]

The unfinished business of modern secular culture, along with the embarrassment of theology referred to above, must be faced. We can begin by noting that whatever faith deals with or theology reflects on, a future tense is involved. The obscure evidence of our faith is awaiting a final vision. Whether we talk of Christ, the Trinity, of grace or the sacraments, it is clear that all such matters have a bearing on what is coming about. However limited and fragmented such tokens of faith might be in the present, they are essentially looking to a future evidence. Indeed, they presuppose, if not a grip on the future, at least some intimation of what is to come.

Yet, though we are always living toward a future, it does not mean that we are living in it; what is present is usually the engrossing concern. 'Now is the acceptable time' is not only a biblical summons; it makes good psychological sense. Still, when we do not take time to see what future is in the making, and explore how to make best sense of the direction of Christian life, a strange muteness enters into conversations. Loved ones die, and we are left with only stumbling expression—perhaps an optimistic construction put on a regrettable state of affairs, but hardly an inspiring language of hope. The world runs on, careering close to catastrophe of one kind of another. Any response to this can often be facile, either a kind of optimism that expects everything to sort itself out; or, at the other extreme, an inarticulate acceptance of doom and despair. Here, too, our received language seems to lack both bite and imagination. We might summon up a variety of religious words, but they do not sound as though they come from one whose native language is meant to be the language of hope.

It is true that we can't say everything all at once. Especially when we address ourselves to the last things, the rule of there being a time and place for everything has a special force. Speaking about death too much would naturally evoke from our listeners the suspicion of morbidity. And yet, speaking too readily about the glory of the resurrection to someone who is grieving the tragic loss of a child can also appear obtuse. Because, too, when our rapidly changing lives are engrossed in trying to keep some sort of routine balance, the last things can be left to wait their time. Ultimate things are an ungainly intrusion into our busy dealings with the immediate. The penultimate keeps us occupied. We are simply not always living at the uttermost limits of life.

And yet, the limits are there: death, intense suffering, the tragic fate of millions, the ecological state of our planet, the dangerous state of international relations, the precariousness of the economy, a deep sense of restlessness or of guilt looking for absolution and healing. Uncanny limits, leaving us at a loss for words: why are the most noble human values so vulnerable to cynicism and violence in the real world of our days? Was it all worth it? What hope is there for us? How does the faith we are living suggest a hope for what might be?

The limitations of the tradition

Theology has always been familiar with the existential limits just referred to. Perhaps, we suspect today, too familiar. Though theologians could give clear and definite answers in terms of death, judgment, purgatory, heaven and hell, there were often unnoticed problems. Chief among these was that the great last things of human existence were left to last, as rather fantastic additions, considered only after everything important had been said.

At best, speculations on the *eschata* (the last things) were fitted in at the end of theology—once God, Christ, grace, Church, sacraments, the moral life and so on had received due attention. The last things gave the impression of being a somewhat mystifying, sometimes lurid, appendix to the real work of theological reflection. What was an accident for St Thomas Aquinas, since he died before he could complete the great *Summa*, seems to have become the norm. The *Supplementum* dealing with the last things, *de Ultimis*, is appended to his great unfinished synthesis, but does not quite fit. There is something symbolic in the fact that Aquinas' treatment of the resurrection of the dead and the situation of the soul after death immediately follows on his treatment of illegitimate children![2] The well-meaning compilers of the supplement have to be blamed for that peculiar little sequence.

The result was that a whole series of eschatological questions follow in a rather unhappy isolation from the great parent body of the *Summa*. The synthesis breaks down. Thomas had no chance of extending the great principles he had established in his treatment of the beatific vision of the divine essence, the trinitarian missions, ultimate human destiny, grace, the theological virtues and so forth, into a well-rounded eschatological treatise. The compilers of the supplement had to be content with supplying material drawn from his other, less magisterial, writings.

That is just one example, and I do not wish to exaggerate its importance. What is difficult to exaggerate, however, are the unhappy consequences for eschatology when the last things are left to last. For they have ended up isolated from the central mysteries of faith. Admittedly, the creed imposes its own sequence, ending with 'the resurrection of the body and the life everlasting'. Also, one must concede, there is a certain logic in naming the *eschata* the last things in terms of human biological and historical experience, as what we know least about, that which is the most removed from our experience, and the most threatening to it! On the other hand, if the last article of the creed is an authentic expression of Christian faith, in more ways than one is it too important to leave it until last. The final, culminating communication of God is not a divine afterthought, but primary in the divine intention in creating the world. All the articles that precede it represent phases in the overall divine design; even as the incarnation is part of the divine self-giving to all creation. As one of the earliest axioms of theology expressed it, 'God became human that the human might become divine'.

But the problem remained, at least in a practical form, and remains to this day in theological courses. There is still plenty of evidence that eschatology is either left until last, or, more generously, is designed to be a dimension of all theological utterances. Theology continued to explore the central mysteries of God, Trinity, incarnation, redemption, grace, Church along with the complexities of moral life in today's world. But so often there was room for an impression that specific reflection on the *eschata* was a rather weary and embarrassing speculation in which the central mysteries of faith have little relation to our way of imagining what is to come. For, quite simply, the great mysteries of Trinity and grace were left to float free from the forlornly isolated last things of traditional eschatology. In the meantime, history was presenting us with a variety of visions of hell and of the ending of the age; and human beings kept dying. But theology had only a fragmentary and stilted inheritance in which to express its hope.

Still, there is another side to it. As it lurked there, rather menacingly at the end of the theology course, eschatology (*de Novissimis, de Ultimis* in the language of the day) had little to base itself on in terms of explicit Church doctrine. The slender fund of dogmatic teaching was all but exclusively addressed to the questions that relate to the fate of the individual after death. A dogmatic theology had very few dogmas to deal with. Hence, theological reflection on this ultimate dimension of hope became impoverished. It had to await the renewal of theological method, more thoroughly based on scriptural sources; and, from a Catholic point of view, on ecumenical stimulation, as a number of eminent Protestant scholars re-opened the eschatological file.[3]

The language of body and soul

Allied to all the above, were a series of problems relating to the categories to be employed. What Jesus proclaimed as the great mystery of the Reign of God, what the bible referred to as the 'resurrection of the flesh', as the new creation or as the great commonwealth of eternal life, was so often narrowed by a jejune theological use of the body-soul distinction. Theology easily veered toward a superficial dualism in which the individual soul is the only truly personal element and the body merely some material substrate, a transient housing for the spirit. The soul, it was alleged, is spiritual and immortal; the body, material and temporal. The resurrection of the body occurred on the last day as a kind of optional extra, a bonus in the grand plan of God, who basically remained interested in souls only.

Predictably, scholars of scripture and theology have been reacting vigorously against such superficial accounts. Had the basis of Christian hope in the power of the risen Christ been displaced into a kind of philosophical certitude regarding the immortality of the soul?

The debate has gone on, and now a broader view of the matter is emerging.[4] In the first flurry of biblical consciousness, some suggested that the very notion of soul be abandoned altogether. For, it was alleged, it is the whole person who is brought to life. The immortality of the soul represents an extra-biblical philosophical understanding, something essentially alien to the far more corporal emphasis of Christian faith. There is no mid-way between being dead and being raised up: hence the resurrection, it is argued, happens in death, and the resurrection of the body at the end of the world, happens for each individual in the ending of his or her world.

Though such a position has its theological respectability, it is now being challenged by a larger sense of the realism of Christian hope. The two main points against the simpler, seemingly more biblical, more 'Christian' position are these. First, it is not so clear that the notion of soul is such an extra-Christian category, somehow smuggled into Christian theology. For one thing, the bible itself, more concerned with proclaiming the good news of salvation for the whole of our earthly and human reality, was not uniformly averse to using such a notion in its varied vocabulary of hope. Part of the reason for this is that the so-called Greek notion of the immortality of the soul is now understood to be itself a statement of hope,[5] meaning in its own way, and in its own more limited context, what the New Testament would call the resurrection of the flesh. It is not surprising, then, that such an expression of hope for the salvation of the real person had a place in the vocabulary of some of the biblical authors, since it was part of the cultural language of the day. The languages of saving one's soul and of resurrection to eternal life seem to be bear a family resemblance to each other in the larger rhetoric of biblical hope.[6]

Secondly, reflection on the meaning of the faith is an ongoing affair.[7] An adequate account of the hope within us has to make distinctions and explore new categories if it is not be sterile or shy away from the questions that arise. One of these developments was St Thomas' transformation of Aristotle's body-soul philosophy in the interests of Christian eschatology. And one of the most enduringly valuable insights of Thomistic anthropology is the understanding of the soul as essentially 'the form of the human body': only in a body-soul composite can we properly talk about the human person, the 'I', the one who exists; this 'somebody'.[8] For Aquinas, the spiritual principle is essentially and always related to the material principle in our human make-up. For example, even in the highest instances of reflective thought, the spiritual intellect always depends on the matter of sensible images.[9] Hence, from different perspectives, we can say that the human person is an animated body, as spiritualised matter, a 'somebody'; and, at the same time, an incarnate, an embodied, an 'en-mattered' spirit.

When this strong sense of the unity of matter and spirit in human existence was applied to eschatology, it was taught that though the soul was separated in death from its embodied state, and even though it enjoyed the beatific vision, it was still in a kind of incomplete state.[10] For the soul intrinsically looked to be embodied in a material world; it was 'transcendentally related' to matter. Such essential incompletion is overcome only with the consummation of the universe. On the last day, all such separated souls would be re-embodied in the matter of a transformed creation. Only then would the whole person be fully saved in the resurrection of the body.

In different ways, some of the leading theologians of our day have tried to develop this Thomistic position. Karl Rahner, and the many who follow him, would say that the human spirit expands in death to a pan-cosmic relationship.[11] The particularities of the time and space of individual embodiment yield to a more comprehensive and inclusive relationship. What historical life experienced as spiritual openness to the whole universe of being, but as realised only through the mediation of the signs and symbols of one's world, is an index of a far more comprehensive relationship to the whole, the cosmos. It is as though death releases the human person to enter into the simplicity of a pure relationship to everything that is, beyond the restrictions of time, space and biological structure. To that degree, death signals the moment, or process, of a pan-cosmic embodiment.

The consequent dispute has turned on the extent to which this new embodiment can be called 'the resurrection of the body' in the full sense of Christian hope. One might ask, can anyone be fully transformed, fully risen with Christ until the whole of our history is redeemed? Is it more in accord with Christian hope to understand the life of the dead as being involved in a *process* of final embodiment to be completed only when the times have run their course, when the whole universe is transformed, when the resurrection of all the elect has taken place?

Of course, those sensitive to any dualistic tendency in understanding human existence remain suspicious of anything that suggests a shadowy half-life of semi-embodied spirits on this side of full resurrection. Yet, there remains the other side of the matter: either we are saved with the whole of our world, as agents in the whole of human history, or we are understood to be simply escaping into an unworldly spiritual existence.

Hence, there is room for a process finding its completion in our embodiment in a world made whole by the divine Spirit. We can still be with God, with Christ and yet be involved in a larger process of cosmic transformation. We do not die out of such an unfolding, but into it. It is, therefore, a larger expression of hope to give due allowance to such a cosmic and historical process.

Within such an understanding, the human soul appears most of all as the foundation of our distinctive human relationship to the original mystery from which all things come. At every stage of existence, in life, in death, and after death, the reality of the soul is actualised as a subsisting relationship to God, as the origin and end of our creaturely existence. The distinctiveness of the human being is to exist in a dialogical relationship with the divine. This is realised in many ways in this life, and even in the process of death itself. One can even speak of the souls of the damned: the original dialogical relationship with God remains even while he is being rejected.

When all is said and done, a Christian theology of hope does not seem to be able to manage its fullest and most realistic expression without using such a fundamental word as soul. That was precisely the anxiety expressed by the letter of the Congregation for the Doctrine of the Faith on 'Certain Matters of Eschatology' in 1979. Even though I find Rahner's notion of a kind of embodiment in the cosmos in death a plausible theological hypothesis, and even if it is quite evident that Christian hope centres on our resurrection in Christ, it would seem that a judicious use of the notion of soul makes space for a comprehensive historical and cosmic understanding of the process of transformation. For this does not lessen the reality of the resurrection of the body, but enhances it. Also, one might add, in passing, that the notion of the soul is valuable in dialogue with Eastern religions, as it is with modern scientific exploration of the mystery of human consciousness in the mind-brain-body relationship.[12]

The point to make here is that the old simplicities of the language of body and soul now need to be placed in a much more sophisticated biblical, theological and philosophical context.[13] While I do not think we can do without such a language, we cannot do much with it, unless it is placed within the more comprehensive and normative field of scriptural data, and in the emerging context of a theology in dialogue with philosophy, comparative religion and modern science.

A wrong proportion?

Then there is the question of a persisting wrong proportion, far more deeply injurious to an account of hope than the linguistic or categorial problems referred to above. For, what truly is *the* last thing in the last things of traditional spirituality and theology? It is not an exaggeration to suggest that the fate of the individual, precariously balanced between heaven and hell occupied centre stage. The central drama in such a version of the last things, is that of the individual's personal choice. Human freedom edges from the stage the truly 'last thing': the ultimate character of God's love 'willing all men to be saved and to come to the knowledge of the truth' (I Tim. 2:4). This is made to appear all but peripheral. The good news of the Father's unconditional love in giving to our world what is most intimate to himself, his Son and Spirit, has to share time with an equally present threat, the bad news of God's dire and impending judgment on human sinfulness. The divine love that gives its all for our salvation somehow, in the end, changes its character. The final truth is that, in reality, there will be a fearsome confrontation with the divine. Death is the dark limit at which the all-recording God lies in wait for each of us with the menace of a rather capricious divine judgment.

How much damage was done to the Christian psyche by this misplaced, distorted, evangelically mean kind of eschatological language is hard to estimate. It is not uncommon to meet dedicated and cultured believers who recoil from the ultimate implications of their faith. To them, the ultimate reference of what they believe in has been so subject to distortion that questions bearing on our final destiny are perceived as not worth raising. They inspire not 'an account of hope', but a fearful bewilderment best kept to oneself. In such a mood, what is worth communicating about the ultimate? And so the puzzled believer, quite reasonably, given the lurid, doom-filled images associated with past answers, tends to ask, first, What is there to be said? And then, is bothering about the final outcome just a form of egotism? Fantastic eschatological assertions have been made so often in the form of sanctions against the 'bad conduct' of struggling men and women (and even children), that the whole matter is best laid to rest as bewildered Christian people, however inarticulately and privately, resign themselves to God's mercy to let the whole matter work itself out as they get on with the business of living.

The problem implicit in this state of affairs is considerably illuminated by modern developmental psychology. No special breadth of human experience is required to accommodate motivations of reward or punishment in the complex unfolding of the moral life. Yet, as developmental psychologists point out, inspired by the researches of, say, Piaget, Erikson, Kohlberg, Fowler and others, a fixation on extrinsic motivation can seriously retard human growth.[14] In the present instance, if our final hope was limited to promises of future heaven or the threat of a future hell, there would be grounds for thinking that Christian conscience was being locked into a very early stage of human development. The problem is intensified when such sanctions are unconditional and absolute: hell is eternal!

A properly developmental expression of eschatological hope would need to show some awareness of the stages or 'life-cycle' of a person's development. There are different phases calling for different expressions of hope. If, at an early stage, the question of unique identity is the issue, the eschatological question is likely to be: 'how can I save my soul?'. If later issues centre on intimacy, in affective crises of relating to others, the question of hope is: 'How do I ultimately belong?'. If a developing wisdom leads into the other-centred ways of generativity, our hope would be for an unbroken and expanding life-giving relationship to others. If life mellows into a serene wisdom radiating a conviction of the blessedness of life and the radical goodness of the universe, hope would express itself as a longing for a consummation in which, to quote Julian of Norwich, 'all shall be well, and all manner of thing shall be well'.

In the light of these simple observations it would be easy enough to classify various expressions of eschatological hope in reference to the various levels of personal development to which they are addressed—or from which they came. Even more obviously, it is easy to see how so much of our talk about the last things could be at cross-purposes. For, in the total context of communication, different eschatological languages are appropriate. But, there the difficulty and the risk of human communication begin. The New Testament itself bears ample witness to this complexity when one inspired writer can exhort believers ' to work out your salvation with fear and trembling' (Phil. 2:12), while another can assure us 'that there is no fear in love, but perfect love casts out fear' (I Jn 4:18).

Atheist critique

Add to this problem the fact that Christian sensibilities have been deeply affected by the great masters of suspicion, Marx, Freud and Nietzsche—the great demystifiers of the modern world, whose influence has deeply penetrated modern culture.[15] The result has been that a certain kind of systematic atheism has been the premise, at least implicitly, of any understanding of human life and history.

For Karl Marx, religious hope is a displacement of our best worldly energies into other-worldly and essentially illusory expectations: once people have tasted the real truth and felt their real freedom, religion is revealed as the illusion it is.[16] For Freud, religious hope is a psychomythology. Hope is wish-fulfilment, an infantile projection expressing itself in the fantasy of the hereafter. It is a symptom of a neurotic flight from the pain and burden of a genuinely adult existence. Basically, such religious hope is an effort to manipulate reality so as to escape our authentic responsibilities. To this end, it forms the image of a father-figure who will keep us safe, and save us in the end. And then, with all the resources of his literary genius, Friedrich Nietzsche gave repeated expression to his humanist conviction that Christianity was the cult of negativity. He saw the Christian conception of God:

> *as degenerated into the contradiction of life, instead of being its transfiguration and eternal Yes! God as the declaration of war against life, against nature, against the will to live!—the formula for every slander against 'this life', for every lie about the 'beyond'!*[17]

Who could doubt that there was an abundance of evidence in our Christian history to justify such radical diagnoses? But the diagnosis of the disease can presage a recovery of health; and recent decades have seen the emergence of a healthy Christian hope in ways that the great atheists of a former era could scarcely have imagined. The Church's commitment to the poor, its championing of human rights, its work for peace, its new concern for the environment, to say nothing of its daily spiritual ministry of prayer and liturgy in a culture starved of transcendence, are all signs of a more genuine hope—stimulated, in no small measure, to a new vigour by its searing experience of atheism.

For instance, Vatican II was especially sensitive to the reactionary anti-humanist image of the Church. As it stressed the genuinely earthly and secular character of the Christian vocation, it presented authentic Christian hope as enhancing rather than diminishing the quality of secular involvement. It concluded that 'there is no question of the Christian message inhibiting people from building up the world or making them neglectful of the welfare of their fellows. They are even more strongly bound to do these very things'.[18] Pope John Paul II expressed himself even more boldly: 'The human...is the primary and fundamental way for the Church, the way traced out by Christ himself, the way which leads invariably through the mystery of the incarnation and the redemption.'[19]

In its discernment of the signs of the times, Vatican II has given valuable expression to the totality of Christian hope:

> *We know neither the moment of the consummation of the earth or of the human, nor the way the universe will be transformed. The form of this world, distorted by sin, is passing away, and we are taught that God is preparing a new dwelling and a new earth in which righteousness dwells, whose happiness will fill and surpass all the desires for peace arising in the hearts of men. Then with death conquered the sons of God will be raised in Christ, and what is sown in weakness and dishonour will put on the imperishable: charity and its works will remain, and all of creation which God made for human being will be set free from its*

bondage to decay.[20]

Such a statement considers the risen life in a far more collectively embodied manner than was customary in ecclesiastical documents, so often restricted to the state of the individual soul. History and creation have a place in this definitive and transformed human life. Such expressions, even if they could be dismissed as eschatological flourishes in an otherwise this-worldly document, indicate a valuable perspective in which to explore the more particular themes of the last things.

Emphasis on liberation

The turn to the world in Christian hope has achieved its most dramatic and problematic expression in what has become known as Liberation Theology. This style of theological thinking has been quick to expose the escapist elements in past eschatologies.[21] Believers start thinking differently when they are confronted by the institutionalised economic and political violence that keeps millions in poverty. Hope searches for a deeper realism when those expressing it are assassinated, tortured, imprisoned, exiled. A theology born of such an experience of struggle has no use for any notion of heaven which could function as a distraction from a present commitment to one's neighbour, as well as any conception of hell which remains unaware of the infernal character of present social conditions. Nonetheless, the basic concern of Liberation Theology is to make eschatological hope an effective force in the oppressive situations with which it has to contend. It is designed to inspire hopeful action: solidarity with the poor in the hopeless conditions which structure society in forms of economic, political and cultural oppression.

In speaking for the hopeless of the world—those whose destiny has been confined to the underside of history—theologies of liberation aspire to express the practical meaning of Christian hope in a way that is both credible and critical.[22] A Good News which is the church's exclusive secret and without consequences in the secular world can hardly be a blessing on the struggling, conflict-ridden human reality of things. A hope that can be indefinitely deferred, that offers no hope to the world's most hopeless situations, that lacks any present realisation, appears, in fact, as no hope at all. In the same way, a morality which draws its only commitment from the rewards or threats of an afterlife is hardly likely to show either imagination or compassion in the dramatic struggles characterising the historical present.

There is an inescapable risk involved in the recent Christian search for a more comprehensively human hope. When the Church makes its often heroic option for the poor it thereby exposes itself to all the accusations of being political, of being the pawn of sectional economic interests. We are clearly under the necessity of finding a new kind of language in which to express our ultimate hopes. It is no small challenge to express a critical social hope without sounding utopian, a transcendent hope without sounding escapist, an historical hope without being dismissed as partisan. To be stirred to a greater secular responsibility and immediate concern for our neighbour, is to risk diminishing the full scope of the Gospel. In any case, hopeful action is more important than another theology of hope. Besides, everything cannot be said all at once. Any account of hope needs to take its own time in its own place: those involved in the drama of violence and confrontation know, more than most, that what is not yet can get lost in what is, and that the mystery of the new creation is often concealed in the violent spasms of the old.

The practitioners of liberation theology are, of course, not alone with that problem. The global dimensions of feeding the starving, healing the sick, freeing the prisoner, welcoming the stranger, educating the ignorant, slowing the arms race, defending the environment and recognising human rights, leave us all not a little tongue-tied when it comes to the promise of eternal life. The trauma of momentous confrontations, humanly speaking, does not readily expand into a hope for an ultimate reconciliation of those engaged in all these varieties of human conflict.

It is nothing new in Christian life to suffer temptations. At times, Christians may feel that they can gain most acceptance perhaps as agents of social change, or as an international welfare agency, perhaps as a therapeutic community for the troubled, or as an institution of higher culture for the spiritually inclined. But without radical and ultimate hope, we will find that in the end we have nothing to say to an agonising world. For all human living keeps on touching those dark limits of mortality, transience, guilt, pain and failure. These simply do not go away.

The ultimate question is always there. There would be no liberation for anyone if there was no hope for the martyrs who laid down their lives in their service of the great human causes, if there were no hope for the millions who died before the cause of justice could be served. And we who have lived in Utopia, with perhaps only an occasional exposure to the drama of struggles elsewhere, know well enough by now that there has to be something more than *this*; that the political and economic freedoms to which the millions of the poor and oppressed aspire brings a final accounting: what do we really want? What do we really hope for? In these closing years of the twentieth century, perhaps in the closing stage of Western civilisation itself, it is not being especially elegiac to echo the feeling of St Paul, 'If for this life only we have hoped in Christ, we are of all men most to be pitied' (I Cor. 15:19).

All in all, it is a matter of grappling with a new kind of question. How is Christian existence a way of hope? How does such a hope find its appropriate form in the cultural and political situation of the day? How is it a truly incarnate hope, a truly embodied anticipation of the Kingdom of God, an exodus into the promised land of transformed humanity?

To articulate such a scope of concern while, at the same time, doing justice to the traditional theme of the last things presents no small problem. One senses in theology a time of gathering energy, of drawing in its breath before making the more comprehensive attempt.

The place of our world

Underlying the conflicts just referred to are profound differences in the way we experience the world itself. For most of human history, the world was simply, massively, fatefully *there* as the arena in which we human beings worked out our lives. But the technological mind of modern culture has seen it as something like a quarry from which we mine the materials for building the future, so greatly has human power increased. Or, to change the metaphor, the world provides the stage props for the acting out of the human drama. For human freedom, not fate, occupies centre stage at the expense of all the tyrannies of time and space and physical limitation which structured the past. Both such images are, of course, far too lurid to be taken as a critical statement on the character of the modern world, and our growing ecological awareness suggests an even greater caution in taking them too literally.

Still, whether we experience the world as a quarry, a stage or a garden, the history of human freedom has become the all-determining factor. What formerly resisted human freedom is now transformed by it. Nature is subsumed into history. Everything is touched and shaped by our technological powers. As nature is shaped by the human decision to serve a cultural design, space shrinks with our capacities for communication, transport and travel. Sight, hearing and touch are electronically extended. The human memory stores and retrieves information in the computer. The secrets of nature are unlocked to harness energy for human use. The traditional maladies of our forebears now yield to the marvels of modern medicine, and the healthy problem of longevity brings about its own social dislocation.

As environmental pressure groups make clear, even the experience of unspoilt nature is largely a result of political and economic policies. National parks and world heritage areas are 'reserved' from exploitation for other purposes. All that world which previously surrounded us with its beauty or terror to manifest the *vestigia Dei*, as 'traces of the divine', is now a thoroughly trodden area revealing only the *vestigia hominis*, 'human footprints'. The technological mind and hand has possessed, penetrated and shaped the earth. In an often perverse sense, the biblical command to fill and subdue the earth has been conspicuously obeyed. Though ecological violence is now revealed in its tragic proportions, still, there is no way back. We live in a human world penetrated by human reason and pressed into human service. The accompanying nightmare is the speedy degeneration of our planet, increasingly populated by de-natured earthlings, rootless and alien beings more inclined to haunt the earth rather than inhabit it.[23]

Painting in bold strokes on a large canvas as we are, still we come back to the simple questions: what is the human future we are envisaging and forming in the world? Does it anticipate some end-point of fulfilment for the whole of human history, and for the universe itself? How is God acting in it all?

Unlimited hope?

There is one further complication for the traditional theology of the last things. How universal can hope be? In every age, theology had to account for the biblical conviction that 'God wishes all men to be saved and to come to the knowledge of the truth' (I Tim. 2:4). But its judgment on the likelihood of salvation for all or most was usually expressed in a severely qualified manner. The Christian experience of persecution and heresy, together with the apparently obvious rejection of Christ through all forms of human malice, tended to make theology concentrate on human freedom as the really last thing in theological consideration. This, too, had its abundant scriptural support, Chapter 25 of St Matthew's Gospel for instance. Such a theologically restricted Christian hope, and, indeed, the human realism behind it, was hardly invited to further expansion by the onslaughts of systematic atheism as a refined, deliberate, politically powerful world-view. Hence, a theology, intellectually respectable within the contexts of its tradition and the culture, was compelled to emphasise that salvation without or against human choice could hardly be thought of as salvation at all. The tragedy of the human situation inherently resisted any attempt to impose a hopeful construction on it.

Still, any harsh or exclusive view always had to be tempered by the biblical injunction against judging anyone (Lk. 6:37; Mt. 7:1). Likewise, the practice of the Church, so creative in its beatification and canonisation of the saints, knows no instance of damning any individual to a realm beyond the reach of salvation—with the exception of the devils. Nonetheless, the outlook for universal salvation was grim. The most generous theology was caught in a bind: either God saves us without our consent or with it. If without it, then human freedom is destroyed. If with it, then such freedom must be really free to make its choices.

Apart from this main stream of conscientious theology, the Christian tradition held within it, not so much another theological view,[24] but something larger than theology—the lived hopefulness of Christian witness.

As I say, it is neither a more benign theological theory, nor an optimistic conviction that everything will turn out all right in the end; nor, for that matter, simply a more morally tolerant attitude. Rather, it is a kind of assurance that can only arise from living hope itself. For hope, as distinct from a theology of hope, deals, as it were, directly with God, in the immediacy of Christian consciousness, rather than through the complex mediations of theological thought. As such, it does not so much set itself up in opposition to a more restricted theological assessment, but implicitly refuses to let the freedom of God be contained in any theological or philosophical theory. Hence it acknowledges that our knowledge, above all our theological knowledge, is always limited, always this side of some ultimate synthesis, even as it knows our hopes need not be: only within the limitless mystery of grace is the final synthesis to be realised. Where theology was forced to retire before the impenetrable mystery of divine grace and human freedom, hope kept going, and accepted no limits to the mystery of ultimate mercy.

As an indication of this living tradition of unlimited hope, let me quote at some length from Hans Urs von Balthasar's reflection on the mission of Thérèse of Lisieux:

In the official theology of the West, since Augustine at the latest, unlimited hope finds itself shackled by the certitude that a certain number of people will be damned, and, in a still more disastrous way, by the doctrine of double predestination erected into a system. But it is significant that, from the Middle Ages up to the modern epoch, a whole series of women saints have silently protested against this masculine theology, and, being strong in their heartfelt boldness and having a direct access to the mystery of salvation, they have expressed a boundless hope. Limiting ourselves to the

> *greatest names, let us mention Hildegarde, Gertrude, Mechtilde of Hackeborn, Mechtilde of Magdeburg, Lady Julian of Norwich, Catherine of Siena, to whom could doubtless be added Catherine of Genoa and Marie of the Incarnation, and Mme Guyon. But the theology of women has never been taken seriously nor integrated by the establishment. Nevertheless, after the message of Lisieux, thought must finally be given to this in the current reconstruction of dogmatic theology.*[25]

Perhaps, the subversive question such a tradition poses for a theology intent on being intellectually respectable is this: has Christian theology been *theologically* respectable? The time-honoured description of theology has been 'faith seeking understanding'. It might be that the time has come to see it as 'hope seeking its most inclusive expression', or even as 'love searching for its true poetry'. The unrestricted hope of these great mystics is looking for a theology, even if no theology can ever replace hope's surrender to the mystery of God with its own assurances. For God, not theology, is the foundation of hope.

In its pastoral concern, Vatican II provides an impetus toward a more hope-animated theology. With its vivid sense of the mystery of salvation at work in the world, with its encouragement to dialogue between Christians and members of other religions, and even with non-believers (including explicit atheists) it exhibits a less anxious and a far more hopeful approach regarding the mystery of human salvation. It is true that we have here no definition of faith; but what we find in these recent Church documents is the presence of a humble, reverent and compassionate hope:

> *All this* [the saving grace of Christ] *holds true not only for Christians but for all men of good will in whose hearts grace is active invisibly. For since Christ died for all* (Rom. 8:32), *and*

> *since all men are in fact called to one and the same destiny which is divine, we must hold that the Holy Spirit offers to all the possibility of being made partners,* in a way known only to God, *in the paschal mystery.*[26]

'In a way known only to God...', a way not known or comprehensible to our necessarily limited theologies. This wider, deeper, more engaged tradition of Christian life confronts any account of the hope within us with the question, what, in the theology of the last things, is really the last thing? Is it the capacities of human freedom to accept or reject the grace that is unconditionally offered, or the inexhaustible capacities of divine grace to win our assent in the end? Is our final account of hope to be defeated by the appalling evidence of human tragedy? Or, may we still remain open to what only a limitless love can bring about?

As a theological virtue, hope need have no limits in its scope. There is nothing within its immediate contact with God to provide a positive reason to fall into despair about anyone. The fundamental ecstasy of hope is soberly expressed by St Thomas in the words, 'The good we should chiefly and rightly hope for from God is an unlimited one, matching the power of God who helps us. For it belongs to his limitless power to bring us to a limitless good.'[27] Theology does come up against limits as it turns to the various themes and particular questions of eschatology, but the incalculable freedom of God cannot be fitted into any system; nor, indeed, can freedom be reduced to a coherent philosophy of nature. There is always an excess, the limitless mystery of God's grace, which remains the native element of hope. This is what made Thérèse of Lisieux set herself in a great tradition that refused to be defeated by any experience of evil, as she proclaimed, 'My hopes touch upon the infinite.'[28]

The shortcomings of the older eschatology, the atheist criticism of Christian pathologies, the new hopeful energies which are finding expression in a deeper Church commitment to peace and justice, all make for a changed eschatological situation. Yet the complexity and the novelty of the situation hardly justify a defeated silence. Certainly, the older schematisation of the four last things has been greatly complicated; but the complications come from a more comprehensive expression of hope. So, the challenge remains: if our Gospel does not keep on being good news in the face of death, suffering, failure, human malice, the precariousness of human history, even in our native confusions and fears about the final state of things, is it really the genuine Gospel in the first place? How can grace keep on being grace at all limits of our experience of life? A 'faith that seeks understanding' would be a faith resigned to intellectual timidity if it did not explore the ultimate bearing of the mysteries it holds to. A hope in God's grace and mercy, if it recoiled from imagining the promised fulfilment, would be a hope that has lost its self-confidence. A love that 'believes all things, hopes all things, endures all things' would fail in its essential ecstasy if it remained unconcerned with how 'love never ends' (I Cor. 13:7–8).

Hence, there is nothing indecent or unduly speculative in exploring fresh ways to keep Christian hope alive, so to make Christian life truly hopeful.

However, in an obvious sense, we are left with a special darkness. No amount of hope can conquer the future, and drag it into the present as something controlled, grasped, a secure possession. As Paul would put it, 'hope that is seen is not hope' (Rom. 8:24). In all the meanings of the word, what we hope for is *provisional*. Divine and human freedom, divine creativity and human history, are not exhausted in their respective capacities to surprise us with the new and unexpected.

We will now go on to that experience of God which gives Christian hope a particular standpoint and outlook.

1. Jaroslav Pelikan, *The Melody of Theology. A Philosophical Dictionary*, Harvard University Press, Cambridge Mass., 1988, pp.76f.
2. *Summa Theol., Supplementum* q.69.
3. *See*, for instance, A. Yarbro Collins, 'Eschatology and Apocalypticism', *The New Jerome Biblical Commentary*, Geoffrey Chapman, London, 1989, pp.1359–1364; and Phan, *Eternity in Time...*, pp.26–31, where he refers to some nine eschatological approaches associated with such names as Schweitzer, Werner, Barth, Bultmann, Dodd, Culmann, Pannenberg, Moltmann and Metz.
4. *See* Ratzinger, *Eschatology...*, pp.140–157, 241–270, in response to Gisbert Greshake, *Auferstehung der Toten*, Essen 1969; and Gisbert Greshake and Gerhard Lohfink, *Naherwartung-Auferstehung-Unsterblichkeit. Untersuchungen zur christlichen Eschatologie, Quaestiones Disputatae* 71, Freiburg, 1982; Heino Sonnemmans, 'Soul, Afterlife, Salvation', *Communio* 14, Fall 1987, pp.248–261. The matter is further complicated by the 'Letter on Certain Questions of Eschatology' issuing from the Sacred Congregation for the Doctrine of the Faith, May 11, 1979 in which the following statement is found:

   > *The church affirms that a spiritual element survives and subsists after death, an element endowed with consciousness and will, so that the 'human self' subsists. To designate this element, the church uses the word 'soul', the accepted term in the usage of scripture and tradition. Although not unaware that this term has various meanings in the Bible, the church thinks that there is no valid reason for rejecting it...[n.3]*

   The puzzling point here for Catholic theology formed so massively by the Thomistic tradition is that 'soul' is made to mean the same as 'the self'. This is, of course, to contradict St Thomas Aquinas for whom the human self always meant a soul animating a body! (*See Summa Theol.* I, q.75, a.4)
5. *See* Heino Sonnemans, 'Soul, Afterlife, Salvation', *Communio* 14, Fall 1987, pp.249–256; and, with his masterful comprehension of the history of culture, Eric

Voegelin, 'Immortality: Experience and Symbol', *Harvard Theological Review* 60/3, July 1967, pp.235–279. For a most interesting and informative account of the history of this topic: *See* Simon Tugwell, *Human Immortality and the Redemption of Death*, Darton, Longman and Todd, London, 1990, pp.3–72.
6. Case by case, of course, this is a question of great complexity: *See* Joseph A. Fitzmeyer, 'Pauline Theology', *The New Jerome Biblical Commentary*, Geoffrey Chapman, London, 1989, pp. 1406–1407; also, 'Soul' in *Harper's Bible Dictionary*, Paul J. Achtemeier (ed.), Harper and Row, San Francisco, 1985, pp.982–983
7. Theological understanding does develop: fresh discoveries, new cultural and historical contexts, differing mentalities all play their part. See N. Max Wildiers, *The Theologian and His Universe Theology and Cosmology from the Middle Ages to the Present*, Seabury, New York, 1982.
8. *See* St Thomas Aquinas, *Summa Theol.*, I, q.75–76; II–II, q.83, a.11 ad 5.
9. *ibid.*, I, q.84, a.7.
10. For a fuller discussion: *See* S. Tugwell, *Human Immortality...*, pp.128–155.
11. For a convenient summary: *See* Phan, *Eternity in Time...*, pp.46–47, 85–88.
12. Ernest Joós, 'What If We Have a Soul?', *Science et Ésprit* XXXVI/2 (1984), pp.211–232.
13. Michael J. Scanlon 'Anthropology, Christian', in *The New Dictionary of Theology*, Joseph A. Komonchak, *et al.* (eds.) Michael Glazier, Wilmington, Del., 1988, pp.27–41.
14. For a comprehensive and balanced statement on the developmental model and human and Christian existence: *Walter Conn, Christian Conversion: A Developmental Interpretation of Autonomy and Surrender*, Paulist Press, New York, 1986.
15. *See* Hans Küng, *Does God Exist? An Answer for Today*, Vintage Books, New York, 1981: for Marx, pp.217–260; for Freud, pp.262–337; for Nietzsche, pp.343–423.
16. For a thorough-going theological confrontation with Marx: *See* Nicholas Lash, *A Matter of Hope: A Theologian's Reflections on the Thought of Karl Marx*,

Darton, Longman and Todd, London, 1981.
17. *The Portable Nietzsche* ed. G. Kaufmann, Viking; New York, p.585.
18. *Gaudium et Spes*, par. 34; *Lumen Gentium*, par. 18.
19. *Redemptor Hominis*, par.14.
20. *Gaudium et Spes*, par.39.
21. For the most mature and profound account of this type of theological thinking: *See* Gustavo Gutierrez, *The Truth Shall Make You Free: Confrontations*, Orbis, New York 1990.
22. Johann Baptist Metz, *Faith, History and Society: Toward a Practical Fundamental Theology*, Burns and Oates, London, 1980, is a bracing European sketch of a theology earthed in the political and social experience of suffering and hope. For a useful survey of ecclesiastical documents: *See* Brian Johnstone, 'Eschatology and Social Ethics. A critical survey of the development of social ethical theory in ecumenical discussion 1925–1968', *Bijdragen* 37(1976) pp.47–85.
23. Thomas Berry, 'The New Story: Comments on the Origins, Identification and Transmission of Values', *Cross Currents* Summer/Fall, 1987, pp.187–199. For similar remarks: *See* Vincent Donovan, *The Church in the Midst of Creation*, Orbis, Maryknoll, 1989, pp.35–48.
24. Here we refer to the doctrine of *Apocatastasis*, a final, universal restoration and salvation of all in Christ, as was propounded by Origen, Jerome (at times), Clement of Alexandria, Theodore of Mopsuestia and Gregory of Nyssa. This was strongly attacked by Augustine, and condemned by the Council of Constantinople in 543 (DS 411). The point to emphasise is that it was condemned as a theological hypothesis and as a statement of fact—not as an expression of hope. *See* Phan, *Eternity in Time...* pp.155f; and, for a more stringent view, Leo Scheffczyk, 'Apocatastasis: Fascination and Paradox', *Communio* 12, Winter 1985, pp.385–397.
25. Hans Urs von Balthasar, 'The Timeliness of Lisieux,' *Carmelite Studies* (1980/1), pp.117f.
26. *Gaudium et Spes*, par.22, my emphasis. *See*, too, par.16 for a more extensive statement.
27. *Summa Theol.*, II–II, q.17, a.2.
28. Quoted by von Balthasar, *op.cit.*, p.117.

3 The Ground of Hope

Even though we have listed the numerous factors affecting our former, too simplistic treatment of the last things, theological reflection has its humble service to offer as it ponders on how best to express the ultimate range of Christian hope. For theology can never be too far removed from eschatology: the *logos,* 'the meaning' of both *Theos,* 'God', and of the *eschaton,* 'the last' are necessarily interconnected.

True, no theological eye is able to look into the face of God, and no theological ear has yet heard the whole message of the Word, just as no theological mind, however enlightened its methods, can comprehend the mystery. All that is possible for theology is to explore the character of the future in a way inspired by the present data. These are literally *data,* the 'givens', the grace of the divine self-giving in Word and Spirit into human hearts and history. From such givens, theology works out its account. It serves the life of hope by extrapolating what is to come from what is present. There is no possibility of giving a guided tour of the world to come. Humility, a somewhat forgotten virtue for theology, places us firmly on the ground of the present moment of God's saving action, as it is given to us out of the past and opens into what is to come.

Now, the fundamental *data,* the givens, of hope are all reducible to what is given in the grace of Christ. In the Gospel story, this is narrated in the sequence of the various 'mysteries' of the life, passion, death, and resurrection of the Lord. In its totality, this mystery of Jesus Christ is the point in our world from which the horizon of hope unfolds. In such an horizon, the truly ultimate is the Father's original and unconditional love (Jn 3:16). So it is that theology, in its eschatological mode, is always extrapolating from what is given in the fundamental mystery of Christ: 'Christ has died, Christ is risen, Christ will come again!' Everything that can be said is implicit in the original Word of Christ 'the Alpha and Omega, the First and the Last, the Beginning and the End' (Rev. 22:13). Whatever the particular themes we might consider—death, judgment, purgatory, heaven, hell and so forth—their Christian substance is rooted in the one who 'is before all things, in [whom] all things hold together' (Col. 1:17).[1]

With such a focus in Christ, theology expands to consider the trinitarian God present as the mystery of our future. God, 'who is Love' (I Jn 4:8,16) is irreversibly involved in our history.[2] The Word, declaring this love, is incarnate in Christ, the Son, the one nearest the Father's heart (Jn 1:18). The Spirit, dwelling in the hearts and communities of believers, energises a movement into the future with Christ 'our brother' into the mystery of God 'our Father'. The Spirit of the Father and the Son is not 'the spirit of slavery, to fall back into fear' (Rom. 8:15) but the Spirit of trusting intimacy with God, our true future. Hence the Spirit, working in our minds and hearts, will 'declare the things that are to come' (Jn 16:13).[3]

The God who is love is thus revealed as a hope-inspiring, compassionate mystery. For God's self-giving in the Son and through the Spirit is directed to human beings locked in an apparently insuperable problem of evil. The Son empties himself into suffering human history as Jesus of Nazareth. The Father empties himself into the vulnerability of having no self-disclosure in this world other than Jesus, the only Son. Similarly, the Spirit is exposed to human rejection by witnessing to no power and no truth other than the love that is shown forth in the crucified. Such a God, such a love, is a light for our darkness because the divine has known our problem of evil and freely entered into it. God has acted within human history to open our self-enclosed defeat into what alone can give it hope.

Hence, divine love, communicated as Father, Son and Spirit, has to contend with all that resists it. The accumulated absurdity of the 'heart of stone' is dramatically documented by Paul (Rom. 1:18–32); and described by John as a refusal of the light (Jn 3:19–21). The Word incarnate is uttered into a world of human conversation in which the new commandment appears as an absurdity. The Spirit has only the power of love to counter 'the principalities and powers' (Eph. 6:12) of this world, be these the familiar demons that infest the human condition and impel toward self-destruction, or massive, rather more neutral, influences structuring human existence. The presence of the Father, intimated in an unlimited horizon of grace and mercy, is obscured by the self-projections of existential idolatry.

Nonetheless, this divine love refuses to be anything other than itself. The Son, precisely in the moment of experiencing the demonic intensity of the world's evil, gives himself for the life of the world. The Spirit is not changed into one more worldly power, but empties himself into the vulnerability of love. The Father is not set above the world as a patriarchal idol legitimating oppressions that promise no future. Rather, he is revealed as the subversive mystery of unconditional love incarnate in the Crucified. This love comes to its own victory in the resurrection of the Crucified, and in the history of the self-sacrificing ways of hope it energises.

But it is a victory which appeals to human freedom and does not suppress it. God continues to have time for our whole history. The immediate radiant evidence of the Risen Lord, and the vision of the invisible God must wait to the end. Only in the energy of the Spirit, inspiring the faith and hope and love which abide (I Cor. 13:13) is love's victory communicated, as it transforms human lives, individually and communally, into anticipations of what is to be. The excess of evil calls forth the excesses of the 'never ending' love that 'bears all things, believes all things, hopes all things, endures all things' (I Cor. 13:7f.).

The manner in which God has entered human history to draw it into his own future is a communication to free beings. We are still living a history of freedom. And that distinctively human mode of existence needs time, takes time to unfold to its full proportions. Though God is present in the incarnate and personal manner we have described, such a presence creates a 'free space' around it to make room for our full human history. This is the space of the Spirit, inspiring our searchings and our hopes, stimulating desire and longing, impelling toward dialogue, and all the witness of different vocations and different gifts.

The Word of God, irrevocably incarnate though it is, does not kill the ongoing conversation of human history. As a word meant for all, as all-comprehending in its original meaning, it demands all the creativity of dialogue among peoples and even faiths to come to its full human expression. Heard and told within human history, the Word becomes a story.[4] And as a story, as fundamentally the expression of the autobiography of God, it is open to include the life-stories of individuals and communities, or societies and cultures, the great cosmic story of the universe itself. Everything we are in this corporeal, 'earthed', communal and individual historical existence is now part of the story of the incarnate Word. Or, as Karl Rahner would say it:

> *The whole is a drama, and the stage is also part of it. It is a dialogue between spiritual and divinised creatures and God, a dialogue*

> *and a drama which has already reached an irreversible climax in Christ.*[5]

Our entire existence is addressed by the Word of the 'One who is to come',

> *For it is within history and not alongside it that there takes place the event of God's self-communication to creatures and the history of the free acceptance of the infinite God.*[6]

And yet, even though the last word on our future is addressed to the inconclusive and fragmented reality of human history, it does not lose its definitive character. For, as a whole, it has been claimed and possessed by God. As a whole, the human race has a divine future. Though, as we mentioned in the last chapter, theology has no right to utter judgments about the particular fate of individuals, it is within its capacity and responsibility to speak of an assured future for a whole humanity. Again, Karl Rahner has put this point in a striking manner:

> *For since we are living in the eschaton of Jesus Christ, the God-Man who was crucified for us and who has risen for us and who remains forever, we know in our Christian faith and in our unshakeable hope that, in spite of the drama and ambiguity of the freedom of the individual persons, the history of salvation as a whole will reach a positive conclusion for the human race through God's own powerful grace.*[7]

Hence, all the particular issues of eschatology are expressed, not as the disconnected themes of an abstract or inconclusive hope, but as extrapolations made from the burning centre of what is already occurring within our history. For where we are and how we are has already been penetrated by the divine. Through Christ, the reality of our world is already claimed and owned by God. The death and resurrection of the Lord has occurred as a mutation within the sphere of human existence.

But to stress such a point is not to underwrite an unimaginative fundamentalism. For the mystery of Christ is communicated essentially in the form of a story. As such, as Gospel, it is told and retold in all the variety of contexts that make up our human condition. It is meant in its innermost meaning to be addressed to the longings and fears and hopes that make up human history. Whilst the story of Christ is always at the centre of our accounts of hope, the human telling point can be anywhere in a vast and expanding circumference. The Christian hope of, say, the dying, the ageing, the young or the old, the condemned, the guilty, the threatened, of those oppressed by hopeless poverty or menaced with political violence, of those who have wakened to ecological wonder and responsibility, of those have dedicated their lives to making peace among nations, will express itself in differing accents and in different keys.[8] The ever changing human condition will not let us be fundamentalist too long! For fear of being either an absurd or fantastic answer to an unasked question, Christian hope demands a new imagining in every age and in every human context.

Yet, however varied the accounts of hope might be, there are constants in any authentic Christian hope. These reduce to two: first of all, the grace, the givenness of the mystery of Christ; and secondly, the ever questing, ever unfinished thrusting of our lives toward an ultimate wholeness and a final homecoming.

What, then, are the last things that eschatology fundamentally deals with? The traditional answer was clear: death, judgment, heaven and hell. The answer, far more fundamental, that I have suggested here, can be indicated under the following headings:

(i) God's Original Love

The ultimate purpose of the universe, its essential character, derives from the *eschaton* of the love of God.

This comes to its victory in the glory of a universe transformed by the grace of God's self-giving in Christ. As St Paul expresses it:

> *He destined us in love to be his sons* [and daughters] *through Jesus Christ according to the purpose of his will, to the praise of his glorious grace which he freely bestowed on us in the Beloved.* (Eph. 1:5 f.)

This original and universal will of God, the mystery of creative and redemptive love, finds its consummation at the point of ultimate communication when 'God may be everything to everyone' (I Cor. 15:28). In this context, the eschatological prayer is, 'Thy Kingdom come!'

(ii) Christ, the Ultimate Form

As the ultimate form of the transformed universe and redeemed humanity, Christ himself is the *eschaton*. Again, the words of Paul express this kind of finality:

> *He is the image of the invisible God, the first-born of all creation; for in him all things were created, in heaven and on earth...all things were created in him and for him. He is before all things, and in him all things hold together*' (Col. 1:15–17).

In such a context, the eschatological prayer is the oldest Christian prayer recorded in the New Testament: 'Maranatha, Our Lord, come!' (I Cor. 16:22).

(iii) Spirit: the Ultimate Life

As the energy impelling everyone and everything to achieve its ultimate form in Christ, and uniting all in him, the *eschaton* is the Spirit:

> *If the Spirit of him who raised Jesus from the dead dwells in you, he who raised Jesus from the dead will give life to your mortal bodies also through his Spirit who dwells in you* (Rom. 8:11).

Here, the prayer of hope is to join with the 'sighs to

deep for words' of the Spirit praying in all the hopeful prayers of the Christian (Rom. 8:26). This finds expression in the invocation, 'Come, Holy Spirit...'.

(iv) A Transformed Humanity

The last thing in terms of our human history is the resurrection of our humanity in a transformed universe. Neither the world nor our humanity is sacrificed in God's gracious design. The groaning of all creation in its cosmic activity of giving birth, the groaning of those who hope for our full redemption (Rom. 8:22f.) envisages, not the destruction of our humanity or our world, but a creation rejoicing in the 'glorious liberty of the children of God'. Here, the eschatological prayer is 'Abba', '*Our* Father...'

Up to this point, the three steps in our account of hope have been, first, a brief reflection on the character of hope in general; secondly, an overview of the complexities and limitations of our traditional language about the last things; and thirdly, as in this chapter, a brief statement of the great theological principles ideally governing any talk about our ultimate destiny: here, as will be frequently stressed in what follows, the first and last reality to be affirmed in any expression of hope is the mystery of God's self-giving love. We will soon tease out this fundamentally hopeful viewpoint in terms of the paschal mystery and the eucharist, the focal parable and basic symbol of Christian hope; and that will lead into a range of special questions.

But at this point, I think, it would be most healthy to pause, in the space of the next two chapters, for a kind of meditation on the dark mystery of death. For this essential boundary to human existence invites hope to its authentic seriousness. It will lead us to a kind of telling-point at which the full hopeful story can be told with less illusion and more healthy defiance of the despairs that, often unnoticed, gnaw at Christian confidence.

1. *See* Phan, *Eternity in Time...*, pp.64–78.
2. See Tony Kelly, *Trinity of Love: A Theology of the Christian God*, Michael Glazier, Wilmington, Del., 1988, especially pp. 3–6; 139–145; 174–180 and *passim*.
3. *ibid.*, pp.107–113; 163–169; 195–202.
4. *ibid.*, pp.39–45; and *The Range of Faith: Basic Questions for a Living Theology*, St Paul Publications, Homebush, 1986 (US edition, The Liturgical Press, Collegeville, Minn.), 1989, pp.17–25.
5. Karl Rahner, *Foundations of Christian Faith*, tr. William V. Dych, Crossroad, New York, 1978, p.446.
6. *ibid.*, p.446.
7. *ibid.*, p.435.
8. For example, Jürgen Moltmann, 'God and Nuclear Catastrophe', *Pacifica* 1/2, June 1988, pp.157–170; Brendan Lovett, *Life Before Death: Inculturating Hope*, Claretian Publications, Quezon City, 1986.

4 The Dead End

As we have been stressing, modern consciousness, either in hope or dread, or any mixture of both, is being tugged into the future. We are changing into something that is not yet, at a rate that is too quick for any assured controlling sense of what is happening; and the changes are irreversible. There is no going back.

The range and speed of electronic computation extends the capacities of the forecaster. Sophisticated planning can sketch its various scenarios. Depending on whether trends develop or dwindle in the variety of possible economic and political contexts, different forms of probable outcomes are projected. Still, no matter how rich the possibilities nor how varied the impending dooms, no matter how accurate the forecasting, nor how determined the planning, how comprehensive the list of possible scenarios, how positive the trend, how confident the development, or how favourable the environment, a terminal factor is present. This, quite simply, is death.[1]

The inescapable fact of mortality, takes us to the edge of an inevitable chaos. Here no philosophy, no therapy, no theology is in control. We come to the limits of our human resources. Death is the unique datum that swallows any construction put on it.

Death as limit of future

Planners and those for whom they plan will die, and

dying, if the planning is to be a realistic projection, must be factored in. Longevity may be a trend; but death is a constant.

Utopian visions may indeed present us with the possibilities of marvellous developments in human life and culture. Such is the poignant aspect of the problem for many people living today in the more advanced parts of the world. They are living in the Utopia that their forebears envisioned. Human life is freed from the dull weight of much of the misery and limitation brought about by isolation, drudgery, illness, hunger and insecurity. Even if such comparative well-being is concentrated in little more than a fifth of the world's population, the human race 'has never had it so good'. And yet...death: *Et in Arcadia ego*, 'Also in Arcady am I present'.

Technological advances in medicine tease our mortality with possibilities of extending the span of human life for a few more years: the medical miracles of blood transfusion, organ transplants, artificial joints and limbs, refined surgical techniques, new wonder drugs. Death comes to figure in the cultural imagination formed by social medicine as a disease to be dealt with, rather than our inescapable fate. It has been organised out of the bustling exchanges of modern urban life as something alien, to be banished from the consciousness of the living. Those nourished on health foods, health fads, comprehensively insured against any adversity, are as unaware of the houses of death—the modern nursing homes and hospices—as they are of the precarious fate of most of the world.

The elderly retire into growing isolation, often to attract attention only as an economic problem as their number grows, birth rates fall, and the question arises, who is to pay the bills? As medical resources and life-support systems are stretched, then *their* death is discussed as a social problem, for us, the living.

Makers of public policy find themselves in a quandary: the quantitative cost of death gives rise to a strange language about the quality of life. As it turns the dying into disposable objects of public policy, they are removed further from our care, and we from any emotional connection with them, as from any sense of our awful solidarity in the mystery of death. Our common mortality withdraws further from the social imagination.

The morbid imagination

When the reality of death is so alienated from cultural life, our imaginations take a strangely morbid turn. They are affected with a constant state of dread by the daily news of death as catastrophe: murders, natural disasters, accidents, epidemics, wars. Insatiable media networks seem to play eternally around the darkest and oldest of all human mysteries.

As death is turned into a catastrophe happening to others, it is not surprising that death as the most predictable fact of human existence returns as something of an obsession.[2] Safely distanced by the media, we become death-watchers, voyeurs of what has become culturally obscene; news-worthy death seems to bear the whole weight of our sense of mortality. The obsession degenerates to voyeurism when death-dealing violence becomes so integral to what has come to be regarded as entertainment, as thrillers in pulp literature, the terror movie, the TV crime series. If such titillation should turn to disgust and begin to touch on real questions about human fate, it can be assured in the commercial break that in the real world populated by the beautiful and successful, no one ever dies. In the cult of death-as-catastrophe, our common mortality lies buried.

The impenetrable fact

Though the madness of such a situation may seem obvious, we can hardly pretend to look at life from some vantage point impervious to the fragility and transience of life. No deathless gaze beholds the human tragedy. No single person, no one generation knows the full story of a society or culture, nor even the full story of a single life. None of us can tell a whole life story. Death interrupts the telling. Autobiography eventually fails. And even the most inspired biographers are incapable of fully comprehending the full impact of the lives they have written. History sets both life as it is lived and life as it is written about in the larger movements of culture's progress or decline. Life is always unfinished business with death interrupting both our living and our efforts to make sense of it:

> *The death of each individual keeps breaking the threads of history...is there no longer any salvation, not even for those who have handed on the torch of history, and kept it burning among the living, and have perhaps met their deaths for that very reason?*[3]

In the face of death, hope has to be 'a hope against all hope'. It is the point at which naive optimism collapses, where plans reach their limits, where all utopias reach their moment of truth.

Two deadly intensities

The deadly edge of death cuts sharply into soft, easy hopes. It is honed to further degrees of sharpness from two angles. The first is that of the cultural atheism of modern consciousness. A Nietzsche, a Marx, a Freud, have banished from the modern mind the 'God' of oppression and repression. If life has been so liberated from such a God, death has been too. But in a Godless world, death is immediately experienced as a limit in a more intense manner. With nothing and no one to receive one's last breath, culture is bereft of its traditional ways of coping with death, let alone celebrating it with a final rite of passage. A passing into nothingness hardly inspires any confident ritual expression! The best way to cope with our mortality is silence and repression. Each human being simply dies out; there is no longer any shared assumption about 'going to God'. The banality of simple ending replaces the drama of judgment; there is no passing on, no passing over; no possibility of an entry into life, higher and eternal compared with this. With death reduced to a brute biological event, there is nothing further, and no one there, to save either body or soul. Death is terminally deadly.

In the experience of death, the cultural atheism of our day cashes its cheques. Acceptance of mortality demands heroic acceptance of absurdity in a defiant gesture toward the universe which promised so much, but now, with the finality of death, delivers...nothing. In such a courage, both Freud and Sartre accepted death. Nonetheless, in the God-less worlds of meaning that each created, fundamental questions still stir: is death the destruction of the rich worlds of meaning both these geniuses explored? Is our release from repression nothing more than a release into a world in which every human life is finally meaningless, and utterly alone as each one faces extinction? Is all the brave creativity of human freedom nothing but a futile posture against the onset of the final darkness?

Along with the lack of transcendent meaning, the modern world feels another terminal intensity: the possibility of collective death. For mass death now appears as the lethal possibility of a self-destructiveness unimaginable in its proportions. The prospect of self-inflicted global mega-death is a factor in contemporary consciousness. Though human history has always known its catalogue of natural disasters: famines, earthquakes, plagues—'acts of God'—we now live with the eerie possibility of a 'human act' which could amount to planetary suicide. The possibilities are there: biological warfare, thermo-nuclear incineration, ecological collapse. These are not the fantasies of a morbid imagination. They are the products of human freedom, the dire, doom-laden capacity to end significant human life on this planet. But this time, a 'non-existent' God cannot be blamed. Acts of God have been replaced by human acts as the chief threat. For human activity has enlarged the dimensions of death beyond anything previously imagined. Compared with this sense of impending global death, individual death might appear to be almost insignificant.

As the global precariousness of life pervades human consciousness, those symbols of immortality deriving from nature and race, science and art, religion and spirituality are no longer palpable. For the vast intricate eco-system of nature seems to be going through a gigantic spasm which could lead to extinction. The human race *can* self-destruct. Science, on which Western culture has so pinned its hopes, has been revealed as not necessarily user-friendly; or, more seriously, not necessarily accompanied by values proportionate to the earth-transforming power it wields. In such cultural distress, art might be only a cry of pain, religion merely a naive projection, and mysticism nothing but a regression to the innocent ignorance of the child.

So it is that death occurs in our imaginations with a more deadly edge. With 'God' gone and human life threatened with extinction, our mortal fate cannot rest in some higher principle. Anything 'other', anything 'more' is lost in the opacity of deadly threat. For that 'something more', either in terms of a transcendent reality, or a life-thrust to further fulfilment, have, in a radical way, ceased to exist in the dominant secular culture. In the face of death, there is no salvation, no saviour. However subterranean its influence, death enters modern sensibilities as an all-engulfing emptiness.

In this context, the AIDS epidemic has served as a focus of special anxiety. Apart from the evident epidemic proportions of this disease, it appears as especially lethal for three related reasons. First, because modern medicine has so far been revealed as defeated in its regard. When there is no scientific hope offered, it cannot but appear as more dramatically deadly than any other kind of dying today for it is experienced as a symbol of a wider cultural defeat. Secondly, the victim is forced into a peculiar isolation. The AIDS sufferer or carrier has become an object of fear to the general public, and even to medical practitioners anxiously protecting themselves from this mysterious infection. Thirdly, it is a disease, originally at least, transmitted through different kinds of sexual activity. When it seemed that sex had been liberated to come into its own as promoting intimacy in human relations, it has now been revealed as a potential carrier of death. A deeply eroticised culture has seen the most obvious instance of the joy of life and intimacy go wrong. Isolation, fear and mistrust have come to be associated with what was thought of as most natural. In times and places where death had become an abstract possibility, it has returned with the AIDS virus as a power defeating the expertise of the modern scientist, to isolate the sufferer as an object of dread, and to call into question what seemed most life-affirming and ecstatic.

Two conflicting views?

Though we know death is there, that it will happen, discussing it is a peculiarly complex matter. How complex and many-sided is indicated in the titles of two remarkable modern books, each a classic in its own genre. The first is Ernest Becker's *The Denial of Death*[4]; the second is Ladislaus Boros' *The Moment of Truth: Mysterium Mortis*.[5]

As Becker deals with the repression of death in modern consciousness, his book is a powerful point of reference. He expresses his main thesis thus:

> *The idea of death, the fear of it, haunts the human animal like nothing else; it is the mainspring of human activity—activity designed largely to avoid the fatality of death, to overcome it by denying in some way that it is the final destiny for man.*[6]

The book highlights the primordial terror experienced in the human psyche in the face of death. What it summons us to is a radical acceptance of creaturehood, to an attitude of true humility in the face of a mysterious and threatening universe. At that point of trembling and surrender, is human authenticity realised.

Becker feels that it has now become clear how religious experience, as a 'creature feeling' in the face of the massive transcendence of creation and the crushing and negating miracle of Being, ties in with psychology. This is 'right at the point of the problem of courage'.[7] Faced with the immensity of the universe and its impassivity in regard to individual fate:

> *...man had to invent and create out of himself the limitations of perception and equanimity to live on this planet. And so the core of psychodynamics, the formation of the human character, is a study in human self-limitation and in the terrifying costs of that limitation. The hostility to psychoanalysis...will always be a hostility against admitting that man lives by lying to himself about himself and about his world, and that character, to follow Ferenczi and Brown, is a vital lie.*[8]

Becker generously accepts the enormous influence of Freud in the understanding of psychopathology, but he is critical, too. Relying on the insights of Søren Kierkegaard and Otto Rank, he lays bare a certain inconclusiveness in Freud's approach when it touches on the matter of death and the deep terror that it strikes into every human being. For his part, Becker argues that the fundamental repression or denial in human life is not sex, as Freud had taught, but death. Whatever therapy might be brought to bear on human problems, it is only freeing us to live with the most radical fear of all: that which has its origin in our mortality. The courageous acceptance of one's creatureliness is the only authentic way open:

> *By being or doing we fashion something, an object or ourselves, and drop it into the confusion, make an offering of it, so to speak, to the lifeforce.*[9]

Becker's conception of the human condition demands a renewed collaboration between science and religion. Science improperly absorbs all truth into itself. It is the role of religion to stand for a larger version of truth, enabling human beings to:

> *wait in a condition of openness toward miracle and mystery, in the lived truth of creation, which would make it easier to survive and be redeemed because men would be less driven to undo themselves and would be more like the image which pleases their creator: awe-filled creatures trying to live in harmony with the rest of creation. Today we would add...they would be less likely to poison the rest of creation.*[10]

To live with a genuinely creaturely consciousness is, for Becker, a condition of 'relative unrepression'. Those who have accepted how puny they are in the face of the overwhelming and majestic nature of the universe, aware of the unspeakable miracle of even a single living being, and in some measure open to the 'panic' and the immense, inconclusive drama of creation, have come to a point of healing.

Becker likes Frederick Perls' analysis of the four protective layers which structure neurosis. The first two layers are the mundane, everyday layers of cliché and role. But:

...the third is the stiff one to penetrate: it is the impasse that covers our feelings of being empty and lost, the very feeling we try to banish in building up our character defences. Under this layer is the fourth and the most baffling one: the 'death' or fear-of-death layer; this...is the layer of our true and basic animal anxieties, the terror that we carry around in our secret heart. Only when we explode this fourth layer, says Perls, do we get to the layer of what we might call our 'authentic self': what we really are without shame, without disguise, without defences against fear.[11]

If there is a healing at such a depth, it is because we begin to live in humility—a sense of our radical finiteness, our creatureliness.[12]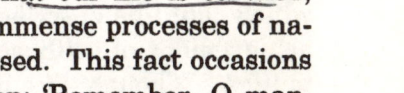

I see the great value of Becker's work as a revaluation of humility, in the most original sense of the word. It has to be the basic mode of any authentic human consciousness. As a word, humility derives from the Latin *humus*, meaning the 'earth', 'soil', 'dirt'. It points to the existential fact that our life is earthed, grounded, bound up with the immense processes of nature in which we are all immersed. This fact occasions the ancient liturgical injunction: 'Remember, O man, that thou art but dust, and unto dust thou shalt return.' The virtue of humility—for it is a *virtus*, in the moral sense, a quality of freedom and self-determination—enables human consciousness to deal creatively with the dread of death. Death is permitted to emerge from its subterranean place of influence, no longer able to sap our energies or drive us to the frenzy of illusory immortality-projects.

Out of this still fearful acceptance of our mortality comes wisdom. Life remains a question, within an overwhelmingly questionable universe; and because each of us is a question what is most clear is that none of us is the centre of that universe. We have emerged out of a vast cosmic process and are dying back into it. When we begin to ask about the true centre, the true life-force of this overwhelming universe, an acceptance of self as mortal and finite begins. With that, if not precisely adoration, at least a surrender to the unnamed, incomprehensible Whole can be realised. Only a de-centred self can live meaningfully. It is the task of religious faith and theory to articulate the relationship between accepting ourselves as creatures and experiencing the presence of the Creator. What Becker has done is to deal with the denial of death that undermines both faith and the authentic quality of human life. What he has not done, is explore with the same imagination, the life to the full that this living consciousness might anticipate.

The polar opposite of Becker's book is Ladislaus Boros' *The Moment of Truth*. Boros concedes that, in terms of experimental science, death implies dissolution and destruction. But a more philosophical view of human existence can ask the question 'whether the complete removal from self which we undergo in death does not conceal a much more fundamental process which could be described...in terms of the progressive achievement of selfhood, of actively initiating the self to life.'[13] Though, like Becker, Boros purports to be exploring human consciousness, he highlights rather the dynamics of self-transcendence in our actual living. Life anticipates a fulfilment in, and even through, death:

> *Death gives man the opportunity of posing his first completely personal act; death is, therefore, by reason of its very being, the moment above all others for the awakening of consciousness, for freedom, for encounter with God, for the final decision about his eternal destiny.*[14]

Death is the final step into the completion of personal life. If Becker leads us back to the psyche's primordial terror in the face of mortality, Boros bids us yield to the unfolding of the human spirit into some form of cosmic homecoming.

The initially unmanageable aspect of any discussion is that both treatments aim to explore human consciousness. More simply, they both appeal to reasonably accessible human experiences. Yet one uncovers a fundamental terror bringing about the massive denial of death, while the other presents the thrust of life as somehow positing death as the door to a final self-possession or self-surrender to the infinite. *NB*

Becker is, by his own admission, more morbid in his analysis of what death means, or is allowed to mean, in our self-understanding.[15] Indeed, he can establish a strong case that a lot of our positive views of death illustrate the acrobatics of the mechanisms of denial. Boros, on the other hand, is vigorously life-affirming. Death belongs within the life process. There is no morbidity here, rather a more ecstatic sense of life.

Another point of contrast: Becker concentrates on the archaeology of the human psyche. The fear of death is bred into us in the earliest stages of infant consciousness. It issues forth in an illusory life-project. We attempt a kind of futile heroics in a culture more or less intent on forgetting its animal nature and inherent limitations. So bound up is the formation of human character with the mechanisms of denial and the promotion of illusion, that, in consequence, it becomes a vital lie. Thus, human character is seen as a complex of strategies intent on sustaining the image of the self as immortal. Only by unlocking such a repression so as to let the truth of our mortality emerge, can personal and cultural integrity be won. What this new self-possession as a relatively conscious mortality might mean, remains only austerely intimated in Becker's work. One has to wait for the light in the darkness. Living in such a state of relative unrepression will be a hard-won matter; it is not to be glossed over by any available religious or philosophical solution.

You could say that Becker's analysis ends where Boros' begins. Boros is not much concerned with the archaeology of psychic terror in the face of death. His approach is more teleological, for it looks to a goal—the final unfolding of what spiritual consciousness already shows in its performance. His basic model is not the terrorised infant in an incomprehensible universe, but the thrust of creative consciousness in its exploration of meaning. Examples of this can be found in the artist, the mystic, the lover, the thinker...[16]

In his meditation, Boros seems to assume an integration of the feelings and symbols of psyche into the dynamics of the spirit. I imagine he would find an example of this in the courageous scholarly integrity of Becker's own analysis of humankind's primitive terror in the face of death. In other words, he would take as his data both the psychic fear of death and the hopeful meaning-seeking activity that confronts it.

One must suppose, had Becker read Boros' book, that he would see it primarily as an instance of denial—terror displaced into spirituality. Boros would reply, I presume, that Becker's performance was a striking example of the spirituality he was uneasy about, and that he was ignoring his best data! For Boros, the philosopher-theologian, Becker is giving a perfect account of death in the context of an experience of original sin, that historical and cultural state that closes human consciousness against the transcendent.

But who is to say? As it is, these two books collide, and seem to inhabit not only different conceptual worlds, but different worlds of feeling and faith. Both books allow for dialogue and collaboration in a larger wisdom, but their respective concerns are so extremely contradictory that a synthesis would not seem likely.

Of course, that is not exactly the point. For we are not about bringing two contradictory realities together, but two different interpretations of the one reality. More poignantly, the concern here is not for some neat textbook synthesis. The issue is *you*, *me*, *us*—our human consciousness. That there is some kind of duality is clear enough: a psycho-physical dread of death, and the impulse of the human spirit to transcend it. The <u>problem for a realistic hope is how to live with such a duality</u>.

The complex language of death

In the complexity of physical, neural, psychic, cultural, philosophical and theological considerations related to any effort to speak of death, the fundamental experience of our mortality can easily get lost. Confusion engenders its own kind of existential panic. We are tempted to jump from one consideration to the other; or better, to displace the archaeology of the psyche into the dynamics of the spirit, or to allow the openness of spirit to be reduced to the terrors of the psyche. It seems to me that if we are intent on giving death its due, both modes of human consciousness have to be respected in the untidy business of what we are as human beings.

For what we directly experience is not death, but the self in its stratified consciousness. I do not directly experience my death, but I do experience my self as mortal. The problem in interpreting death is that of interpreting the self's experience of limitation and mortality, of dread and hope. Unless we give the complex consciousness of self its due, with its many vectors of experience, the meaning of death will remain either an unassimilated image of terror or a too-easily possessed symbol of transcendence.

What Becker concludes and what Boros assumes, is that our notion of death is actually the outcome of reflecting on data from three levels of our complex consciousness.

First, there is the primitive psychic level, the spontaneous flow of our feelings, the strange language of our dreams, the early conditioning of our childhood, the interiorisation of the bias of our culture. Here Becker is the authority.[17] How the psychic level enters into consciousness, to what degree it is irretrievably subliminal to consciousness in the bundle of neurones and physical dispositions of a given psyche is, of course, one of the great concerns of clinical psychology. To speak generally, it is consciousness of limits, above all those associated with being physically embodied, subject to biological limits, and located in time and space, the product of a certain culture—the person as 'some-*body*'.

Secondly, then there is the level of spirit, the self-transcending conscious self. Here Boros gives his impressive account.[18] We interact with a world; we ask questions about its meaning; we make judgments of fact and probability; we deliberate on our responsibilities. It is a restlessness that knows no quiet until all the data are in, all the questions asked, all the reasons considered, all the values scrutinised. As a trajectory, it faces us with ultimate questions: why is there something rather than nothing? What is the meaning of everything we have found meaningful? What is the sufficient reason for everything we judge to be true? What is the worthwhileness of everything we have treasured as valuable. This trajectory intimates an horizon of meaning, of truth and value which is, in principle, unlimited. We can of course stop this ultimate range of questions with a definite position: our consciousness is really a self-transcendence into nothingness, into meaningless, into a totally indifferent universe. Life is not a promise to be kept but simply a contingent phenomenon to be lived.

Then there is a third vector, that of faith.[19] The struggle of intelligence and moral concern upward, beyond itself into the objectively true and valuable and beautiful is met with new data: that of an ultimate mystery communicating itself. The love of God has been poured forth in our hearts by the Holy Spirit (Rom. 5:5) The Word has become flesh and dwelt among us. The ultimate mystery is revealed not as simply responding to our spiritual efforts, but as the grace, the inspiration, the love making self-transcendence possible, and promising its fulfilment.[20]

Given the polyphony of these three levels of consciousness, the problem is one of dissonance within ourselves. In any reflection on death, how is each voice given its due? How is the data on each of these levels of experience to be respected? For there is the dread of death as the psyche experiences it in the fragility and limitation of our embodied existence. There is the persistent longing of the spirit for ultimate meaning, absolute truth, universal good, supreme beauty which, while unattainable in this life, cause us to experience this life as a promise to be kept. Then, there is Christian hope in an ultimate Love revealing its transforming power in the death and resurrection of Christ. It is possible to understand each of these as contradictory, any one suppressing one or both of the other two, in something like a cacophony rather than the polyphony of the living work of art which each of us might be.

For, culturally speaking at least, we are the battle ground of conflicting ideologies. Each, with its own powerful mechanisms of repression and self-justification, works to insulate consciousness from the full experience of what we are. For example, a dogmatic religious hope that finds in death only the meaning of resurrection without registering any sense of the experienced deadliness of death, is hardly convincing. Is it really hope against hope, hope that knows the dark, deadly limits of life? A hope that has never wept, suffered, grieved the loss of loved ones, or known the fragility of life and the collapse of cherished projects looks like an escape from the human world rather than a hope for it. It would be a hope fleeing from the dread that occupies the psyche.

Similarly, a fundamentalist religious hope that does not know how to address itself to the human spirit, to the mind looking for meaning, to the heart longing for love and value, to the imagination searching for beauty and expanding in wonder, offers only an exotic, even alien, heaven instead of life to the full. In both cases, the question is inescapable: how can you be so hopeful about death when you have not lived?

If theology can provide its own repression of the deadliness of death, so can the human sciences hide it away. Philosophy can make its distinction between body and soul; and, in so doing, reserve death for the body only. The spiritual soul is immortal. The experience of death as the dark, obscene limit to personal existence is thus kept well under control. When the experience of death migrates from classical metaphysics to a more existentialist mode, philosophy highlights the creativity of human freedom. We are self-making beings in the drama of history and distinctive creativity. But here, too, the power of death can be all too neatly transcended. Personal courage is, of course, a desirable quality of life, but the only solution it offers in the face of death is defiance. An arrogant dismissal of death to the realm of non-meaning is no solution either.

Perhaps a transcendental type of philosophy, like that of Boros, fares better? There is a trajectory of the human spirit that thrusts forward to an unrestricted self-realisation in death. But why is life a promise to be kept? Is it all that clear that such a philosophy is not a flight from mortality, a kind of personal schizophrenia eschewing recognition of the obvious limits of our humanity? Further, such philosophies are very evidently expressions of hope. There are no qualified consultants on the experience of personal death. Thanatologists may indicate how the human person unfolds in various stages and new births. But in the end we are left with a theory or a reflection to trust in which purports to be a way of mastering death. The cosmic question which death poses remains unresolved.[21]

Thirdly, as Becker himself points out in his searching analysis of Freud,[22] a purely psychological approach can be immersed in its own immanent explanations of our morbid self-preoccupations. Because it sees the degree of our evasiveness and denial in the face of death, it wants to rub our noses in the reality of decay and limitation. The spiritual or the transcendent which are also part of given human experience are methodologically excluded. With its archaeological preoccupations, such reductionist psychology makes psychic health consist in a spiritually depressed way of life. Death, one way or another, becomes the absolute. The fear of it has to be managed if we are to lead a healthy life. Spirituality or faith are merely escape mechanisms for the terrified animal.

These are caricatures, obviously. They point to a more dialectical gathering together of the interpretations of the significance of death. Then, each of these elements would need to be given its due if the reality of death is to be given its due, and if the whole reality of human existence is to be acknowledged. What is required is to be fully converted to the human reality, so as not to disown any aspect of it. In this larger and more courageous acceptance, we begin a realistic owning of our mortality.

In the following chapter, we move on to a more concrete meditation on death.

1. For useful documentation: *See* Pierre Delooz, 'Death and the Hereafter', *Pro Mundi Vita: Dossiers*, 4/1985, pp.1–20; and the chapter, 'Dying with Human Dignity' in Hans Küng, *Eternal Life? Life after Death as a Medical, Philosophical and Theological Problem*, tr. E. Quinn, Doubleday and Co., New York, 1984, pp.150–175.
2. There is a huge amount of recent writing on death. *See* the most comprehensive, Albert J. Miller and Michael J. Acri, *Death: A Bibliographical Guide*, The Scarecrow Press, Metuchen, NJ, 1978.
3. E. Schillebeeckx, *Christ: The Christian Experience in the Modern World*, tr. J. Bowden, SCM Press, London, 1980,

p.642.
4. Ernest Becker, *The Denial of Death*, The Free Press, New York, 1973.
5. Ladislaus Boros, *The Moment of Truth: Mysterium Mortis*, tr. G. Bainbridge, Burns and Oates, 1962.
6. Becker, *The Denial of Death*, p.ix.
7. *ibid.* p.50.
8. *ibid.* p.51.
9. *ibid.* p.285.
10. *ibid.* p.282.
11. *ibid.* p.57.
12. *ibid.* p.58. *See also:* Andras Angyal, *Neurosis and Treatment: a Holistic Theory*, Wiley, New York, 1965, p.260.
13. Boros, *The Moment of Truth*, Burns & Oates, London, p.viii.
14. *ibid.* p.ix.
15. Becker, *op. cit.* pp.15–24.
16. Boros, *op. cit.* pp.31–35; 42–48; 62–68.
17. Becker, *op. cit.* pp.11–93.
18. Boros, *op. cit.* pp.1–23.
19. This is illuminated by Becker in his chapter on Kierkegaard, in *The Denial of Death*, pp.67–92, and expressly treated by Boros in his 'Theological Discussion', in *The Moment of Truth*, pp.81–171. For a critical presentation of Rahner's theology of death: *See* Peter Phan, *Eternity in Time*, pp.79–115.
20. For a fuller account of the religious dimension of self-transcendence: *See* Bernard Lonergan, *Method in Theology*, Darton, Longman and Todd, London, 1971, pp.101–112.
21. For a searching critique of various modern 'positive' approaches to death: *See* Bartholomew J. Collopy, 'Theology and the Darkness of Death', *Theological Studies* 39/1 (1978) pp.22–54.
22. Becker, *op. cit.* pp.93–124.

5 Meditation on Death

Hope must give death its due. It is not forearmed with philosophical, theological, or therapeutic consolation. An account of hope in any way repressive of the sadness and grief inherent in our lives ends by trivialising itself, perhaps communicating a kind of good news, but one that does not really allow a hearing for the bad news of our common mortality. The language of hope can never impatiently exclude all expression of grief from the human conversation.

Now these remarks on death are not the preface to a new theory. All I am saying for the moment is that faith, before it issues forth into a statement of hope, must pause for a very time-honoured meditation on death.[1] Hope has to begin with reality, and occupy the point where ordinary optimism or finite hopes come to an end. To be genuine, hope must be familiar with the whole experience of death. It must allow the range of darker symbols their proper psychological resonance.

Let me start with a few simple observations. Death is always integrated into a view of life. Even at our most morbid, life is going on, and the discussion is taking place among the living. For death is always experienced in the context of life and a view of life and the world it forms.[2]

Secondly, no one has ever experienced death personally. Near-death experiences are 'near death': but they might also be a long way from it, since those who live to tell the tale are now securely among the living.[3]

Nonetheless, if Christian hope is to avoid appearing as a repressive ideology, the imagination must befriend the dark, tragic, terminal reality that death is. We must go to the edge. Only at that limit where words run out and theories appear paper thin, can any stirring of hope escape delusion. Not to confront our mortality is to leave it buried, unnamed, beneath layers of frenzied optimism, perhaps to surface from time to time in recurring bouts of depression. We can, indeed, take refuge in work or thought or art or religion. We might even try to keep death at bay by drugging our sensibilities, or by the sturdy securities of home and family. But finally, it draws near; and all the utopias, or plans, or theories the human brain can spin out eventually stand forth as provisional against the day on which we die.[4]

With such a concern, a healthy hope knows how to meditate on death. In all the varieties of such imagination, the following points are always present:

First, death is an end. It is final. We die and we stay dead. There is no coming back to this life, no resuscitation. It is over. Whatever the hopes we might have, there is no hanging back, no holding on. Death does have its own deadly finality. It is the termination of the only existence we have experienced. All the seasons and cycles, developments, achievements, relationships, plans and commitments, in a piercingly obvious way, come to an end. No one comes back. Any attempt to feel for that reality or to express it would be awry if it did not or would not use the symbol of the end point, the termination, the full stop, the dead end.

Secondly, death is alien and violent. No matter what our faith might be in a gracious and nurturing universe, at the moment of death that larger reality, even though it has engendered and nourished us and housed our whole being, swallows us up into something incomprehensibly alien and impersonal. It all turns against us in some total way. It has no more room for this living being, nor knows any demand that it should keep on living. What was most friendly and supportive now occurs as alien, weird, destructive in death's dreadful otherness.

Thirdly, death is dark. There is no practical or theoretical way of mastering the reality of death, no comprehension to place it as a specific object in some larger scheme in which it might be solved as a problem. No faith, myth or theory can guide the mind or heart into the impenetrable darkness of the end. It terminates consciousness in the one who dies, and leaves the minds that watch in bewilderment.

And then, fourthly, death is silent, the realm of non-communication. The dead enter into an ultimate aloneness. There, no human voice can reach them, just as they have irreversibly dropped out of the human conversation. In that realm of utter isolation, they neither speak nor hear. They cannot be reached. Hence the symbol of death is that silence into which all human words fade.

Fifthly, death has its own overwhelming power. It leaves us radically impotent. Against its force no human authority or expertise can prevail. It can never be faced 'professionally'. All the competence and capacity of human life are brought to nothing; no security or status can hold out against it. The brute power of death allows for no solution, no manipulation, no therapy, no inspired human inventiveness—no way out. It leaves us in an utter poverty against which there is no security. In the presence of death, we are all amateurs.

Finally, death is ugly, obscene, repulsive. The forces of an irreversible collapse undermine all the reality of life as joy, beauty, pleasure. The golden grace of youth and the wise, gentle attainments of age are eaten up. The corpse, intact for only a short time, mocks the abundance of life that once was. No cosmetic art can conceal the essential decay. History might make its monuments, but what was, has irreversibly collapsed.

Even if the records of words and deed are now enhanced by recordings of the living voice and moving form, they are even more poignant reminders of our powerlessness in recalling those who have gone: images can be stored in files to be retrieved at will, but there is no retrieval of a living presence. Each generation has its day, only to be swallowed up in the dust of the earth.

The deadliness of death resides in what we have termed its alien, dark, silent, violent, ugly finality. Even as we evoke such experiences, we will probably find that our hope is busy about their refutation. Death is not the end, but an entry into true life; not something alien but a birth into a new existence; not an ultimate isolation but a final relationship; not an obscene fact but a surrender to the mystery of existence: surely death does not have the last word, but love, life, hope, surrender...?

But that is precisely the point. For this present earthly existence, death, in an obvious, inevitable sense, *is* the last word. Hope, however it might reach beyond death, must never deny the fact of death nor minimise the grief and the mourning of the world. Though hope inspires surrender to a mystery beyond this world, there is no mastering of death within it. A hope familiar with death must let the ultimate have its way with us in all the darkness of life's dissolution.

Such a meditation on death does not aim to excite a morbid sense of dread at the expense of the quiet patience of hope. On the contrary, the purpose of such a meditation is to release the hopeful consciousness into a deeper authenticity in the face of death: if death is given its due, hope is free to be itself. In short, in the presence of death, when life is grasped as 'being-towards death',[5] we are all brought back to the starting line. If the race does not start from scratch, it is not a true contest. Christian hope, or any other kind of religious hope, does not have an unfair advantage; it is not spared the reality of death, it has to go the whole distance, covering all the territory from the extreme point of darkness to the further limits of the light that it declares is already shining.

Meditating on death reminds one of those baroque pictures of saints with a skull in their hands. The skull objectivises an undeniable aspect of human reality. Such a melancholy symbol is meant to energise life, so that with less illusion, less attachment to what cannot last, it might go forward with greater freedom and intensity.

Meditating on life

Still, a discerning appropriation of one's consciousness finds more than a skull. I am more than a body inevitably given over to a process of decay and eventual collapse. Indeed, the realistic courage of anyone meditating on death is itself evidence of a self capable of transcending illusion and destructive obsessions: it points to a self beholden to a larger world, however demanding that world might be. Meditation on death provokes a more comprehensive meditation on the wonder of life. An examination of conscience in the presence of death opens the way to an examination of consciousness in the light of life.

Such an examination of consciousness discovers the ever-present, dynamic, unfolding of a living self. For it begins to reflect on the data of the actual, accessible experience of the conscious, acting, human self that each of us is. This is not to rely on some prior theory of the soul with its various faculties, but to tune into the experience of the living self, to the self as an 'I', not as an 'it', to the personal subject. This conscious 'I' is present in the actions of any one of us, in the shared 'we' realised in any instance of the shared life and community belonging. Here we are not dealing with abstract 'human nature', but the particular conscious self, not as morbidly self-absorbed, but as vitally pushed and pulled into the attractive and demanding reality of what is other, of what is most meaningful, most plausible, most appealing, most worthwhile, most real, in our world, and in ourselves.[6]

The examination of consciousness aims to catch us in action, as it were, in that ongoing self-transcending movement which makes for genuine human living. Technical philosophy, as it investigates the basic phenomenon of human consciousness, draws attention to the manner in which this expands through all its inter-related levels of sensing, feeling, understanding, judging, deciding, loving and praying. It is all there in a usually unnoticed manner: we experience, feel, think, ask questions, reflect further, judge, decide, always being drawn out of ourselves in wonder, responsibility and self-surrender.[7] To be a self is to self-present as a mystery of relationship, of openness, of movement within a limitless horizon. It is to exist within a world of becoming, within an uncanny universe of being.[8]

This, along with all the evidence of dissolution and decay, is an accessible given in our living awareness—the self as ever transcending itself towards what is another, a fuller, a richer, a more expansive self-realisation. It is a movement fuelled by a universe of meaning, truth, value, beauty. For everyone is a self ever in the process of becoming, ever in the making, intimately involved with the inexpressibly larger emergence of the universe itself.

Admittedly, it is not an uncomplicated upward and outward trajectory. For the self experiences many deaths in its process of becoming: the hard decision, the narrow way, the demands of self-sacrifice, failure, guilt or disgrace, starting all over again, the weight of sickness, discouragement and exhaustion—all the familiar experiences of dying many times, compared to which our eventual real death might well appear as a happy release.

But to return to the point: meditating on death is set in the larger context of meditating on life. We own not only our mortality, but the whole restless, insistent dynamism of our lives. This manner of meditating on life discloses a radical, hopeful thrust in our existence. Our real self is always ahead of us, yet to be more fully realised. Not to decide, is to settle for a self less than what we feel we are meant to be. Not to love more generously is to fall back into a willed isolation. Not to ask uncomfortable questions opens the way to mere conformism or defensiveness. Not to be open to the great challenges of the day is to bury one's head in the dangerously shifting sand. Not to refine our perceptions of the splendours of art is to be barbarian in regard to all the beauty that human beings appreciate and create. Not to risk all, at the dramatic juncture when all is demanded, is to live with a sense of self-disgust and guilt.

On the other hand, to give ourselves into the ongoing challenge to transcend a present self-realisation by being more attentive, more aware, more objective, more intent on pursuing real values and caring for real people is to be creative selves in an expanding horizon of life. Our world is understood, explored, and even transformed, by the manifold creativity of self-transcending action. In the hopeful thrust of actual living, such acting selves are ever renewing the world grown old in nonsense, deceit, malice and ugliness with meaning, honesty, forgiveness and beauty. They respond to the questions that life poses with all the supremely meaningful works of science, art, philosophy, religion and politics. Further, it is a world that is not only analysed or interpreted, but a world that is being increasingly directed in its histories, great and small, by human activity. For it is always within us to ask not only: What is the explanation for the way things are? but also: What is to be done?; not only: What may be done? but: What should be done in accord with everything we value in ourselves, in others, in the world, in the universe itself?

Such a real world is a free world, at least in the

sense of facing every human person with his or her personal conscience: reality is so complex, and the dimensions of human responsibility so daunting, that the temptation to allow oneself to become a rootless nomad, a conformist, or even an automaton, is quite real. To be more, is to break out of the closed circle of private satisfactions and fears into a solidarity with others in the pursuit of a radical commonwealth of values. Only in this way can an elemental justice be possible, in the family, city, society, nation, and in the emerging planetary society of our day.

This world which we meaning-makers and value-seekers find and form is one which is continually taking us to the limit: limits to human life in death, failure, guilt; all the limitations of time and space and energy. To find these limits in our consciousness, is to live, even if not to formulate, a whole series of questions: Is our self-transcendence, with all its struggle and many dyings, a movement into death, into ultimate defeat, into cosmic worthlessness? Are we simply at the mercy of a history and a universe ultimately indifferent to what we find within ourselves to be the direction of true life?

There are, too, inextricably tied up with all the experience of negativity, of the limits that close us in, the positive experiences of limits of another kind, the frontiers of something else. Events occur in which we are taken out of ourselves in the direction of what the dull eye of routine, the deaf ear of preoccupation, the numbed heart of too much calculation has failed to notice before : these are moments of wonder, joy, the experience of great loves, the strange grandeur of moral achievement. In such moments, there is an uncanny 'more' in the experience of the mystic, the artist, the martyr, the prophet, the great thinker. Such people dramatise what all of us feel, perhaps more tentatively, as the direction in which we are called.

The great question of the universe itself throbs within our consciousness as it nourishes us with its wonder and invites us into our freedom. Is the world of our varied and problematic experience the ultimately real world? Is our meaningful world lost in an ultimately meaningless universe? Is our moral world ultimately pointless in an indifferent universe? Is the world of our dramatic human history finally insignificant as a minor moment in the unfolding of an impersonal universe? Are all hopes gesticulations in a world that holds no promise? Wherein lies the hope of the following wise advice?

> *If you surprise the world with your life, the world will surprise you at death. Don't think of death as extinction; such uninspired speculations are simply too prosaic to be true. Your dull imagination insults the very grandeur and staggering wonder of the universe...embrace your death. It will serve you.*[9]

The human self is thus a question, a hope embodied in the uncanny universe of all that is. Only by expanding into the domain of religious faith and hope do we find an answer. In the judgment of religious faith, we find the assurance that our lives are a promise to be kept.

However religious hopes are expressed, they at least affirm this: the horizon of life is no longer a blank signifying nothingness, not a mere screen on which human beings project futile desires in a doomed search for meaning and worth; not a black hole swallowing up the whole human endeavour into some final, unwitnessed extinction. Rather, such an horizon of life, even though it can never be fully expressed, is experienced as filled with the all-fulfilling presence we commonly name, 'God'—the ultimate reality in which we live and move and have our being.

The homing of the self

How the homecoming of our deepest self is best expressed will always remain a challenge. The world of religious experience indicates a field of life occurring within this world but is not of it:

> *There is in the world, as it were, a charged field of love and meaning; here and there it reaches a notable intensity: but it is ever unobtrusive, hidden, inviting us to join. And join we must if we are to perceive it, for our perceiving is through our loving.*[10]

It is the 'peace the world cannot give', a 'joy that no one can take from you', a hope leaving the conviction that what we shall be has not yet fully been revealed. That it occurs seems clear, in the faith and hope and love of millions of people who inhabit this planet. For they live in a field of new ultimate awareness with its implications of loving familiarity with the mystery of the universe, self-sacrifice in the face of suffering and death, new hopeful patterns of belonging to the human community, of participating in human history, of facing all the ills bedevilling the world.

So it is that a meditation on death is set within the larger process of meditating on life as an insistent orientation to further, and even absolute, fulfilment. The objectivity of death is thus integrated into the continuous unfolding of the self-transcending subject. In this style of reflection, the fact of our mortality comes into our consciousness as a final act or mode of self-transcendence. Death is now a matter of dying into the ultimate mystery of life. It is a necessary moment in the unfolding of the human self to yield itself into infinite mystery as the ground and goal of all our being and doing.

It is hardly surprising then, that those who have entered most deeply into this process of progressive self-realisation, and extended it into eschatological contexts, see the moment of death itself as a final act or moment of freedom in which the human spirit achieves its relationship to the whole universe; thus, to enter into a final form or process of embodiment in the universe.[11] Since our consciousness is ever expanding through all the activities and stages of life, it is argued, why not see death as a moment of maximum expansion and realisation? The emphasis here is not morbid in Becker's sense, but hopeful. This hope is born out of the basic thrust and direction of our conscious life in the unfolding of our lived experience.

The passion of Christ

But to return to the problem. How can we anchor a theology of death that is neither depressive nor schizophrenic? Forcing our meditations to the consideration of the skull risks a tragic forgetfulness of the positive hopeful direction of our lives in this world. But concentrating on that hopeful fullness might find us out as repressing the piercing tragedy at the heart of our existence. The mystery of death has to integrate both the negative and the positive dimensions of our experience. Yet these extremes don't simply meet. How then, can they best be held in hopeful realistic tension?

As we turn to the mystery on which Christian hope bases itself, we find a symbol which can allow both meanings to exist, and to illumine each other. This has to be the crucifixion and death of Christ himself.[12] The meditation of the Christian is not fixated on a skull, but on the cross of Jesus. For the Crucified has taken into himself the deadliness of death as a brutal ending, as a realm of darkness and isolation, as an overwhelming power stretching him before human gaze in the obscenity of torture and public condemnation.

But, to Christian faith, the death of Jesus crucified manifests the ultimate form of life as self-surrender. Jesus' unreserved dedication to the Kingdom of his Father in solidarity with the poor and the lost leads him through many testings to a final point of self-offering. In this ending, God is now free to be revealed as a love stronger than death. There will be no resuscitation to this life, no return to what has to be left behind. Only a transformation of human existence can answer the hopes written into a life of all-inclusive love. Faith will always recall that love's victory is not a cure for death, but its transformation into an act of ultimate love. For the one who is our way, our truth, and our life bears forever the stigmata of his death. If 'by his wounds you have been healed' (I Pet. 2:24), it is because his wounds were first borne in compassion for our common humanity in all that most terrifies and defeats us:

In the days of his flesh, Jesus offered up prayers and supplications, with loud cries and tears to him who was able to save him from death (Heb. 5:7).

Before the cross becomes a symbol of hope as a way through death and beyond it, it is first of all a way into it. The followers of Christ must go with him into the dreaded darkness; there to wait with him for the light to shine: 'Since therefore the children share in flesh and blood, he himself likewise partook of the same nature, that, through death, he might destroy him who has the power of death' (Heb. 2:14–18).

Hope, then, remains hope. It is never immune to the darkness of life. In the patience that waits for the whole mystery of love stronger than any death, even the New Testament writer takes us to a point of sober realism:

As it is, we do not yet see everything in subjection to him. But we see Jesus who for a little while was made lower than the angels, crowned with glory and honour because of the suffering of death so that by the grace of God he might taste death for everyone (Heb. 2:8f.).

Our meditation on death has now led us to a meditation on the passion, death and resurrection of the

Lord.

1. A classic of this genre is St Alphonsus de Liguori, *Preparation for Death*, Eugene Grimm, (ed.), Redemptorist Fathers, Brooklyn, 1926.
2. How the theme of death and dying might be integrated into a contemporary spirituality is well explored in 'Spirituality, Death and Dying', *Studies in Formative Spirituality*, 11/2, May 1981.
3. See Hans Küng, *Eternal Life?...*, pp.1–20.
4. See B.J. Collopy, 'Theology and the Darkness of Death', *Theological Studies* 19/1, 1978, pp.22–54. I am indebted to this fine article in what follows, especially to the section, 'Lineaments of a Dark Model', pp.39–47.
5. Heidegger's phrase. For one of the most influential and searching philosophical reflections on mortality: *See* Martin Heidegger, *Being and Time*, trans. J. Macquarrie and E. Robinson, Harper and Row, New York, 1962, pp.279–358.
6. Especially in *Method in Theology*, Darton, Longman and Todd, London, 1971, pp.3–25; 104f.
7. For an extraordinarily stimulating analysis of the experience of self: *See* Walker Percy, *Lost in the Cosmos. The Last Self-Help Book*, Farrar, Straus and Giroux, New York, 1983.
8. *See* Zachary Hayes, *Visions of a Future...*, pp.71–88.
9. Brian Swimme, *The Universe is a Green Dragon: A Cosmic Creation Story*. Bear and Co., Santa Fe, 1984, p.117.
10. Bernard Lonergan, *Method in Theology*, p.290.
11. For more on Rahner's theory: *See* Peter Phan, *Eternity in Time...*, pp.79–134; and, on a more popular level, Marie Murphy, *New Images of the Last Things*, Paulist Press, New York 1988, pp.13–19.
12. Gustave Martelet, *L'au-delà retrouvé: Christologie des fins dernières*, Desclée, Paris, 1975, pp.33–98.

6 The Paschal Mystery: the Parable of Hope

In what follows, we will be exploring how the heart of hope is formed in the heart of darkness. Only when hope is familiar with death's darkness and silence, when it feels death's lethal power, can hope come into its own. When death is neither denied, nor mastered, hope is freed to be itself in surrender to the mystery of ultimate life.

Both the heart of hope and the heart of darkness are found in the paschal mystery of the passion, death, burial and resurrection of Christ. In the agony of the crucified Jesus, our hope is prevented from denying the deadliness of death. In his death and burial, hope is forced to make time for all the dimensions of human grief and dread. In the resurrection of the crucified one, it surrenders to the mystery of our transformation in God.

As it meditates through the 'three holy days', the *sacrum triduum* of Good Friday, Holy Saturday and Easter Sunday, Christian hope is given time to expand into its authentic proportions.[1] The manner in which an ultimate love times itself through three days invites our hope to attend to its fundamental parable. The teller of parables becomes, in himself, God's supreme parable of the last things. If the other parables of the Gospel upset the usual world of our experience and draw us into the universe of grace, the cross and resurrection of Jesus do this with maximum intensity.

The whole drama of human existence is enacted in the happenings of these three holy days. The 'passing over' of Jesus through death to resurrection is not merely a time remembered, nor merely a story told. As the fundamental form and movement of our world, it is the mystery given to engage every aspect of our personal, communal and cosmic existence.

So, as hope's timing, as its parable and as its present mystery, the 'passing over' of Christ provides the primary symbolism of hope's eschatological expression. The analogical imagination finds its proper creativity within such a time and space and structure. All particular questions about eternal life are interconnected here.

By locating the expression of hope in the paschal mystery, we escape any tendency either to displace our hopes into an evolutionary myth or to distort it by fundamentalist fantasy. If the former tendency results in reducing Christian hope to a minor variant of evolutionary optimism, the latter, more often than not is bent on manipulating it to some unredeemed purpose.

So let us go on to meditate on these three holy days as a brief exploration of our hope's fundamental form and direction.

Good Friday

In any language, the cross is an obscene and tragic event. To confess that God could allow the crucifixion of his chosen one, was for the Jews a scandal, and for the Greeks a folly, to say nothing of its subversive implications for the imperial authority. Yet Paul integrates this 'foolishness of God' into his hope in the transcendent power at work: 'for the foolishness of God is wiser than men, and the weakness of God is stronger than men' (I Cor. 1:25).

Indeed, the Gospels evidence a kind of divine necessity regarding the cross: 'The Son of Man *must* suffer many things...and be rejected...and be killed...' (Mk

8:31; Mt. 16:21; Lk 17:25). But this necessity does not make Jesus the victim of either a blind fate or a capricious divine will. Rather, his passion and death result from his unreserved commitment to what was ultimate in his life: the saving will of his Father. His crucifixion is the outcome of his solidarity with the poor and the lost. For the all-inclusive Reign of God is the great central symbol of Jesus' imagination. As such, it enables him to present himself as agent and embodiment of the incalculable grace of God at work in human history. Through his preaching and symbolic actions, the Reign of God implies a field or 'state of grace' into which all are summoned. In the dramatic unfolding of his career, through conflict and temptation, Jesus stakes the whole meaning of his life and his whole identity as Son on the ultimacy of the Reign of God.

Hence, Jesus' acceptance of the cross, in dying disgraced, abandoned and condemned, is not obedience to some kind of arbitrary, external divine will. It is bound up with his identity and vocation as Son. His involvement with the Kingdom brings him to this tragic and obscene conclusion. John puts this in more human terms: 'Having loved his own who were in the world, he loved them to the end' (Jn 13:1). The end that came in the cross was the outcome of who he was and what he stood for: a universe of grace exploding the boundaries of a self-enclosed world.

The will of God was the fundamental nourishment of his existence (Jn 4:34). The inevitable extrinsic connotations of doing the will of God are helpfully refined when we realise that this came to him above all through the interior inspiration of the Spirit which possessed and empowered him.

For in this Spirit he is conceived (Lk 1:35) and anointed (Lk 4:18; Acts 4:27; 10:38). The Spirit that descends on him is the force in which he moves to his mission (Mk 1:10–12). As such, it is the fundamental instinct of his life (Lk 4:14,18; 10:21). The Spirit acts through him as the power of the new creation (Mt. 12:18–21, 28). In the power of this Holy Spirit, he is led to confront Satan and the evil spirits in all their variety—all the forces of the anti-realm which enslave human beings and tempt them to settle for a world less than the universe of God's grace (cf. Mk 1:12f., 21–28; 3:11f.; 3:2–30; Lk 4:1–13; 11:22). Indeed, this Spirit is not only the fundamental instinct of the life of Jesus, but also the last breath of his final self-offering in death. In this 'eternal Spirit', he surrenders himself on the cross into the mystery of God (Heb. 9:14). And, in his last moment, Jesus breathes forth his Spirit to be the source and witness of eternal life (Jn 19:30).

Led by this Spirit, Jesus comes to the crucial moment of the cross. It is literally the *crux* of the meaning of his mission and identity, for in his suffering and death, the character of ultimate reality is tested: will his Spirit be revealed as truly Holy? Will he be confirmed in his identity as Son of the Father? Will the Kingdom come? Will God, can God, still be the true God in the real world of this terminal encounter with the power of evil?

Such questions can be more deeply posed in their trinitarian form: how will God prove himself to be the Father of Jesus? How can Jesus live his completely filial existence even in failure and rejection? How is the Spirit the power of ultimate life even in the shocking vulnerability of this death?

The concentrated eschatological significance of Good Friday is anticipated in various themes related to the day before, the Holy Thursday. First, there is the eminently Johannine theme of the 'hour' of Jesus.[2] This hour is the absolutely decisive time. It will include all the moments of Jesus' glorification (Jn 12:23), of the world's judgment and of the expulsion of its ruler (12:31); when, in showing his unreserved love for the world, he will pass out of this world to the Father (13:1); when his followers will be scattered and he will be left alone, save for his mysterious union with the

Father (13:32). The hour of Jesus waits on the disclosure of ultimate love: 'Father, the hour has come; glorify thy Son that thy Son may glorify thee... to give eternal life to all whom thou hast given him' (17:1f.).

This meaning of this hour is enacted in Jesus' washing of the feet of his disciples. Out of this action comes the command to love as he has loved. Such loving is thereby presented as the ultimate form of life, even if it is experienced as powerless within the world of darkness. It draws its energy from the promise of the other Counsellor 'to be with you forever, even the Spirit of truth, whom the world cannot receive...he dwells with you, and will be in you' (Jn 14:17).

The crucial intensity of what John describes as this hour and in the new commandment of love is portrayed in the second anticipatory theme, what the Synoptics portray in the eucharistic self-giving in the Last Supper. The covenant history of God with his people culminates in Jesus giving himself as food and drink in the bread and wine of the meal: 'This is my body given up for you...the new covenant in my blood which is poured out for many for the forgiveness of sins' (Mt 26:27). Such words draw their force from the impending reality of the cross. By surrendering himself to the all-demanding will of the Father, Jesus is giving himself into the depths of the human crisis: 'Do this in memory of me'.

Later, Paul will correct the euphoric amnesia of the Corinthians with the words, 'As often as you eat the bread and drink the cup, you proclaim the death of the Lord until he come' (I Cor. 11:26). History is brought to its eschatological point by the self-giving of Jesus unto death. For the eucharist is the memorial of the sacrificial character of Jesus' existence as it reaches its conclusion in the cross. He is both with and for 'the many', in all their worlds of alienation. Communion with him must express a similar compassion if it is to be celebrated in its authentic meaning.

The Gospel narratives add further intensity to these

themes in their various presentations of the 'Agony in the Garden'.[3] With different stresses these depict Jesus' agonising awareness of the eschatological denouement. In Mark, above all, Jesus experiences an agony of isolation in the heart of darkness. He is offered the cup of complete earthly failure. The world bears down on him as utterly opaque to the light of God. It has become pure resistance to the Kingdom, as the Son and the prophet of God's Reign, is left at the mercy of the world closed against its only future. There is no sign of the Father's presence: 'His soul began to be greatly distressed and troubled' (Mk 14:33). He falls to the ground, praying that the hour might pass. So much does he feel the pressure of the infinite weight of the world's fate that Luke will add the graphic detail of the bloody sweat (Lk 22:44).

In this state of utter collapse, with his disciples asleep and the triumph of his enemies impending, he is stripped of everything except his character as Son. There is no remaining psychological possibility of the 'vital lie' (Becker). Yet this terminal moment wrings from him an act of ultimate, hopeful self-surrender to the will of his Father at its most dreaded and impenetrable point: 'Abba...all things are possible to thee...remove this cup from me; yet not what I will, but what thou wilt' (Mk 14:36). The existential drama of this hour is cryptically summed up in the Letter to the Hebrews, 'Son though he was, he learnt obedience' (Heb. 5:8).

Though John presents Jesus as the Lord of life moving serenely in the eye of the storm, the Synoptics present him drawn into the vortex of eschatological crisis. His whole being is in spasm as his mind is possessed by an appalling vision: the nullification of everything he had lived for. He is left in the heart of darkness with nothing except what the Father can be. In the Father, for whom all things are possible, now lies hope's only hope. Jesus is not a Jewish martyr, like the Maccabees suffering for Israel. He is not a post-resurrection Christian following the way of his crucified and risen Lord. He is the Son, emptied of everything, become pure prayer, total surrender to the possibilities of God. 'Not as I will, but as thou wilt' (Mk 14:36). His words, 'Rise, let us be going' (v.42) express the freedom of an absolute hope which trusts, even at the most impenetrable moment, that the Kingdom will come on its own terms and in its own evidence. He refuses to commit himself to anything else but the mysterious conditions of the Father's will which, in essence, demands that this Son be, indeed, truly human:

> *Put your sword back into its place. For all who take the sword will perish by the sword. Do you think that I cannot appeal to my Father and he will at once send me twelve legions of angels? But how then should the scriptures be fulfilled that it must be so?* (Mt 26:52ff.).

In such nakedness, Jesus is one with the hopeless of the world. He realises an agonising solidarity with those lost in a world estranged from the only God they know, for whom God has to be God in a way they have never known before. He is the victim of a world in which grace has no worldly power, where evil is the most obvious reality, and God merely a remote possibility.

The once all-affirming, life-giving presence of the Father now seems a massive absence, just as the Spirit seems extinguished within him, and all his relationships corroded by desertion and betrayal.

How the disciples themselves experienced this ultimate darkness is strikingly evoked by Sebastian Moore as he imagines a disciple speaking:

> *There is nothing left of the magic dream which Jesus conjured up and persuaded us to step into with both feet, that dream which became for us the world.* (Yet) *it was not like a dream; on the contrary it was the most real state of*

*mind and feeling we had ever known. We had
been schooled from our earliest years to believe
in God. This was as though all that we had
believed about God was coming true. It was
the uncanny feeling of stepping through the ancient words and images into the thing itself.
These words and their images appeared to us
now as the creation of men: in the company of
this man, they seemed like the discarded toys of
an earlier age. Yet nothing was thrown away.
It was not a case of believing something different. It was a case of believing more; of
believing more because now we saw. All that
we had ever believed, our whole past as pious
Jews, came miraculously alive...*

*Now all this has gone. Everything has gone.
It is not merely the absence of God, an experience known so well to our people and our
prophets, but the death of God.*[4]

One of his disciples, Judas, betrays him to the parties who have been plotting for months to destroy him.
They hand him over to the Jewish leaders. From the
Sanhedrin he is taken to the Roman governor. Pilate
passes him along to the local puppet king. Herod
sends him back to Pilate. The Governor offers him to
the mercy of the mob. Betrayed by one of his own,
denied by the leader of those he had chosen to walk
with him, left for lost by the rest of them, despised now
by his own people, libelled by false witnesses, he is
condemned in the courts of the secular and religious
authorities alike.

Then, after being tortured by the police and soldiers
guarding him, he is taken to be executed in the
hideous manner of crucifixion. He had spoken little in
his defence, and in the end remained completely silent.
What he had to say, had all been said. In all this the
'power of darkness' carries him on to his fate, as a
demonic force rejecting in him the world's only hope.

In all this, we glimpse the eerily intractable power of evil. No one is exclusively to blame; but, in the dark conspiracies of self-justification, no one is innocent.

His death is a shrouded in many darknesses. All he had lived for was ending in obvious defeat. He is found guilty by both the religious and secular authorities of his world. He has been betrayed by a disciple, abandoned by friends, rejected by his own people. Prolonged, obscene, humiliating torture is followed by the most hideous form of execution known to the ancient world. At this point of intense isolation, he feels the most dreadful darkness of all: the One whom he has so lovingly and easily invoked as his Father is now an abyss of absence.

The cross is the climax of the power of darkness. God appears as banished from his good creation, just as that creation appears as a self-enclosed world. In condemning the Son to the cross, the injustice of the world appears as just; and the crucified Son, far from being accepted as the bringer of the Kingdom and the true form of our humanity, appears as a criminal. He is 'counted among the wicked' (Mk 15:28), 'made sin' (II Cor. 5:21). He 'has become a curse for us, for it is written 'Cursed be everyone who hangs on a tree' (Gal. 3:13). As the Gospel invites its readers, in Pilate's words, to 'behold the man' (Jn 19:5), it implies a judgment on our standard versions of humanity: the projections of human pride collide with the humanity of the Word incarnate.

In the cross of Jesus are concentrated all the enigmatic experiences that make for the problem of evil: the defencelessness of the good, the absence of God, the immorality of 'morality', the destructive perversity of preferring to cause death rather than allow for life. The Cross stands as the sign of a world of a humanity disowning its own grace and promise. It wrings from the crucified an agonised prayer, 'Eloi, Eloi, lama sabacthani? My God, My God why hast thou abandoned me?', and culminates in his loud last cry as he breathes his last (Mk 15:34,37). Mark does not let us forget that this hope is built on Jesus' experience of the stark deadliness of his death in that real world where infinite love appears as the most defenceless, the maximally unreal of truths.[5]

Still, in other Gospel accounts, the cross is the realisation of the freedom of Jesus in his ultimate surrender: 'Father, into your hands I commend my spirit' (Lk 23:46), and 'It is finished' (Jn 19:30). He yields himself into an incalculable mystery of grace that it might still be grace even at this most impenetrable point of the world's darkness. To meditate on the passion of Christ is to be drawn into the drama of his naked self-surrender.

As death looms, his progressive silence in the face of questions, accusations and unbelief, anticipates the silence of death. If love has brought him to death, only love can prove itself stronger than death. By letting matters take their course, he is letting the Kingdom come on its own terms: '"Where are you from?" But Jesus made no further answer so that Pilate wondered' (Jn 19:9). The new creation is beyond human expression.

The cross is thus presented as provoking the disclosure of the eschatological reality of God. The power of evil challenges, as it were, the mystery of God to reveal itself, to declare its essential reality. God would not be God if he were defeated. And he would have been defeated if the transcendent mystery were reduced to the level of worldly powerplay, answering evil with evil, making an eye for an eye and a tooth for a tooth a cosmic law binding even the reality of God himself.

Yet there is no divine vengeance. God is not changed into violence or revenge. He is no mere worldly power. He sends no legion of angels. For the Father refuses to have any presence in the world save that of the crucified Son. And as this Son prays for the forgiveness of those who have crucified him, he rejects any worldly identity, any worldly justification or protection save what the Father can be for him. At the point of demonic concentration of evil, he surrenders himself to an all-Holy Spirit as the last breath of his life. This Spirit, inspiring the self-giving death of Christ for the many, has no other identity, works in no other power, than that of unconditional love. The trinitarian communion of self-sacrificing love brings a new crucified humanity into existence.

Human hope can live only from this form of life—and death: 'By this shall all men know that you are my disciples, if you have love, one for another' (Jn 13:35). Hope for the future bears the mark of the cross: '...always carrying in the body the death of Jesus...for while we live, we are always being given up to death for Jesus' sake, so that the life of Jesus will be manifest in our mortal flesh...' (II Cor. 4:11; cf. Rom. 6:3).

The genesis of a new community of crucified hope is represented in various ways in the Scriptures in Simon of Cyrene, the courageous presence of the women, the humble prayer of 'the good thief', Mary and the beloved disciple at the foot of the cross, the Roman centurion, Joseph of Arimathea...These representative figures embody a new hope that 'nothing in all creation, not even the most intense form of the power of evil, death itself, can separate us from the love of God in Christ Jesus our Lord' (Rom. 8:39). The eschatological parable of the crucified has opened a new horizon for human existence.

Significantly, too, for eschatological reflection, the event of the cross is accompanied by the apocalyptic signs of the appearance of the dead, darkness over the land, the rending of the temple veil leading to the Gentile confession of the identity of Jesus: 'Truly, this man was the Son of God' (Mt 27:51–54). Such signs must be taken as a biblical perception of the universal significance of the new order of reality which has occurred in the death of Jesus. An ultimate love has given itself for the world and a new creation is coming to birth. In the momentous tragedy of the cross, something happens at the heart of the universe.

Holy Saturday

This middle day of the paschal mystery is often passed over by theology without comment, just as the descent of Christ into 'hell' continues to be a puzzling article of the creed: 'crucified, died and was buried. He descended into hell'.[6] But authentic hope needs to take its time. It must have the freedom to dwell on this day when Jesus is truly dead among the dead—dead and buried, cut off from the land of the living, with all relationships sundered, gone down into the dread place of death. The patience of hope must replace the impatience of a repressive optimism. There is no room for automatically interpreting the cross as resurrection.

Not to have time for this day means repressing the horror and the mystery of the real death of Jesus. For making his death simply *mean* resurrection is a serious denial of the deadliness of death, and one more effort to master it. To leave out this day, to reduce the paschal mystery simply to two days, is to leave too much out. It takes the endurance and patience out of hope (Rom. 5:3ff.) to hurry past the fact that Jesus, in his surrender to the divine will, experienced the full death in its starkest reality. Neither for him nor any other human being did death simply mean resurrection!

Leaving space and having time for this second day, when liturgically no Alleluia is sung and the altars are stripped bare, acts as a corrective to any hope hiding from the true agony of life. For, to repeat, it is the day when Jesus lies in the tomb, buried, dead among the dead, the day when death means death, not life.

We dare not prematurely smuggle into his experience an anticipation of resurrection—as though this were the automatic consequence of going down into death's darkness. The cross meant that Jesus was stripped of everything save what God can be and what love can do. It meant being emptied into the mercy of the divine freedom. Human time now had to yield to 'God's good time'. Death is not prematurely robbed of its sting. So, before death means life, before death leads to life, death means...death! Jesus was crucified, died, and was buried. His tortured corpse lay in the tomb. This day contemplates him as shrouded in the silence, darkness, defeat and isolation of the world of the dead.

Sebastian Moore has the disciple expressing the experience of Holy Saturday in these words:

It is the day after the day which saw the end. Sleep came to us, the heavy stupid sleep of overwhelming shock and loss. After sleep, refreshed, we experienced the world without what till recently we had. The world awakes, and we with it, empty. There is a settling. The emptiness of the world without God, now we realise, has its own voice, different from the voice of shock and grief. Everybody knows that curious comfort which is in bereavement, of a weight lifted. However intense the love, the loss is a weight lifted... There is no God for the emptiness; for the emptiness is his denial. When people feel it, they feel there is no God. No one will ever know how we feel it today.[7]

Jesus' descent into hell is an article of the creed from the Fourth Century. As such, it at least expresses the full human character of Jesus' death. He is one with us not only on the surface of life, not only in the experience of life's mortal agonies, but in going down into the underworld of the dead. To the degree that we are prepared to enter more deeply into the grief in which Christian hope is born, we can begin to catch the realism of Christ's radical solidarity with human fate.

It is not only a matter of letting this Saturday have

its place before Easter Sunday, but of letting death in general, and this death in particular, leave us bereft of easy philosophical and theological preconceptions. The brute experience of death provides no vision of a departing soul or of a glorious union with God! To distance ourselves imaginatively from such convictions, which in the long run are hopes, makes room for the full grace of hope. Such hope only comes into its own when death which has swallowed Jesus up, is itself drawn into the larger mystery of a love stronger than death.

The realism of hope demands that we be prepared to feel the hopelessness, the isolation, and the grief attendant upon his shocking death. Perhaps, very simply, it is a matter of contemplating the brutalised corpse of Jesus while allowing the imagination to recall the remains of the dead we have known. For this 'middle day' was originally not experienced as being the middle of anything. It was the day of God's obvious defeat and removal from the world of our experience, of his being finally reduced to silence. The hearts of his disciples were benumbed in a universe suddenly turned grotesque. Jesus, on whom they had pinned all their hopes for something radically new in human affairs, is condemned, violently removed from life by a brutal execution, and buried as a corpse to lie in a stranger's tomb.

To ponder the meaning of Holy Saturday requires a special effort for Christian imagination. We need to recapture the pre-Christian sense of death. This is not to indulge in anachronism. But it does mean allowing hope to enter into the utter darkness of the cross. Only there will the light of Christ began to shine. In the depths of this darkness is the underworld into which Jesus descends. He is no glorious victor at this point. For he has been subjected to the power of death. He is no emissary sent into the realm of death with an announcement of victory. Simply, in utter vulnerability, he has gone down into the heart of darkness, into hell.

What is this hell which Jesus goes down into?[8] 'Hell' translates the Greek *Hades*, the god whose name is 'Unseen', ruling over the underworld. This name, in turn, is often used to translate the Hebrew *Sheol*, meaning literally 'the place of questioning'. For the realm of the dead has always left the human mind wondering, appalled at the fate of those who have gone from this life. It is described as the abode of 'darkness', 'silence', 'dust', 'the place of no return', a total separation from life and, indeed, from God (cf. Job 7:9). It was an underworld of inaction and complete passivity (Eccles. 9:10), of sadness (Sir. 14:11–17), of powerlessness (Is. 14:10), and even of no praise of God (Ps. 6:5; Ps. 88:3–6, 16). Linked with the Canaanite imagery of *Mot*, the god of death, it was the place where the dead were 'swallowed up' and 'devoured' (Is. 5:14). Death's appetite is never satisfied (Prov. 30:16). All life's radiance and power come to nothing (Is. 14:10f.). As von Balthasar remarks:

> *Being dead is not merely the antithesis of human life but also of the living God himself; therefore, a vaguely felt, unanalysable connotation of guilt, punishment and curse clings to it forever.*[9]

After the exile, Israel's hope had, indeed, become more differentiated: at the end of time, God's power could extend even into death to rescue the just and restore them to life, as the great vision of Ezechiel portrays it (Ez. 37). Though hope expanded to anticipate a final time of restoration to life, the wicked would be left to a further deadliness (Is. 66:24).

This outer limit of existence was expressed as a 'Gehenna', depicted in terms of a symbolism related to that 'valley of the son of Hinnom' (Jer. 7:31; 32:35). It is recalled in the history of Israel as a repulsive place of idolatry and human sacrifice by fire, and apparently used as a garbage dump at different times. Historical and geographical symbolism conspire to describe the fate of those who, dying alienated from God, have lost their chance of grace in the land of the living. In Hebrew imagination, *Gehenna* stood for the place of dread where any human hope was powerless and reduced to silence. No divine mercy was known to penetrate into those depths. Hence it was portrayed as a region of utter horror and torment.

The question begins to form itself: did Jesus simply go down into the world of the dead; or into that further region of despair and alienation? Did the death he died make a difference to the damned of Gehenna?

The Latin of the creed, *inferna, inferos* seems to mean simply 'the lowest places' that human imagination can depict. It denotes that limit of God-forsakenness for which we have no human hope. Whether it means the abode of the dead (*Sheol*) or something more akin to *Gehenna* can not readily be resolved. The very vagueness of this term invites further exploration.

But then, when we translate all such multi-layered symbolism by the word 'hell' in modern English, while it adds its own ominous resonance, it still leaves the meaning vague. The use, if not the choice, of this word stirs hope to probe more deeply into the extent of God's mercy. Certainly hell points to Jesus' descent into the regions of ultimate dread, the point most distant from God, the darkness that leaves every imagination appalled, where death acts with all the power of our insoluble problem of evil.

Does Jesus go down into that area of maximum alienation from the world of God's creation? In any biblical understanding it would seem so. He dies as one accursed, condemned by the law of Israel, rejected by his own people, abandoned by the Father, with his prayers unanswered. Jesus disappears into the region of utter lostness, into hell.

The sense of this ultimate enigma and dread is conveyed in the fifty or so references that the New Testament makes to Jesus being raised 'from the dead', *ek nekron*. What the mystery of Holy Saturday expresses is Jesus' obedience to the Father's will, in descending into these most dreaded, deepest reaches of human darkness. He is 'sent' into our heart of darkness: death as the final scandal in a world of suffering; death as the focus of the human problem of evil. Jesus goes down, 'goes under', and enters the depths of 'being dead'. He is fettered in 'the pangs of death' (Acts 2:24). His death dramatises the question, Can the ultimate love he proclaimed reach him at this impenetrable depth?

As hope tries to probe this ultimate human darkness, it finds an inevitable question: how and why does the Father enfold this underworld into the way of the Son?

It seems that the Word must become flesh right to the end; that the Word must go down into the world of utter silence. The communion between Father and the Son must be stretched to breaking point as love becomes an infinite compassion allowing the beloved Son to enter the realm of God-forsakenness. It allows the darkness and silence of this 'being dead among the dead' to enter into the communion between the Father and the Son. Only the Holy Spirit of unlimited love can span such a distance. The language of hope seems to imply that Love must first of all survive the deadliness of death before it can promise a new creation.

So the Word becomes truly incarnate. In solidarity with all who have lived and died, he tastes death. He is subject to the power of the 'last enemy'; and goes to that point where all earthly relationships cease, either with God or with anyone else. He is unreachable in the impenetrable darkness of being dead. Not only does Jesus go down into the underworld of death, but into a death shrouded with all the alienation of despair and unredeemed self-enclosure. Von Balthasar leaves us in no doubt on this point:

> *But on Holy Saturday there is the descent of the dead Jesus to hell, that is...his solidarity in the period of non-time with those who have lost their way to God. Their choice, with which they have chosen to put their 'I' in the place of God's selfless love—is definitive.*[10]

Jesus is not going into this world of alienation as a glorious victor, but as one who bears the whole weight of the world's alienation. His surrender to the Father takes him to a point of abandonment to the power of death, 'unto the end'. Jesus' death is not an act of doing something for the dead—as though his dying were the act of an immortal being, as though his cry of abandonment were the beginning of a message of hope. It was first of all an act of radical obedience in unreserved surrender to the Father's will. He is left with nothing but his being dead with the dead, and with what could come out of the incalculable power of the life he proclaimed. The meaning of his last great cry from the cross contains all the inexpressible dread of our humanity in the face of impenetrable mystery. It echoes in all the deaths of defeated, of those who have trusted in an apparently powerless God. Von Balthasar writes:

> *In this finality of death, the dead Son descends, no longer acting in any way, but stripped by the cross of any power or initiative of his own, as one purely to be used, debased to mere matter, with a fully indifferent (corpse) obedience, incapable of any act of solidarity— only thus is he right for any 'sermon' to the dead.*[11]

In this total abandonment, Jesus becomes God's mercy on the dead and the irretrievably isolated. His descent to this depth is the incarnation of the divine compassion: God is giving what is most precious to himself, the beloved Son, to the point furthermost from him. So Love becomes present to ultimate isolation.

The Son in refusing to be anything but the one given for the life of the world is the revelation of the Father rejecting any form of relationship to the world other than that expressed in giving what is most intimate to himself in the beloved Son. Thus, the divine mystery enfolds ultimate darkness into compassionate love. The Spirit fills these extremes to make of them one groaning totality—'the whole of creation groaning in travail' (Rom. 8:22), a people of hope 'groaning inwardly' (v.23), the 'unutterable groaning' of the Spirit (v.26). However unfathomable such a solidarity might appear, it demands to be considered as the act of limitless mercy. The Son dies for sinners by being dead with them.

The reality of ultimate estrangement is now open to another presence, the only presence that could penetrate it, an absolute love giving itself: the Father so loving the world as to give his only Son. Von Balthasar goes on to say:

> *He is, (out of an ultimate love, however) dead together with them. And exactly in this way, he disturbs the absolute loneliness striven for by the sinner: the sinner who wants to be 'damned' apart from God, finds God again in his loneliness, but God in the absolute weakness of love who unfathomably in the period of non-time, enters into solidarity with those damning themselves. The words of the Psalm 'I will make my bed in the netherworld; thou art there' (Ps. 139:8) thereby take on a totally new meaning. And even the cry, 'God is dead' as the self-made decree of the sinner for whom God is something done away with, takes on a totally new meaning objectively established by God himself.*[12]

In this mystery, hope finds its proper depth. However much the philosopher and the theologian may speculate on the transcendent causality of God in relationship to human freedom, here hope is given an image to feel its way toward the inexpressible creativity of love. Human freedom, even in a state of ultimate perversion, organised as a resistance against the power and claims of the sovereign other, now finds that this other is unreserved forgiveness, a final chance within its despair:

> *The freedom of the creature is respected, but it is retrieved by God at the end of the passion, and seized again in its very foundations. Only in absolute weakness does God will to mediate to the freedom created by him the gift of love that breaks from every prison and every constraint: in his solidarity with those who reject all solidarity.* Mors et vita duello...[13]

Guided, then, by von Balthasar's profound but tantalising reflections, we can indeed express Christ's descent into hell in its redemptive significance. The cross and the death of Jesus are the way of love into the depths of all human despair, whether it was called *Hades, Sheol, Gehenna, inferna*. Christ is *inferno profundior*, 'deeper that the lowest place' (Gregory the Great). The divine compassion fills all the dimensions of human existence: 'God was in Christ reconciling the world to himself, not counting their trespasses against them...' (II Cor. 5:19).

The beautiful homily for Holy Saturday's Office of Readings by an unknown author of the third century, presents Jesus' descent into hell as an act of divine compassion on all the dead:

> *What is happening? Today there is a great silence over the earth, a great silence and stillness, a great silence because the King sleeps; the earth was in terror and was still, because God slept in the flesh and raised up those who were sleeping from the ages. God has died in the flesh, and the underworld has trembled.*
>
> *Truly, he goes to seek out our first parent like a lost sheep; he wishes to visit those who sit in*

darkness and in the shadow of death. He goes to free the prisoner Adam, from his pains, and his fellow-prisoner, Eve—he who is God and Adam's Son... 'Awake, O sleeper and arise from the dead, and Christ shall give you light!'.[14]

We can speak only in metaphors and symbols about Jesus' experience of death and his solidarity with the dead. Theology has to grope for appropriate expressions here. But in all the complex symbolism and imagery, the basic intention is to give an account of the fullness of redemption. While Christian hope cannot escape from analogical expressions, it can extend itself into a deeper sense of the love that reaches into all the dimensions of human existence; above all, that radically indescribable state of the dead and the defeated: they are not excluded from the universe of grace. In his death, Jesus has gone down into the realm of the dead, 'right down to the central point of all world connections, the centre of the earth, i.e. the innermost core and heart of the whole cosmos.'[15]

While the image of Hades in classical antiquity, the many myths dealing with journeys into the underworld, and the Old Testament *Sheol* and *Gehenna* suggest the differing but often related ways in which the fate of the dead was understood, the New Testament offers witness of a different kind. From a variety of points of view, the rhetoric of hope will celebrate Christ's solidarity with the dead, and his lordship over what was most dreaded and most closed to experience.

In such a language of hope, the way of Christ is one of descent and ascent, as it fills the heights and the depths of the created world: he 'fills all things', descending even to the 'lower parts of the earth' (Eph. 4:9). He is Lord of the dead, and holds in his hands the keys of death and Sheol (Rev. 1:18). Every knee bows to him, even those 'under the earth' (Phil. 2:10). The Son of Man, three days and three nights in the heart of the earth, is Jesus, the new Jonah (Mt 12:40). Though he is swallowed up in the monstrosity of being dead, though he descends into the abyss (Rom. 10:6–8), against him the gates of Sheol shall not prevail (Mt 16:18ff.; 27:51–53). He has the power to subject death as the last enemy (I Cor. 15:26–29). After his death, he preaches to the mysterious 'spirits in prison' (I Pt. 3:18ff.), and to the dead (4:6).[16] Freed 'from the fetters of death' (Acts 2:24), he is 'the first-born of all creation' (Col. 1:15), and 'the first-born from the dead' (v.18). The transforming compassion of God is extended through him into the whole universe. By descending into the realm of utter darkness, he dies into the heart of the world to open it to grace:

For in him all the fullness of God was pleased to dwell, and through him to reconcile to himself all things, whether on earth or in heaven, making peace by the blood of his cross (Col. 1:19f.).

The silence of Holy Saturday, in its distinctive way, provides a word on three classical eschatological themes. First, the realm of death is not annihilation or ultimate isolation. It is enfolded within the self-emptying of the Son, and in the Father's surrender of this Son into the darkest of our human depths. The point most distant from life and from God is reached by self-giving love. It too is 'in Christ'. His solidarity extends to this ultimate dimension.

Secondly, Jesus descends not into some post-Christian hell of those who have explicitly rejected him, but into the rather more vague pre-christian realm as it was, and is, to those who know no hope of redemption. The hell of the damned does not come into existence as 'the second death' (Rev. 20:14) unless these dead refuse the salvation that is offered through Jesus' presence with them. The God they rejected in the times of their power now comes to them out of the depths of their weakness. To exclude him now would be to imprison oneself in the destructiveness of an ultimate alienation. Josef Ratzinger crystallises this point:

> ...*in his passion he went down into the abyss of abandonment. Where no voice can reach us any longer, there is he. Hell is thereby overcome, or, to be more accurate, death, which was previously hell, is hell no longer. Neither is death the same any longer, for there is life in the midst of death, because love dwells in it. Now, only deliberate self-enclosure is hell, or, as the bible calls it, the second death* (Rev. 20:14).[17]

Thirdly, his descent into hell makes the state of 'being dead', a purgatory: in death Christ is found as pure self-giving love inviting the dead to yield to the energy of true life.[18] This is the meaning of purification as such love becomes both a judgment and a summons: a judgment, as unconditional love exposes human self-centredness for what it is; a summons in that a final self-transcendence into the Spirit of such love is called forth. The fire of purgatory is the reality of love exposing all residual selfishness. There is nothing to prevent seeing this as an instance of Paul's more general teaching: 'For the Day will disclose it, because it will be revealed with fire, and the fire will test what sort of work each man has done...he will be saved but only as through fire' (I Cor. 3:12–15).

To gather all these varied expressions together in the light of various creedal statements about Christ's decent into hell, we could say that his 'being buried' and going down to 'the lowest places' is a statement both of the realism of the incarnation and the inclusiveness of redemption. Because his way went into this lowest place, there is a way out. There, too, 'nothing in all creation, nothing in life or death...can separate us from the love of God in Christ Jesus' (Rom. 8:38).   Love's outreach includes the impenetrable realm of the dead. And hope is supported by the perfect love which casts out even this final fear (I Jn 4:18).

Once more, let me quote von Balthasar, as we try to centre this mystery of Holy Saturday more deeply in the final mystery of the God of love. The mystery of grace is here presented as encompassing our hope's anguish over the problem of evil:

> *Only when the very one who has our monstrous world on his conscience, who had the inconceivable power and fearful courage to unleash this monster, only when he had not merely joined in inflicting the most fearful torment but had subjected himself to it (for only God can know what it truly means to be forsaken by God), only when the maximum coincides with the minimum (both of which are beyond our comprehension) albeit not in indifference, but in such a way that absolute power becomes one with absolute impotence in protective compassion...*[19]

In such a vision, hope become truly as unreserved as the love which inspires it. The self-giving Mystery of the Trinity communicates itself to every dimension of the universe, that all creation might be drawn into the ecstatic life of the three divine persons. God as love realised in the undying communion of Father, Son and Spirit is hope's ultimate foundation:

> *only when God is triune—the same God the Father and Creator of the cosmos and mankind, who in the God-forsakenness of his Son concentrates in the cross every conceivable kind of abandonment, who together in a deeply intense love form the one Spirit, the Spirit of the Father and the Son, the Spirit of the strong and the weak, the Spirit of the same love—only then am I given a key that makes credible and tolerable to me a meaning of existence—though I may not understand him or it.*[20]

The radiance of this hope is strikingly evidenced in the second-century *Odes of Solomon*. Ode 42 depicts the descent of Christ as the messenger of divine compassion going down into the darkness, 'no matter what the depth':

> *Sheol saw me and was conquered. I was like gall and vinegar for them and I descended to them no matter what the depth. I held among the dead a meeting of the living...the dead cried out to me, 'Have mercy on us, Son of God; free us from the bondage of darkness, and open the gates that we may come out to you...I drew my sign on their foreheads and they hence are now free and belong to me.*[21]

We conclude this reflection with a beautiful expression of hope. The unknown homilist of 1700 years ago puts these words on the lips of Jesus as he addresses Adam in the realm of the dead:

> *I am your God who for your sake became your son, who for you and your descendants now speak, and command with authority those in prison: Come forth; and those in darkness, Have light; and those who sleep, Rise.*

> *I command you, 'Awake, sleeper. I have not made you to be held a prisoner in the underworld. Arise from the dead. I am the life of the dead. Arise, O man, work of my hands, arise, you who were fashioned in my image, Rise, let us go hence.' For you in me, and I in you, together we are one undivided person.*[22]

Thus, hope, journeying through the darkness with Christ, comes to its ultimate conviction:

> *The cherubim throne has been prepared, the bearers are ready and waiting, the bridal chamber is in order, the food is provided, the everlasting houses and rooms are in readiness, the treasures of good things have been opened;*

the kingdom of heaven has been prepared before the ages.[23]

How hope emerges from the darkness of the death and descent of Jesus will be the business of the next section treating of the third holy day.

Easter Sunday

Without the event of the third day, hope would have no grounds for understanding Good Friday as 'good' or Holy Saturday as 'holy'. Jesus would have been one more good man, swallowed up in defeat and death. But because of what we have come to call 'the resurrection', Christian hope understands the death of Jesus as the manifestation of God's transforming love touching our existence at its most hopeless point. Such hope understands his being dead as the power of that compassionate love to penetrate the depths of human defeat and isolation in order to engender a new creation.

The Resurrection is the light in which the whole mystery of Christ is grasped.[24] It is the first and last word on the hope Christians profess. Paul underscores the crucial character of the resurrection of Jesus. To deny the resurrection would be to misrepresent God, to leave the dead, dead; the sinful, unforgiven; the believing, victims of futility; and the preachers of the Gospel, 'of all men most to be pitied' (I Cor. 15:12–19). But 'in fact, Christ has been raised, the first fruits of those who have fallen asleep' (v. 20). The new thing that occurred in such irresistible objectivity puts faith's understanding of all that has gone before and of all that will take place after into a universe of transforming grace.

In the light of the resurrection, Christian hope rereads the law and the prophets and psalms of Israel's hopes (Lk 24:44). It penetrates the meaning of 'all the scriptures' and of the sufferings of Jesus (Lk 24:25ff.; cf. also Jn 2:22; 12:16; 14:26). As the resurrection breaks into human consciousness to inspire the conviction that God has acted in an ultimately decisive manner (Gal. 1:1; Acts 2:23, 32), it forms a community of witnesses energised to proclaim salvation in the name of Jesus to all nations (Lk 24:47ff.; Jn 20:21f.).

Jesus appears to the disciples as risen precisely at the time when they are suffering the disillusionment and grief of his shameful death and historical failure. He comes as a light shining into the darkness of apparent defeat: he is self-revealed, in the glory of a new life. The New Testament gives both lists of witnesses (I Cor. 15:3–11), and a variety of accounts of how they came to see and recognise the Lord.[25] Further, each of the Gospels relates this recognition to the discovery of the empty tomb.

Though these witnesses come to recognise the Risen One as the crucified Jesus, no one of them ever pretends to describe what the resurrection was, nor claims to have seen it. They show no inclination to prove the resurrection merely from the fact that the tomb was found by the women to be empty. The reports of the appearances of Jesus evidence an inarticulate groping to express some massive and transforming reality: the crucified one lives; we have seen him. Jesus, from beyond the time and space of this world, revealed himself to particular witnesses in an exclusive form of self-disclosure. He appears from the outside, as living in the vitality of the divine mystery, transcending a world of shattered hopes. Out of the experience of darkness and failure, these first witnesses come to acknowledge him, and to commit themselves to him as the ultimate reality of their lives.

There is a certain imposing objectivity about these reports of the appearance of Jesus. They are marked, for all the expression of dismay, doubt and later confusion (I Cor. 15:12ff.; II Tim 2:17f.), by a sense of overwhelming factuality. They were dead sure about something. While these accounts of faith are not exercises in critical philosophy, they do not lack an array of categories in which to make a differentiated judgment on what has occurred in all its singularity: for they know about visions (Acts 16:9; 18:9; 23:11; 27:23), dreams (Mt 1:20; 2:12f., 19–22), ecstasies (Acts 10:9ff.; II Cor. 12:2–4; Rev. 1:10ff.), even miraculous resuscitations of the dead (Lk 8:49–56; Jn 11:1–53; Acts 9:36–42). But with the resurrection of the crucified, something quite different is in evidence. There is no question of meeting a ghost or of inventing a myth (cf. Lk 24:36–40; II Pt. 1:16). A massive event of a new order of reality had erupted into the world. These appearances of the Risen One, even if they would eventually yield to the blessedness of simply believing (Jn 20:29; I Pt. 1:8), gave rise to a special testimony based on a singular evidence, and to the burden of a special responsibility. Both arose out of the experience of a life-transforming happening. However the earliest witnesses expressed it, they were absolutely certain that the radically new had happened.

The fact of these appearances and the mystery of resurrection they intimate, cut across any preconceptions or expectations on the part of the disciples and the world in which they lived. Though the resurrection of Jesus must be set within one of the traditions of Israel as it envisioned a general resurrection on the last day, no one was expecting it as it occurred in the case of Jesus. Indeed, no one witnessed it in the sense of being able to describe this singular event first-hand. Nor does anyone attempt to describe it. There was, and is, an initial impossibility about the resurrection of the crucified Jesus—a too-good-to-be-true quality—which remains the main argument against it (Lk 24:41).

For the cause of Jesus had collapsed with his condemnation and execution. His disciples were scattered and demoralised. The theology or philosophy of the day provided no hope or expectation that such a resurrection could happen: Sadducees did not believe in the resurrection of the dead in any sense; the Pharisees, only a small percentage of the population, believed in a resurrection of the just on the last day; the prevalent Greek world-view found repugnant any concept of a new physical embodiment after death (See Acts 17:18, 32) What happened in the singular event of Jesus' resurrection, was anticipated in no prevalent mentality or available concept. There were simply no terms and words to express what happened in this transformation of the crucified, and in his new presence to his disciples.

The Risen One is not resuscitated to this life as was, say, Lazarus. He lives in the form and energy of ultimate life and an ultimate love. The evangelists certainly take care to stress that the Risen One really is Jesus of Nazareth, even to the extent of his bearing the marks of his passion. Yet, his humanity is transformed into the ultimate mode of existence. It is affirmed in various ways in terms of the Father's glorification of the Son, or in terms of the transforming power of the Spirit, of the dawn of a new creation, of the deathless energies of a new life embodied and communicated in him.

And in all this, the disciples are not seeing his ghost, but meeting the living person, embodied in a new creation (cf. Mk 12:24f.), yet communicating with them in the symbols and gestures of this world—a point which is the foundation of all sacramental theology.

There are three essential features written into the Gospel accounts of what we term the resurrection. First, the Risen One is identical with, and identified as, the crucified Jesus. Even in the risen life, he is still marked with the stigmata of his earthly existence.

Secondly, he discloses himself, in freedom, to his disciples. He draws them through doubt and hesitation to the moment of recognition, which results in their worship and unqualified commitment (Jn 20:16ff.; Mt 28:9, 17).

Thirdly, the resurrection occurs in a way that has time for human history. While it is the decisive mutation for human history, while it is the eruption of an incalculable grace into the world, it is not an interruption in the history of human freedom. History is not swallowed up in a premature fulfilment. On this point, let me quote G. Martelet:

> *If, then, the Risen Christ wishes to show himself and so confirm his faithful in their faith, in a world whose continued existence he has at heart (since what he came for was to make sure of its direction not to halt its course), then he will appear only within the limits this world can tolerate; and that means keeping very close to what he was, with no more than a discreet hint or adumbration of what he is. It will be something between the two, quite unambiguous in itself, and yet necessarily impermanent...he conforms to the 'rules of the household' (the economy), which is still the world of entropy and death.* [26]

While the resurrection appearances are not the fabrication of the psychological state of the first disciples, they do occur within human consciousness. They disclose a passage from utter desolation and emptiness to a sense of divine presence. They evidence a new kind of encounter with Jesus. He is experienced as the source and form of a new and ultimate life. Only in such a way could the emptiness and darkness of Jesus' defeat and death be replaced. No place is left for lingering doubt. The cross and burial of Jesus scooped out of mind and imagination every vestige of either worldly hope or simple optimism or subtle manipulation of the divine, along with every religious projection of God as a worldly power meting out a worldly justice. Such darkness and emptiness readied the disciples for the sheer originality of God's new creation. Love is free to appear in its own terms, and to inspire its own hope. Again let Sebastian Moore's disciple speak:

Today it happened. We saw him...I saw him with the emptiness I spoke of, as though the emptiness was a kind of second sight... The strange 'other side' of the soul knew him, and knew him for more than the man we thought we knew.[27]

The singularity of this event is like a black hole in the religious experience of the disciples. The ordinary laws and expectations of their religious perceptions have been changed. In his death and resurrection, religious reality has been brought to a crisis of maximum intensity. Is love, that essential being-for-others that leads even to the giving of one's life for the sake of a new existence in God, really the ultimate and decisive existence in this universe, or is it not? Is God the transforming energy that inspires, hallows and fulfils such an existence, or are we dealing with some other power? In the drama of these questions, and in the release that comes from their resolution in Jesus' rising from the tomb, something radically new is brought into our human history.

Human beings now belong together in a new field of life focused in the evidence of this event. Its reality explodes into new meanings and the transformation of old values. The revelation of an ultimate love, victorious even within the space and time of this history, changes the very sense of the universe in which we live, and the manner in which we belong to one another. If the crucified one embodied all the darkness and emptiness of the human condition, his resurrection fills that darkness with the energy of new life.

Love is no longer at the mercy of the destructive powers of the world. For that world is changed at its core and drawn into the universe of a transforming love.

This new sense of the universe and the power of love at work, flows from a consciousness transformed by the Spirit of Jesus. The crucified and risen one *is* the mystery of God embodied and involved with the world in an irreversible and absolute manner. The is the fundamental ground for the disciple's confession of him as 'My Lord and My God' (Jn 20:28). The qualitatively new life invading human experience is connected to the qualitatively new presence of God revealed in him. The rhetoric of adoration is, as are all the early and later efforts to word this new perception, in profound conflict with the disciples' Jewish modes of thinking about this man. The confession of him as Lord, as Son, as the conqueror of death, is hardly explicable outside a profound conviction that, in him, the radically new has happened. As risen from the dead, he is the source of new life. He is doing what only God can do. In this way, the confession of Jesus as Lord and God is the natural language of the disciples' transformed consciousness as it resonates with the overwhelming reality that has taken place.[28] The stock of available religious words had to be stretched to new range of meaning as these first witnesses groped to express what had happened. That much is clear. But it is also clear that he had come back as conqueror from the darkness and emptiness of death, in a way that left available expressions stammering and religious imagination bewildered. In him, they had met the God of the living.

The Risen One comes to those disciples as the bearer and embodiment of new life. He is living with a life of love now proved to be stronger than any death that human beings could conceive of. The light has shone forth from death's absolute darkness—the tomb in which Jesus, his God, his grace, the cause of his kingdom, the hope of the poor, were, seemingly, so finally buried.

The God who has apparently failed his Son, and the followers who had been called to leave all in his name, now appears as the patient, inexhaustible power of mercy and love that has been at work all the time. The deadliest of dark nights of the soul has now seen a glory shine within it: the Mystery that has given of its very own to release the human mind and heart into a new level of freedom and unconditional hope. This God whom Jesus has invoked as Father, whom he had involved in his words and deeds as the lover and healer of humankind, is now identified as the compassion behind the cross and the agent of the resurrection itself.

This compassionate, life-giving love is not only represented in what Jesus has become. It communicates the Spirit of new corporate life. For such love has reached, not only into the tomb, but into the grave of humanity's deepest despair and disillusionment. It draws the disciples into the field of its own energy, to be registered in human consciousness as faith, hope and love: the gifts that remain (I Cor. 13:13). It opens up a new horizon of seeing and hearing, touching and tasting: of seeing, because the crucified is recognised as the Lord; of hearing, because in the silence of the tomb the word of ultimate victorious love has been heard; of touching, since the Risen Lord is now present to all space and time; of tasting, since his whole being becomes our food and drink in the sacraments of a now expectant age. The mystery of love is the light that shines in the darkness, and is not overcome. The risen one is the source of a new atmosphere, a Holy Spirit, which will 'groan' in Christian hope for final liberation, just as the whole of creation now will groan in us in the labour of a great act of giving birth to the full body of the Christ.[29]

The self-disclosures of the Risen Lord are connected in the tissue of the Gospel narrative to another extreme of factuality. Here I refer to the empty tomb, with its temporal reference to 'the third day' and personal reference to 'some women of our company' (Lk 24:22) who discovered it.[30]

How Christian hope is related to this tradition is a complex question. On the one hand, it never was, nor could it ever be, a matter of Christian hope arising out of the mere emptiness of the tomb. Indeed, such emptiness gave rise only to further perplexity and fear (cf. Mk 16:8; Lk 24:5, 11). There was no point in seeking the living among the dead. For the realism of Christian faith was always primarily focused on the Lord of life, now living and life-giving. Such faith does not primarily haunt a grave or linger among the dead. Rather, it confidently expands into a full-bodied connection with the risen Jesus as form and agent of a new and ultimate vitality. The overwhelming experience of living communication with the risen Jesus can never be reduced to the mere fact of his empty grave. Indeed, the disciples' assurance of Jesus' victory over death is in stark contrast to the ambiguity of the empty tomb.

On the other hand, that emptiness does have its place in the fullness of the Gospel narrative. As an index of the radical reality of the resurrection, the blank fact of the empty tomb is lifted out of its original ambiguity. The inclusion of the empty tomb in the Gospel accounts prevents Christian hope from remaining on an idealistic or mystical plane. To leave out the empty tomb is to find oneself veering very quickly into hoping in a theology rather than a transforming divine event—and, incidentally, dismissing the special role of women in communicating the Gospel of new life! A legend would hardly base its case on the testimony of women in a culture that scarcely accepted their credibility.[31]

The empty tomb is a kind of historical marker for a transcendent mystery. It is a demand, set right there in the history of human defeat and failure, that Christian hope be truly eschatological, truly ultimate, truly a matter of dealing with the transcendent power of the Spirit. As such, the empty tomb is a negative sign. For it is an absence pointing to a presence. It is an emptiness inviting to a fullness, challenging faith to its ultimate realism and hope to its radical inclusion of all that is human. Because of it, hope cannot present itself as merely a positive construction of Jesus' continuing significance after his death. The light of the Risen One shines more brightly from the empty darkness of the grave.

Though, of itself, the empty tomb does not make that risen life palpable in this world, it does invite Christian experience to explore how the resurrection is palpable form and presence of new life in our time and space, how hope now lives from the energies of a new order of reality, a new creation among us. It calls forth the realist conviction that God has truly acted in raising up the Crucified in the reality of a world hitherto locked in death. In the conviction that the universe is now different, faith returns to the tomb, but not to stay there. It breaks forth into a new sense of the wholeness of life and of the real victory of the love which has already radically taken the sting out of death (Acts 2:31; I Cor. 15:54ff.).

As a special kind of sign in witnessing to the resurrection, the empty tomb plants the reality of the resurrection in the ground of history as a seed of questions and wonder. And of doubt, too—for those who have settled for a closed-system or vicious-circle view of the world. The empty tomb, so soberly recorded in each of the four Gospels, does not draw attention to itself. We are caught up in the movement from the tomb (first discovered as a puzzling fact) to the mystery of what had happened (in the appearances of the Lord), then back to the tomb (as an index of a new creation), then out into the limitless horizons of the Spirit's creativity.

Through all, the reality of God's transforming action in Christ is the focus. There is no biblical evidence of defensive embarrassment. Nor, for that matter, is there any evidence that either friend or foe thought that the tomb contained the remains of Jesus. The Gospel writer is quite aware of the allegation that the corpse had been stolen as a quite predictable explanation of those for whom Jesus had to stay buried! (Mt 28:1–15).

While the light of resurrection faith shines brightest out of the darkness of the tomb, that dark emptiness is never a simple proof: 'Why do you seek the living among the dead?' (Lk 24:5–7). The resurrection is a divinely wrought fact, explicable not in terms of the emptiness and silence of the tomb, but in the transformative action of a love stronger than death. The silence of this grave is that of the fullness of life into which the Word is gone: 'It is to your advantage that I go away' (Jn 16:7).

The full-bodied symbol of the resurrection touches both those limits of our experience of death referred to in Chapter three. It obviously points to the ultimate self-transcendence offered to human existence: in the power of Christ's Spirit, we die into ultimate life. But it also contends with our experience of death in its objective deadliness, as the collapse and corruption of our earthly existence. It trans-values death's dark symbols: mortality is not only transcended but death is radically transformed; human life is not only fulfilled but human death loses its immemorial sting. Jesus is risen not only beyond this world of death, but within it:

> *In the face of the awful challenge of this time, the Resurrection faith is required to be unusually sensitive to that element of its Good News which is addressed to the numbing power of death-as-corruption over the deep spiritual insight into death-as-climax. God has spoken his resurrection word into the context of universal and nameless decay, as well as into the context of keen mystical expectancy. And for us who easily get trapped in our own necropolis, there is an inalienable comfort in the message of the empty tomb. There, even in the grave, the word has been, the mysterious care has shown itself. And the sentence will be heavy on a theology that, still able to survive in the groves*

of academe, has felt no call to attend to this... I cannot believe with passion in the resurrection without the empty tomb. And, as Pascal says, without passion, nothing significant can be done.[32]

The mystery of the resurrection

Eschatological hope is, then, founded in the resurrection of Jesus as essentially the act of a love stronger than death, confirming everything that is most promising in our humanity and healing the mortal trauma of our being. While the resurrection breaks into human history, it is not contained by previous expectations or present categories. Where the old language was the product of other more limited or more general expectations, its singularity demanded something new. Christian hope had still to seek its proper expression. For, while historical investigation can document all the ways in which the ancient world thought of life beyond death, and the variety and development of Israel's own expressions of hope, while it can make a judgment on the emptiness of the tomb and consider the evidence of vitally transformed community, it can go no further. For the resurrection is a divinely wrought event. As such, it radiates its own evidence in those who can receive it as a divine act. Here it claims its own witnesses to solicit a response proper to the kind of ultimate reality it is.

Hence, as the culminating mystery of God's action in the world, the mystery of the resurrection poses a series of problems for Christian thought and expression. How are we to speak within this world of an event which so profoundly affects this world with the energy of a life not of this world? How can traditional categories be stretched to allow for a hearing of this unique last word? What analogies can our hope find to express what is beyond all human expression and achievement? What other mysteries of faith can be brought into a fresh focus to throw light on this definitive consummation of the mystery of Christ? These questions pose the big problems for Christian hope that is called to give an account of itself. Hence, the ever provisional, always failing, always necessary searchings of theology.

Such a theology finds its centre only in the essential first and last thing, the mystery of God's self-giving love. The love that has given existence, that has given life, and inspired the long journey of history has compassionately reached into the whole human agony of our problem of evil. It has met us at the dread point of death. As such, it is a love that keeps on being love. As one with the mystery of God, it is neither turned into something less than itself by the evil of the world, nor defeated in its essential energy. In the resurrection of the Crucified, it comes to its own victory and shows its own transforming power. In the Risen One, we see the mystery of such love not only as one with us in any darkness we know, not only as opening a way through it or beyond it, but as overcoming it. He appears as the one who experienced the crucifying power of evil and the burying power of death in the transforming power of love. The Son who has borne the world's darkness in himself, is now the light in which the world is transfigured. In the darkness, such love becomes the light that is not overcome (Jn 1:4f.).

To displace the meaning of the resurrection into anything but the triumph of life-affirming and life-giving love, would be to misplace the foundation of our hope. The three-fold character of this love enfolds human life as the ultimate life-source in the Father, as the ultimate life-form in the Son and as the ultimate life-force in the Spirit. The fundamental meaning of the resurrection is thus linked into the love-life of the Trinity itself gathering our world into itself. In the risen Lord, this love-life is finally revealed as the fundamental energy in which the universe finds its unity and wholeness. Love is the *actus purus*, 'the sheer act', the *ipsum esse*, the 'very being' into which the world is being drawn to find its true existence.

For the resurrection is the culminating instance of the fundamental activity of the divine mystery. It occurs in our world as a decisive reversal of all the forces that are hostile to life and its most transcendent meaning, self-giving love. In that act, the world is enfolded into the generative power, into the great womb, of divine love. God becomes the energy exploding open the tomb of the self-enclosed world. Jesus is the stone rolled back. The Spirit is the breath of new life enabling the despairing and the dead to come forth.

The cosmic reality of the resurrection:

In the subversive imagination of Christian hope, the risen Lord is the radiant point of entry into the open circle of divine communion. In him, the new life is embodied, 'en-worlded' as the irreversible beginning of the new creation. The heart of reality has been changed. The cosmic 'heart of darkness' has been transformed into a heart of love: the pulse of new, ultimate life beats there.

Hope properly expands in the resurrection to a cosmic comprehension. Indeed, the risen Christ is the risen body not only of our common humanity, but also of its world. In him, 'the first born from the dead', the first-born of all creation, God's original intention for the world is realised. As Martelet remarks:

> *...we believe that Christ, through his risen body is the principle of a life so absolute that it embodies on the cosmic plane, the ultimate hope of a world that has been created for the resurrection.*[33]

It is customary to remark that, in recent times, Christian hope has often suffered from a very limited notion of its cosmic embodiment. The human body has too often been presented as a somewhat limited personal possession, as a fragment of the universe, a parcel of matter detached from the rest of the world and informed by the individual soul. In contrast to this extreme individualism, is a more relational (hence more personal) more cosmic view. The body is the human person's insertion into the cosmic whole, the individual focal point where each belongs to the whole, and it possesses what each one is. To tease out the cosmic significance of the resurrection of the body, and to appreciate the cosmic significance of Jesus's resurrection, the following points are made.[34]

First, if the resurrection is going to affect the structure of the universe in an ultimately transformative manner, it must be, of course, a divine event. This has been our main theological emphasis. But now the question is, what kind of divine event? How might we envisage the transforming activity of the Spirit of God? The answer lies in understanding this activity as a transformation of our embodiment in this universe. For it is essentially through the body that the human person is related to the universe: 'The body is man's organic root driven into the heart of the universe.'[35] Teilhard de Chardin asks, 'What exactly is the human body?'. He goes on to reflect,

My own body is not these cells or those cells that belong *exclusively to me: it is* what, *in these cells and in the rest of the world, feels my influence and reacts against me.* My *matter is not a* part *of the universe that I possess* totaliter: *it is the* totality *of the universe possessed by me* partialiter.

From this point of view, we see that the world is no longer like an aggregate of interfused elements, but a single sphere with countless centres from which it can be observed and from which action can emanate. It is multiple, not as a heap of stones *is (a sum of juxtaposed parts), but as a* gaseous mixture *is (in which*

> *each gas fills the whole volume of the mixture)—though that is a lamentably crude comparison. Since each element is strictly coextensive with all the others, with the whole, it is really a microcosm.*[36]

Teilhard is casting around for the right metaphor; and I am not sure he has found it in the gaseous mixture! Had he lived, one must suspect he would have been delighted by what modern physics calls Bootstrap theory or the anthropic principle.[37] What modern physics does stress is the essential inter-relatedness of the cosmos in all its dimensions. Particle analysis, so long the prevalent model for physics, is now yielding to a more relational view of the totality. Each individual instance, each particle has its function and identity as a dynamic focus of an incredibly complex network of relationships. The particle cannot be understood without situating it within the complex interaction of the whole; just as the whole has no density if it is considered apart from its myriad foci.

This is to say that, through the body, our human being has a world; and the world owns it. To be embodied is to be en-worlded. This would mean, in turn, that if human existence is to be transformed, then the way in which it is en-worlded must be changed.

First, let us apply this principle to the resurrected reality of Jesus. After all, he remains still embodied in the cosmos, as 'the first-born of all creation', even if he is no longer subjected to it in the conditions of biological and historical life. In a new and ultimate embodiment, Christ possesses the totality of the world in his distinctiveness. As Lord, head, new Adam, 'the first-born of all creation', 'the first-born from the dead', the early documents of faith present him as 'before' all things, the one in whom all reality coheres and find its fulfilment: 'all things hold together in him' (Col. 1:15ff.). With regard to the whole created order, he is the decisive breakthrough into the ultimate form of the universe. In him 'the end of the ages has come upon us.'(I Cor. 10:11). St Ambrose captures this cosmic sense of the resurrection in his statement, 'In Christ, the world has risen, heaven has risen, the earth has risen'.[38]

Admittedly, the universe, even before the quantum leap of the resurrection, knows its own, even if limited, kind of self-transcendence. Through our embodiment in the cosmos, the creativity of human history is continually contesting the world of inevitable entropy manifest in the gradual exhaustion of its energies, and in its slow but everdiminishing cycles of renewal. For the biological cycles of birth and death are taken up through consciousness into a universe of meaning and values. Human groups find common identity in all the variety of cultures. Physical sounds and signs break forth into languages and eventually literatures, in a world of teeming communication. Art transforms the given world of sight and sound, of shape and colour and movement, into the entrancing forms of music, dance, sculpture and painting, poetry and drama. All the variety of pacts and arrangements to ensure security gradually inspire aspirations to a world-order of justice and of universal belonging. Science generates energies to enables human life to transform its physical environment in a thousand ways. The comparative self-enclosure of the primitive world transcends itself in the history of freedom as the human community opens out to the ever richer experience of its dramatic, creative and often tragic course.

Nonetheless, despite all these achievements of art and science, of thought and culture, morality and religion, the transcendence they evidence is only relative. Death continues to mock human achievement, and our highest aspirations have to deal with the overwhelming surd of human evil and self-destruction. Human freedom is continuously being checked, frustrated, appalled by that over which it has no power. The physical laws of mortality, the historical movements of progress and decline assert themselves as ineluctable forces against which we are powerless. The universe can seem so essentially indifferent to human achievement, so uncaring of the individual destiny or cultural attainments that our greatest sages can see it all as vanity with nothing new under the sun. Death as an inescapable biological fact comes to symbolise all that is alien, hostile, radically unappreciative of the varied creativity and the self-realisation to which we might aspire. It is all doomed to an eventual and total collapse. Entropy conquers all.

But the resurrection of the crucified changes the structure of our basic relationship to the universe. A decisive transformation has occurred. What we most cherish is no longer at the mercy of what we value least or of what we most fear. Life has been revealed as stronger than death.

This is a matter of cosmic significance. For the resurrection, as was mentioned above, does not mean that Jesus' embodied relationship to the cosmos has been cancelled, or that he has begun to exist outside the universe. The Risen One belongs to the whole, and contains it in a new form. Into the ambiguity of our relative self-transcendence is uttered the Word of absolute self-transcendence. True life is not subject to the power of death and the destructive forces it symbolises: 'Christ being raised from the dead will never die again. Death no longer has dominion over him' (Rom. 6:9).

In the Risen One, the ultimate mutation in human life occurs. The creative Spirit, at work in the whole creation, and concentrated in the life and being of Jesus, transforms the crucified one into the form and source of ultimate life. Human existence now enjoys, so to speak, a new Spirit-given metabolism. It is not made to collapse into the dark ambiguity of a never-to-be-resolved destiny, but to be transformed into a new, eternal being-in-love. Death itself is no longer the blank wall against which life and all its hopes are shattered, but the door to a fuller incorporation into a universe of grace. Until the moment of resurrection, this cosmos was essentially entropic, being-unto-death, 'subject to the powers of death'.[39] Thus, the Risen One is the absolute negation of cosmic entropy.

The Christ of the resurrection represents a revolution in the emergence of the universe. He is the point of mutation in a new creation from which all things are born anew. In the most comprehensive and cosmic sense, all the promises of God find their 'Yes' in him (II Cor. 1:20).[40] Where, before, death was the cosmic sign of nature's victory over human history, it now yields to the resurrection as the great sign of cosmic hope. For in the Risen One has taken place the ultimate homecoming of our humanity and its world. The 'end of the ages' breaks into human history with the reality of something that history has neither produced nor hitherto experienced. As a result, history is enabled to look beyond itself in hope. What has happened within it already, in the death and resurrection of Jesus, becomes the point from which a new horizon of life unfolds:

If the Spirit of him who raised Jesus from the dead dwells in you, he who raised Jesus from the dead will give life to your mortal bodies also through the Spirit who dwells in you' (Rom. 8:11).

In other words, the human existence of Jesus is expanded, in death and resurrection, to a pan-cosmic relationship. He exists now 'in the Spirit', as in a field of all-pervasive energy drawing the universe into a new totality: 'Our world...has already become essentially heaven.'[41] Though it is still hidden in the ambiguities of earthly existence, the risen Jesus is the pledge and sign of this 'pneumatic universe', a transfigured world whose living atmosphere is the Holy Breath of God's Spirit. Christ is the focus of 'the divine milieu': 'I when I am lifted up from the earth, will draw all men to myself' (Jn 12: 32):

> *Christ's transfigured body is the archetype of the universe already introduced, in a hidden and mysterious manner, into the state of transfiguration, and also of the human race permeated by the Spirit and eschatologically unified.*[42]

The New Testament represents this new relationship to the universe as Christ disarming the 'principalities and powers' which, in biblical terms, ruled the phenomena of nature and the events and forces of history. There is some dispute over whether these cosmic forces are to be understood as evil or as neutral or as good.[43] What all agree on is that these mysterious forces have been the obvious conditioning factors embodied in the transpersonal structures which give our earthly life its shape and momentum—social institutions in their national and international forms, the power of nature, political and cultural movements, the pervasive impact of technology, the massive influence of the media.

But, in the full unfolding of the paschal mystery, Christ is revealed as the ultimate factor for the fate, and even for the form, of creation. All its forms and forces are made subject to him, reintegrated into a new wholeness. Through him, the reshaping of the universe has irreversibly begun. He becomes the ultimate space in which all the becoming of our history and our world takes place, the single absolute point by which all else is measured, the goal finalising all genesis: 'From the metaphysical depths of the universe, new, divinised forces are already flowing into our existential environment in the outer surface of things.'[44]

In the light of Christ's descent and resurrection, the Ascension is the symbolic presentation of his entry, in a final, all-fulfilling manner, into the glory of God.

His journey terminates in his ascent to the Father, in his entry into the realm of ultimate mystery—the tabernacle not made by human hands (Heb. 9:11)—that 'he might fill all things' (Eph. 4:10). Lukan theology presents the phases of the paschal mystery in the time sequence of the 'forty days': the hour of John expanded into a longer duration accommodated to human historical experience. Now, whether we employ the symbolism of the hour or the sequence of the forty days, the message is the same: Jesus has entered definitively into his 'being in the Spirit'. He is no longer a phenomenon at one with us in our earthly existence. Rather, he is with us and we with him, in the field of the Spirit, as communing with him in a new order, drawn after him into a new creation.

Conclusion

The three holy days, the *sacrum triduum*, are the fundamental parable of Christian hope.[45] Any statement on a particular theme, heaven or hell, purgatory or the end of the world, is nothing more than a re-telling of this parable at a particular point of concern.

1. In what follows, the influence of Hans Urs von Balthasar's *Mysterium Paschale* is pervasive. It appeared as chapter 9 in *Mysterium Salutis. Grundriss heilsgeshichtlicher Dogmatik: Das Christusereignis*, Band III/2, eds., Johannes Feiner and Magnus Löhrer, Benziger Verlag, Einsiedeln, 1969, pp. 133–320. *See also* Tony Kelly, *Trinity of Love...*, pp.107–113.
2. *See* Ignace de la Potterie, *The Hour of Jesus*, tr. G. Murray, St Paul Publications, Middlegreen, Slough, 1989, pp.21–39.
3. *See* David Stanley, *Jesus in Gethsemane*, Paulist Publications, New York, 1980.
4. Sebastian Moore, *The Fire and the Rose are One*, Darton, Longman and Todd, London, 1980, p.85.
5. For a good survey: *See* Gérard Rossé, *The Cry of Jesus on the Cross: A Biblical and Theological Study*, Paulist

Press, New York, 1987.
6. *See* the various versions in *The Christian Faith in the Doctrinal Documents of the Catholic Church*, eds. J. Neuner and J. Dupuis, Collins, London, 1982, ns. 4, 5, 17, 20, 23. Hereafter, Neuner-Dupuis.
7. Sebastian Moore, *The Fire and the Rose are One*, Darton, Longman and Todd, London, 1980, p.86. See, too, the concluding paragraphs of George Steiner, *Real Presences*. University of Chicago Press, Chicago, 1989, pp.231f.:

   There is one particular day in Western history about which neither historical record nor myth nor Scripture make report. It is a Saturday. And it has become the longest of days...
8. Wilhelm Maas, 'He descended into Hell', *Theology Digest* 30/1 (1982) pp. 43–47. His seminal work is *Gott und die Hölle: Studien zum Descensus Christi*, Johannes Verlag, Einsiedeln, 1979.
9. Hans Urs von Balthasar, 'The Descent into Hell', *Chicago Studies* 23/2, August 1984, p.225.
10. Hans Urs von Balthasar, *The von Balthasar Reader*, eds., Medard Kehl and Werner Löser, trans. R.J. Daly and F. Lawrence, T. & T. Clarke, Edinburgh, 1985, p.153.
11. *ibid.*, p.153.
12. *ibid.*, p.153.
13. *ibid.*, p.153.
14. The second reading from the Office of Readings for Holy Saturday.
15. Ladislaus Boros, *The Moment of Truth...*, p.152.
16. The precise meaning of these two passages has been much disputed. If William Dalton's exegesis is correct, namely, that 'the spirits' here refer to the fallen angels, then these references only obliquely apply to our theme. See W. Dalton, 'The First Epistle of Peter', *The New Jerome Biblical Commentary*, pp.903–908.
17. J. Ratzinger, *Introduction to Christianity*, tr. J.R. Foster, Burns and Oates, London, 1969, pp.231f.
18. *See* the explicit treatment in Ch.8: Purgatory: The Realism of Hope.
19. Hans Urs von Balthasar: *Einfaltungen: Auf Wegen christlicher Einigung*, Munich 1969, p.130, quoted by A. R. van de Walle, *From Darkness to Dawn: How Belief in*

the Afterlife Affects Living, tr. John Bowden, Twenty Third Publications, Mystic, Conn., 1985, p.217.
20. *ibid.*, p.217.
21. Cited by Hans Urs von Balthasar, 'The Descent into Hell', *Chicago Studies* 23/2, August 1984, p.227.
22. From the second reading of the Office of Readings for Holy Saturday.
23. *ibid.*
24. The works that have most influenced me in this section are: Pheme Perkins, *Resurrection: New Testament Witness and Contemporary Reflection*, Doubleday, New York, 1984; Gerald O'Collins, *Jesus Risen*, Darton, Longman and Todd, London, 1987; Sebastian Moore, *Jesus the Liberator of Desire*, Crossroad, New York, 1989. Raymond E. Brown, 'The Resurrection of Jesus', *The New Jerome Biblical Commentary*, Geoffrey Chapman, London, 1989, pp.1373–1377.
25. Raymond E. Brown, 'The Resurrection of Jesus', *The New Jerome Biblical Commentary*, Geoffrey Chapman, London, 1989, pp. 1373–1377.
26. G. Martelet, *The Risen Christ and the Eucharistic World*, tr. René Hague, Seabury Press, New York, 1976, pp.93f.
27. Sebastian Moore, *The Fire and the Rose...*, p.86.
28. *ibid.*, p.88.
29. *ibid.*, pp.88–93.
30. See Gerald O'Collins, *Jesus Risen...*, pp.121–127; Pheme Perkins, *Resurrection...*, pp.91–95; Sebastian Moore, *Jesus the Liberator of Desire*, Crossroad, New York, 1989, pp.63–70.
31. See P. Perkins, *Resurrection*, pp.94; 126; 130; 172; 177; 196; G. O'Collins, *Jesus Risen*, p.126; J. Jeremias, *Jerusalem in the Time of Jesus*, Fortress Press, Philadelphia, 1969, pp. 374–6; P. Lapide, *The Resurrection of Jesus*, SCM, London, 1984, pp. 95f; S. Moore, *Jesus the Liberator...*, pp.51–60.
32. See S. Moore, 'An Empty Tomb Revisited', *Downside Review* 1981, pp. 245ff.
33. G. Martelet, *The Risen Christ and the Eucharistic World*, p.82.
34. *ibid.*, pp. 82–92.
35. *ibid.*, p. 82.

36. Teilhard de Chardin, *Science and Christ*, tr. René Hague Collins, London, 1965, p.13.
37. For an accessible exposition of the new paradigms in modern science: *See* Fritjof Capra, *The Tao of Physics*, Fontana Paperbacks, London, 1985; and *The Turning Point: Science, Society and The Rising Culture*, Fontana Paperbacks, London, 1984. In this latter book, Capra begins to show some inkling of possible Christian resources in his new paradigm, above all in reference to Teilhard de Chardin, eg. pp.331f.
38. Ambrose of Milan, *De Excessu Fratris sui* I, 2 PL 16, 1344.
39. G. Martelet, *The Risen Christ...*, p.182.
40. *ibid.*, p. 84; and *L'Au-delà retrouvé...*, pp.165–181.
41. L. Boros, *The Moment of Truth...*, p.156.
42. G. Martelet, *The Risen Christ...*, p.157.
43. Exegetes such as Cullman, Schlier, Cerfaux and Benoit have treated this large question. For a biblical comment: *See The New Jerome Biblical Commentary*, p.1403, and for a stimulating contemporary reflection: *See* Walter Wink, *Unmasking the Powers: The Invisible Forces That Determine Human Existence*, Fortress Press, Philadelphia, 1986, especially pp.108–165.
44. L. Boros, *The Moment of Truth...*, p.154.
45. It is true that the New Testament completes its narrative by referring to two other days, Ascension Thursday and Pentecost Sunday. However essential such mysteries are to the integral Christian story, they do not add to the substance of the parable of the three holy days. They serve, rather, to focus Christian time and meaning precisely in the fundamental time and space of the death, burial and resurrection of Jesus.

    For the Ascension, in the narrative of God's dealings with us in Christ, is the sign that the 'economy of seeing' is over now: only by believing and hoping can the *eschaton* be possessed. Pentecost, on the other hand, is precisely that outpouring of the Spirit meant to make this paschal parable the vital form of the Church's life in every generation of its existence.

7 The Eucharist: Sacrament of Hope

If the paschal mystery is the basic parable for Christian hope, the eucharist is hope's fundamental sacrament. Though such hope imagines its future in many ways, its paradigmatic symbol is this sacrament:

O sacred feast in which we partake of Christ: his sufferings are remembered, our minds are filled with his grace and we receive a pledge of the glory that is to be ours.[1]

As hope celebrates 'the real presence of Christ', and communicates in his 'body and blood', the eucharist is the real presence of the Christian future. Thus hope is being continually nourished on what is to come. The eucharistic symbolism not only grounds our images of the future in the real presence of Christ, but releases the imagination to body forth, in word and deed, God's new creation. The manner in which Christ is present in the bread and wine of the eucharist anticipates a universe in which 'God will be everything to everyone' (I Cor. 15:28).

In this shared symbol of the Church's hope, the eucharist is an antidote for any neurotic projection or fundamentalist fantasy regarding the future.[2] The last thing, the *eschaton*, is celebrated in the familiarity of what is already present both in its grace and demand. This real presence of the future engages the present form of life through the worldly elements of the shared bread and wine, in the earthy activities of eating and drinking, within a living community inescapably aware of its imperfections as a pilgrim people.

As a compact expression of Christian hope both within and for this world, the eucharist envisions a future that is more than the salvation of pure spirits. In the same way, it works against any individualistic restriction of hope. For it is the celebration of a community, not as shades haunting the world, but as sharing food and drink in its midst. When Christians celebrate their hope in this manner, they are not engaging in private meditation, nor are they meeting for a philosophical discussion on the afterlife; nor, for that matter, are they being instructed in a theological seminar. They are eating, drinking, tasting, breathing and sharing the real presence of the future that God has given us in Christ.

The Cosmic Christ

The Christ who is present as hope's food and drink is the source, the goal and the form of what the world is becoming. The englobing dynamism of the reality of Christ is expressed in various Pauline and Johannine statements: all things are made through him, in him, for him (Jn 1:3; I Cor. 8:6; Col. 1:16). He is not only the origin and goal, the exemplar and form of all creatures, but their coherence and consistency: 'all things hold together in him' (Col. 1:17). Further, he is the all-reconciling outreach of God toward a fragmented and alienated creation: 'for in him all the fullness of God was pleased to dwell, and through him to reconcile all things...making peace by the blood of his cross (Col. 1:19f.). The possibilities of such spatial metaphors are exhausted in order to centre Christian hope on Christ as the fundamental determinant of its universe.

On the one hand, Christ transcends creation. For, as Son, Lord, Word, he is neither produced nor contained nor uttered by the world. On the other, the Lord's transcendence of creation is the reason for his special immanence within it. As the incarnation of the divine creative Word, he brings a new coherence, a new form to the whole: he is 'before all things', all things are made 'in him and for him', and 'in him all things hold together' (Col. 1: 16–19). In this sense, the mystery of the incarnation extends to the whole of creation. The whole is 'God's body':

> *The mythical understanding of the world sees the whole world as a sacred theophany. In an eschatological sense, this is also what the world is for Christian faith. If the cosmos as a whole has been created in the image of God that appears—in the First-Born of creation, through him and for him—and if this First-Born indwells the world as its Head through the Church, then, in the last analysis, the world is a 'body' of God, on the basis of the principle not of pantheistic but hypostatic union.*[3]

Von Balthasar catches a sense of the dialectic manner in which the presence of Christ must be understood. In terms of empirical experience he is 'in the world', as part of its process and history. In terms of the horizon of eschatological hope, the world is 'in Christ'—the whole, a theophany of the saving mystery.

> *If the first Adam is lord of the world only as simultaneously being its fruit, then in the second Adam this genuine quality of being fruit and originating from within is surpassed by the free act of his incarnation. While the first Adam remains open and accessible to the forces of the formless chaos by reason of his being the fruit of the world, the second Adam has from the outset vanquished these forces of chaos through the freedom of his love. That which is itself formless must submit to his shaping power, and rebellion itself must bend the knee with the rest of the cosmos.*[4]

As the historical bearer of Christian hope, the Church is, of course, a part of the cosmos. More deeply, it is that part of the cosmos woken to the mystery at work in all creation. The mission of the Church, then, consists in being 'the visible sign of [such] invisible grace', the body of Christ formed in history to witness to the cosmic body of its Lord, the sacrament of God's universal grace.

Such is the general context of the sacramental expression of hope. There would be no sacramental significance in the eucharist, (or of the other sacraments) unless it enacted the larger sacramentality of the Church. The sacramentality of the Church, for its part, would exist in a vacuum without reference to the cosmic sacramentality of a transformed creation. However, there would be no transformation of creation unless, at its heart, there blazed the paschal mystery of Christ, and that paschal mystery would be only a mythic form were it not the self-embodiment of trinitarian love in our world.

Eucharistic imagination

As the analogical imagination[5] weaves together the many meanings of eucharistic symbolism, the texture of Christian hope is enhanced. As has already been implied, the mysteries of the Trinity, creation, grace, the incarnation, death and resurrection of Jesus, the Church and the sacraments are all interconnected in it. Add to this, the cosmic dimensions of the 'fruit of the earth' and the historical reference to 'the work of human hands', and we find ourselves dealing with an intensely compact symbol of what Christian hope is about.

In exploring more deeply the eschatological meaning of the eucharist, it is important to give full play to this analogical imagination. Former theologies of the eucharist congealed in the deficient categories of a very un-theological physicalist philosophy. A crude, excessively polemical notion of transubstantiation left little room for theological imagination. The bread and wine were simply the matter of the sacrament. Their substance is simply replaced by the reality of Christ. The eschatologically unnerving aspect of this is that the real presence of Christ ousted the real presence, the substance, of the earthly realities. The heavenly Christ, coming from what was crudely imagined as the 'outside' of the world, replaces the essential form of what was on the inside, the substance of the bread and wine: only the accidents remained. The upshot was that the eucharist was certainly held 'to contain' the heavenly Christ in a mysterious fashion, but that the earthly realities concerned no longer had lasting significance. While not denying the intense realistic thrust of such a version of eucharistic faith, I believe it can be expressed in a far more ample manner, more apt to do justice to the historical and cosmic mode of Christ's presence.

For in Christ, as we mentioned above, 'all things hold together', just as he 'sums up' all creation (Eph. 1:10), and is 'the first-born' and the inner finality of creation. Von Balthasar concludes the long paragraph we have already referred to:

> *But in his definitive form, he* [Christ] *takes up into himself all the forms of creation. The form which he stamps upon the world is not tyrannical; it bestows completeness and perfection beyond anything imaginable. This holds for the forms of nature, concerning which we cannot say...that they will simply disappear, leaving a vacuum between pure matter and man, who is a microcosmic fruit of nature. To be sure, it is only in man that nature raises its countenance into the region of eternity; and yet the same* natura naturans *that in the end gives rise to man is also that* natura naturata, *and the whole plenitude of forms which the imagination of the divine nature has brought forth belongs analytically to the nature of man.*

> *The same holds in greater measure for the creations of man in his cultural development: they, too—they especially!—belong to him as the images he has produced out of himself...to impress upon the world and which have a continued existence in man by reason of their birth even when they have perished in time. The same, finally, holds to a supreme degree for the creations in the realm of grace.*[6]

Such a sweeping and intense statement accents how all reality—the physical world, all forms of life, the distinctive life of human consciousness, its cultural creations, and its transformation in the Spirit—is *in* and *for* Christ.

Set within such a comprehensive vision, the transformation of the fruit of the earth and work of human hands into the body and blood of Christ anticipates the cosmic transformation already in progress. The new substance of the transformed bread and wine anticipates the radical transubstantiation of all creation when the inner consistency and coherence of all things in Christ will be achieved.[7] The bread and the wine, the matter of the sacrament, products of nature and culture as they are, are given back to us in the sacrament as bearing an eschatological form. In this way, the community of hope is enabled to communicate in the ultimate form of human and cosmic reality. The bread and wine are not abolished by the Spirit's action. Rather, they are constituted in their ultimate significance, now food and drink to nourish an ultimate kind of humanity. They are no longer 'the food which perishes, but...the food which endures to eternal life' (Jn 6:27). The eucharist is the 'true bread from heaven' (Jn 6:32), 'the bread of God which...gives life to the world' (v.33), 'the bread of life' (v.35): as nourishing us with the life-giving being of Christ, the food of the eucharist is 'my flesh for the life of the world' (v.51).

In short, the eucharist is the sacramental communication of what is 'food indeed', 'drink indeed' (v.55). Through the transformative action of the Spirit, the eucharistic elements are no longer mere nutrients of biological life ('not such as the fathers ate and died...' (v.58)), but the food and drink of eternal life. In their meaning as real food and drink for the community of believers, the eucharistic bread and wine provide a foretaste of life in a transformed universe.[8]

The real presence of the Spirit

If the eucharist is the sign of the eschatological presence of Christ, filling all things, and drawing all things to himself, it is so within the dynamic field of the Spirit's presence. For the 'Holy Breath' is concealed within the travail of all creation to inspire the prayer of Christian hope with 'sighs too deep for words' (Rom. 8:26). The eucharistic epiclesis is the Church's prayer as it invokes this Spirit over the 'matter of the sacrament' and the assembled community. Let us now set this in the wider field of the Spirit's action in forming Christ and bringing the whole of creation to its completion.

When, in the Spirit, Jesus is conceived, anointed and empowered, and when, possessed by such a Holy Spirit, he preaches, heals, and drives out evil spirits, this does not mean the destruction of his humanity—or that of anyone else. The various temptation accounts underscore the conviction that Jesus' mission entailed no escape from the human condition (Mt 4:1–11; Lk 4:1–13; Heb. 2:18; 4:15). For the influence of the Spirit is to expand the humanity of Jesus into solidarity with the suffering and the lost. Through the Spirit, Jesus becomes the 'man for others', the man of inclusive humanness. This is borne out in all his relations with the men and women and children of his time, and in his conviviality with the sinful and the outcast. The cross can be understood only in terms of a life of inspired inclusiveness.

Further, when the Spirit effects the resurrection of the crucified, the risen Lord is still Jesus, marked with the stigmata of the cross. He is glorified in his identity as Son of the Father, and as brother to all. By the same token, the resurrection of individual believers through the power of the Spirit means not a destruction of personal identity, but its final establishment and liberation:

> *If the Spirit of him who raised Jesus from the dead dwells in you, he who raised Christ Jesus from the dead will give life to your mortal bodies also through his Spirit who dwells in you* (Rom. 8:11; cf. I Jn 3:2).

When, for instance, the Spirit forms the community of the Church out of human society by making it the body of Christ (Eph. 1:22f.), individual identity is not suppressed or lost in this transpersonal embodiment. In fact, it is further differentiated, in the unity of the Spirit, into special kinds of giftedness and vocation: 'To each is given a manifestation of the Spirit for the common good' (I Cor. 12:7). Though each Christian can say with Paul, 'It is no longer I who live, but Christ living in me' (Gal. 2:20a), this does not mean a loss of identity. Rather, that identity is enhanced, as a new level of freedom: 'You were called to freedom' (Gal. 5:13) and personal worth: 'I live in the faith of the Son of God who loved me and gave himself for me' (Gal. 2:20b).

The individual transformation models the transformation of the material and collective dimensions of human existence. This is an instance of the more general conviction of the New Testament that all the promises and prefigurements of what has preceded the coming of Christ finds, in him, through the all-completing act of God, its fulfilment: '...all the promises of God find their 'Yes' in him' (II Cor. 1:20).

This is reason to suggest, then, that the epicletic action of the Spirit in the eucharist exemplifies the eschatological mode of the Spirit's transforming activity. The reality of the world, the meaning of history and personal identity itself, are neither annihilated nor replaced through the action of the Spirit. For the Spirit brings all reality to its fulfilment in Christ. As the ancient axiom has it, 'grace heals, perfects and elevates nature.' The self-communication of the Godhead (grace) does not overwhelm the self-transcending dynamics of creation (nature). Rather, the divine mystery, as Father, Son and Spirit, is the end, the form and energy of creation's self-realisation in God. In the divine mystery, creation comes home. God's self-communication to us is our self-realisation in the divine.

Thus, the eucharist, as the intense sacramental point in the field of the Spirit's universal activity, educates Christian hope to a sense of the Spirit's transforming presence. At the same time, it compactly symbolises, in the most real sense of the word, the identity of the Spirit as the Spirit of Christ: the Holy Breath is given by him and impels toward him, animating creation as the soul of his body. The eucharist calls on the Spirit to make Christ *really* present to the real world of Christian hope, symbolised in 'the fruits of the earth and the work of human hands'—the bread and wine of our embodied, social, historical existence. On these the Spirit is invoked: '...we ask you to make them holy by the power of your Spirit that they may become the body and blood of Our Lord Jesus Christ.' The Church prays to the Spirit to transform these elements of the human world into their ultimate reality: that they may become both 'the bread of life' and our 'spiritual drink'. Then the Spirit is invoked in the wider context of the community of believers, that they may be transformed by what has become present among them: 'Grant that we who are nourished by his body and blood may be filled with his Holy Spirit, and become one Body, one Spirit in

Christ.'[9]

Thus transformed by the Spirit into the Body of the Son to the glory of the Father, the Christian community is established in its eschatological hope. However dismembered the world, such hope anticipates a universe transformed 'in the unity of the Holy Spirit'.

We are now in a position, after these general remarks, to tease out the eschatological meaning of the eucharist. We have set the eucharist in the context of the cosmic transformation implied in the mystery of Christ, and placed in the field of the universal activity of the Spirit. Some further points can now be made to delineate the concrete character of Christian hope.

Features of Eucharistic hope

(i) The Paschal Form of the Eschaton: the Eucharist as Sacrifice

The eucharist expresses the paschal dimension of hope: as often as you eat this bread and drink this cup, you proclaim the Lord's death until he comes' (I Cor. 11:26). The present moment of hope is enfolded into the 'sacrifice of Christ', so that the community of believers, in the individual, collective and cosmic dimensions of its existence, is drawn into his dying and rising. Indeed, the eucharistic sacrifice not only signifies the paschal character of the mystery of Christ, but is itself an instance of the world's passing over into the new creation.

In shedding his blood on the cross, Jesus actualises his existence as unreserved self-offering to the Father. As dying into the new creation, he yields himself to the Father, and to the incalculable creativity of the Spirit, 'for the life of the world'. His dying becomes the dynamism of the world's transformation. As it sacramentally symbolises such a self-offering, the eucharist embodies the character of our hope as it experiences the travail of creation: '...we rejoice in our sufferings, knowing that suffering produces endurance, and endurance produces character, and character produces hope, and hope does not disappoint us...' (Rom. 5:3ff.). Hence, this sacrament sustains the believer in Christ's sacrificial mode of being: 'And I when I am lifted up from the earth, will draw all men to myself' (Jn 12:32). Being drawn to Christ, means being drawn into his paschal mode of existence. Celebrating the eucharist, the believer participates in the paschal mystery.

In this context, the Spirit's transformation of the earthly elements of the bread and wine in the eucharist is itself an image suggestive of the universality of the paschal mystery. As we have already mentioned, a traditional theology of transubstantiation would state, in Aristotelian categories, that the 'substance' of the bread and wine are changed into the body and blood of Christ, with only the 'accidents' remaining. When this doctrine is set in a more eschatological frame of reference, it becomes possible to understand such a transformation as an index of the paschal movement of the whole of creation. The bread and wine have ceased to exist 'in themselves', as physical and cultural elements serving only the reality of this present mode of existence. For now, as the sacramental reality of Christ's body and blood, they have passed over into their final reality—even though the 'accidents' remain: that is, they are Christ's presence to the as yet unconcluded history of this mode of time and space. Yet, because these worldly elements have passed over into him, to be 'in him, through him, for him', Christ is uniquely 'in them' to nourish our hope into its final vision of the world. For what is so basically 'of this world' now exists as the bearer of an exclusively eschatological purpose, as 'trans-finalised', to anticipate, in its sacramental form, the transformation of the universe in Christ. The eucharistic bread and wine are now the food and drink of everlasting life—offered and consumed for an eschatological purpose: to draw those who receive this sacrament into the great paschal act of 'passing out of this world to the Father' (Jn 13:1).

Nourished on the food and drink of such a paschal form of existence, hope understands itself as dying into a new creation. Death is not a mere cessation, a falling away into the world's past. It is surrendering to the Spirit of the future. Dying with Christ, yielding into the wholeness of God's universe, human existence is extended into its full relationality. We are drawn out of the limited, defensive individuality of this form of life into the ecstasy of truly personal, relational existence. We die out of ourselves and into the sphere of the Spirit. Self-giving love is the ultimate life-form. For existence has to be re-centred by participating in the death of Christ if it is to be re-centred in Christ, re-animated by the Spirit, reintegrated into a new creation. Thus, the transformation of the material elements of the bread and wine into the body and blood of Christ enact, as an image and instance, the 'pasch of the universe'—that groaning and travail of all creation until the new is brought forth.

(ii) The Communal Form of the Eschaton: Holy Communion

As the sacrament of Christian hope, the eucharist is 'holy communion'. Nourished on the reality of this sacrament, hope cannot but be hope for all. For the eucharist always occurs in a communal form.[10] There is no validity in a 'private eucharist'. For this sacrament is celebrated by a given Christian community, with others, for them, as they represent the wider communities of Church and world. In 'holy communion', the Christian receives the whole of his body, the whole of his cosmic incarnation. It is the paradigm instance of that genuine co-existence described by the Swedish poet, Tomas Tranströmer when he wrote:

> *Each man is a half-open door*
> *leading to a room for everyone.*[11]

This communal principle has always been the basis

for discerning an authentic Christian celebration of this sacrament. A self-enclosed individualism has no place in the time and space and mood of the eucharist: 'Because there is one bread, we who are many are one body for we all partake of the one bread' (I Cor. 10:17). The eucharistic cup is not 'private communion' with Christ but a reception of the new covenant in his blood poured out for 'all', the 'many' (Lk 22:30). The effect of the eucharist is to form believers into the one body of Christ. In so doing, it unites unite them in the eschatological solidarity of being members of one another in the new humanity of Christ:

> *For just as the body is one and has many members, and all the members of the body, though many, are one body, so it is with Christ. For by one Spirit we were all baptised into one body...and all were made to drink of the one Spirit* (I Cor. 12:12f.).

This sacramental realisation of our eschatological co-humanity in Christ establishes its own kind of communication and compassion:

> *If one member suffers, all suffer together. If one member is honoured, all rejoice together. Now you are the body of Christ and individually members of it* (I Cor. 11:26ff.).

In other words, the dynamism of the eucharist is to incorporate those who celebrate it into the ever larger community: the body of Christ in a universe of grace. The hope it embodies is essentially corporate. In the words of Teilhard de Chardin:

> *When the priest says the words* Hoc est corpus meum, *his words fall directly on the bread and directly transform it into the individual reality of Christ. But the great sacramental operation does not cease at that local and momentary event...but these different acts are only the diversely central points in which the continuity*

of a unique act is split up and fixed, in space and time, for our experience. In fact, from the beginning of the Messianic preparation up till the Parousia, passing through the historic manifestation of Jesus and the phases of growth of his Church, a single event has been developing in the world: the incarnation, realised, in each individual, through the eucharist.

All the communions of a life-time are one communion.

All communions of all men now living are one communion.

All the communions of all the men, present, past and future are one communion...

In a secondary and generalised sense, but in a true sense, the sacramental species are formed by the totality of the world, and the duration of the creation is the time needed for its consecration. In Christo vivimus, movemur et sumus.[12]

(iii) The Eucharist as Judgment: Real Presence and Real Absence

In its eschatological character, the eucharist anticipates the character of the divine judgment. As the kingdom is often depicted in terms of a banquet (Mt 22:1–10; Lk 12:37; Rev. 3:20), the eucharist is a sacramental anticipation of such final conviviality of life given and received in the mystery of God. To the degree our lives have been nourished on the 'junk food' of false individualism, or on the 'fast food' of life that does not know how to wait and hope, the eucharist is apt to provoke an allergic reaction. It is too rich for the sickly constitution of human selfishness. As such, it is distasteful to the unhealthy palate, and occurs as a judgment on our condition.[13]

In this sense, the eucharist is a form of protest against the forces that compromise the genuine health of the human community. Self-absorption, isolation, and the injustice and greed to which they give rise, are anti-eucharist. To the degree that the human condition is structured in an anti-eucharistic form, the real presence occurs as the *real absence* of our true humanity. Instead of being the sacrament at the summit and source of the life of the Church, it is an empty ritual.

Since violence and injustice dis-member the one body, and make the real presence a real absence in the real world of self-centred calculation, the biblical injunction to 'eat and drink worthily' (I Cor. 11:29), is a continuing call to conversion. Hence the need to 'discern the body'. To profane the body and blood of the Lord is to eat and drink judgment on oneself (cf. I Cor. 11:27–32). Thus, the eucharistic community, experiences itself as being brought to judgment. The eucharist prizes open the closed circle of inward-looking, comfortably exclusive community. It is a judgment on any foreclosure on the membership: 'There is neither Jew nor Greek, there is neither slave nor free, there is neither male nor female; for you are all one in Christ Jesus' (Gal. 3:28; Col. 3:11). In more senses than one, the eucharist 're-members' the body of the crucified one, to form, beyond the alienations and boundaries, the polarities and classes of the given society, the authentically open community of hope.[14]

In celebrating the eucharist, hope acknowledges the sobering fact of a world not yet set free. In the midst of such ambiguities, it is both a judgment upon us 'for falling from [our] first love' (Rev. 2:4), and a promise inspiring hope: 'Behold I stand at the door and knock. If anyone hears my voice and opens the door, I will come into him and eat with him, and he with me' (Rev. 3:20).

(iv) The Eucharist as the Form of Eschatological Grace: Thanksgiving

As the eschatological sacrament *par excellence*, this sacrament is a continual reminder to Christian hope that our ultimate future always remains a mystery of grace. For it instances the manner in which God's transforming love occurs in our world to summon forth human co-operation. There is no eucharist without the antecedent grace of the Father who 'so loved the world' (Jn 3:16) in sending the Son, and in pouring out the Spirit. There is no eucharist without the prior grace of the creation of the world, without a prior history of God's saving action culminating 'in these last days' in the coming of the Son (Heb. 1:1f.). Similarly, there can be no eucharist without the grace of the Church inspired to celebrate its hope in the lives of the apostles and saints, martyrs and prophets, teachers and reformers, mystics and pastors through the ages. Such a sacramental consciousness founds the conviction that 'all is grace' (Thérèse of Lisieux, Georges Bernanos).

As a celebration of such grace, the eucharist is *eucharistia*, thanksgiving for the already-present character of the mystery at work. As responding to such grace, as working with it, 'getting with it', where 'it' is the great field of the Spirit's action, the eucharist is the sacrament of hope. It is the act of expectant collaboration, stretching out to that which is not yet, to that which is truly present, but still only in its sacramental form in the midst of an unconcluded and struggling history.[15]

If hope loses its sense of grace as a present reality, when it cannot 'abound in thanksgiving' (Col. 2:7), it begins hoping in mere hopefulness, with no substance, with no thrust born out of actual Christian life. Though an abstract, doctrinaire valuation of the future might spin out some kind of thin optimistic ideology, it would lack a gracious experience of the present, and relate to both past and present only with dissatisfaction and rejection. On the other hand, if hope is truly eucharistic, it arises within a fundamental thankfulness for the whole grace of life manifest in the wonder of creation, in the coming of Christ, in the gift of the Spirit, in the whole corporate tradition of Christian living. Out of such grace, hope reaches wholeheartedly into the future as a fulfilment of what is already present. The future is neither an ever frustrated human project; nor a dreadful mystery indifferently devouring history by the force of some absolute power that has not shown its face. It is grace which will keep on being grace, ever surprisingly, ever more wonderfully, true to itself: 'I came that they might have life and have it more abundantly' (Jn 10:10).

(v) The Eucharist as the Presence of Eschatological Love

The eucharist is the real presence of God's love as the ultimate life-form and fundamental energy of the new creation: 'love remains' (I Cor. 13:8).

The sacrament of Christ's body given up, and of his blood poured out for the many, enacts the mystery of the God who is love (I Jn 4:8,16). This God has 'so loved the world' as to give what is most intimate and personal to himself, his Son, for the world's salvation. The Son, as both the self-revelation and self-communication of the Father, expresses this love by 'loving his own who were in the world', and loving them 'to the end' (Jn 13:1f.). The Son's self-sacrifice for others becomes in turn the way, the truth and the life for those who believe in him. These, in turn, hear his new commandment 'to love one another as I have loved you' (Jn 13:34).

The eucharist is the living memorial of such love. It invites hope to imagine the world being drawn into its ultimate 'love-life'. For the love embodied in the eucharist nourishes human existence into its final form: 'If anyone eats this bread he will live forever, and the bread that I shall give you is my flesh for the life of the world' (Jn 6:51). Love communicates itself into the body of this earthly existence: for the Word is with us not only in the 'flesh' of the incarnation; but in the eating and drinking basic to our earthy conviviality. By assimilating the eucharistic bread and wine, we are incorporated into the transfigured humanity of Jesus:

> *The cup of blessing which we bless, is it not a participation in the blood of Christ? The bread which we break, is it not a participation in the body of Christ? Because there is one bread, we who are many, are one body* (I Cor. 10:16f.).

So incorporated into the transformed reality of Christ's body, the eucharistic community lives an eschatological life which promises its own fulfilment:

> *Amen, amen, I say to you, unless you eat the flesh of the Son of man and drink his blood, you have no life in you: he who eats my flesh and drinks my blood has eternal life, and I will raise him up on the last day* (Jn 6:53f.).

As it intimates the ultimate life-form of creation, the eucharist unfolds in the consciousness of a mutual indwelling of Christ and the community of hope: 'He who eats my flesh and drinks my blood abides in me, and I in him' (Jn 6:56; 15:4). This co-inherence of Christ and the faithful is, itself, understood in terms of the communion between the Father and the Son: 'As the living Father sent me, and I live because of the Father, he who eats me will live because of me' (Jn 6:57). Jesus' presence to the disciples is, by implication, an extension of this communion, and a way of offering it to the world: 'As thou didst send me into the world, so I have sent them into the world' (Jn 17:18). When such a communion opens itself to the world, it works to enfold all believers into an eschatologically consummated union...'that they may be perfectly one' (Jn 17:23); 'That they may all be one, even as thou, Father, art in me, and I in thee, that they also may be in us...' (Jn 17:21).[16]

The intense consciousness of mutual indwelling and communion expresses what the eucharist suggests can only be understood in terms of two great desires. The first is the desire of Christ that we might be where he is: 'Father, I desire that they... may be with me where

I am to behold my glory which thou hast given to me in thy love before the foundation of the world' (Jn 17:24). The eucharist evidences the continuing eschatological prayer of the risen Jesus. Even though this sacrament occurs within the pilgrim history of hope—a real presence and a real absence, a 'now' but 'not yet'—this prayer is already being answered. Each eucharist is the answer to the prayer of Jesus, 'that they may be one even as we are one' (Jn 17:11).

Corresponding to, and, indeed, resulting from, this prayer of Christ is the desire of the Church for the return of the Lord. In 'announcing the death of the Lord until he come' (I Cor. 11:26), the eucharist embodies this desire to be united definitively with Jesus as the full realisation of the mystery of saving love: 'Maranatha!'...'Come, Lord!' (Rev. 22:20; I Cor. 16:22). The eucharist expresses this desire that Jesus as Lord will enter fully into this world as his domain, establishing his lordship, filling all things, bringing all things to completion in a transfigured universe. In the meantime, it is celebrated in an adoring, expectant openness to the mystery of ultimate love at work, a living memorial of the ultimate reality: 'This is my body given up for you. Do this in remembrance of me' (Lk 22:19).

For this sacrament of God's self-giving resonates with deepest symbols and experiences of love: desire, union, mutual self-giving, the ecstasy of the self sacrificed for the other's good, the self nourishing the being of the beloved other... All such forms of love are subsumed into the excess of the divine love which the eucharist enacts. Such an enactment of love does not occur merely in the domain of piety or personal mysticism or romantic sensibility. For what is presented in its sacramental form is the original and ultimate character of reality itself. It offers itself in sober objectivity as the substance of all existence to be literally eaten and drunk, tasted and felt, heard and seen (cf. I Jn 1:1–4).

Thus, through the eucharist, hope envisions its future as ultimate being-in-love. This appears as folly, of course, to a culture in which the experience of love has been so drastically disenchanted and its physicality so trivialised. As subverting all our cultural attempts to reduce love to mere consumption, the eucharist expresses in our world that special excess which every form of love we know obscurely recognises. It is an emblem of the passionate nature of the new creation in which the lover's extravagant rhetoric becomes a statement of real life: 'my flesh is food indeed, and my blood is drink indeed' (Jn 6:55). The sacramental reality predictably contests all our types of psychic numbness, not least within the Church itself. Yet still, the passion and fundamental physicality of eucharistic love-language shocks hope out of any vision of the future that would reduce it to the habitation of bloodless, disembodied, unfeeling and isolated pure spirits.

(vi) Foretaste of eternal life:

Finally, the eucharist is the foretaste of the future. It gives hope a taste of what is to come.[17] In this sacrament of hope's passionate longing and present communion, the language of taste has a certain emphasis in evoking the presence of the future within Christian experience. For the believer is one 'who has tasted the heavenly gift', 'become a partaker of the Holy Spirit', and 'tasted the goodness of the Word of God and the powers of the age to come' (Heb. 6:4f.). In the eucharist, the psalmist's exhortation to 'taste and see that the Lord is good'—Ps. 33 (34):8—attains an intense sacramental realism in eating and drinking the body and the blood of Christ. In his commentary on this, St Thomas Aquinas remarks on the metaphor of tasting in an arresting manner:

One experiences a thing by means of sense, but the experience of a thing present differs from the experience of something absent. One experiences an absent [distant] *reality by sight,*

> *smell, hearing. Whereas one experiences a present reality by touch and taste. Still, touch attains this present reality in an extrinsic way; while taste attains what is present in an interior way. Now God is neither distant from us nor outside us...and so the experience of the divine goodness is called tasting.*[18]

The eucharistic extension of this principle is obvious enough: in the eucharistic meal we taste the object of our hope as present within the body of our experience. It is not the taste of death, but of life. If hope has new eyes to envision the future, new hearing to catch the ultimate promise of the Word that is spoken, if it inhales the Spirit as the atmosphere of the new creation, in the eucharist it tastes the reality of eternal life. In the earthiness of the sacrament, our hope has a fundamental grip on the reality of its future as it handles the tokens of a transfigured creation. It eats, drinks and savours eternal life; so to relish in anticipation, in the hesitant conviviality of what we are, that which will be offered us in the end as a banquet.

Conclusion

We have been focusing on the eucharist as *the* eschatological sacrament. In traditional terms, it is the *signum efficax gratiae*, the 'symbol efficacious of the grace it represents'. It is a sign, certainly, for it employs the very earthly realities of the human world, bread and wine. But it brings about, through the power of the Spirit, the eschatological embodiment of Christ in our midst. In him, crucified and risen, our humanity is passing over into its eschatological fullness. Admittedly, we have expanded the meaning of the eucharist in the analogical imagination of hope, in order to appreciate its reference to the whole of cosmic and human reality. For the celebration of the eucharist is not meant to be a liturgical episode isolated from the universe of our Christian experience.

Rather, it is the intense, compact index of the Spirit's activity throughout the world, as it christens the whole of reality, and brings creation to its ultimate coherence and consistency as the body of Christ.

All this is to say that the eucharist is the radical orientation of the life of Christian hope. From the earliest times, the eucharist was celebrated as a literal *orientation*, as the worshiping community turned toward the rising sun as a symbol of the risen Christ.[19]

Such a tradition of facing east has a contemporary relevance. For the celebration of the eucharist turns us toward the light of our world and its history, to welcome the presence of what will rise out of the depths to fill creation with its radiance.

After these extended reflections on both the focal parable and fundamental sacrament of hope, we are now in the position to address more freely a number of particular questions. Even if we cannot escape from an essential provisionality in our answers, the parable that illumines our hopeful existence and the sacrament that nourishes it will give a scope and momentum to our words, allowing them to rest in what cannot ever be fully expressed—in the ever-obscure, but peaceful assurance of hope itself.

1. Antiphon from the Vespers of *Corpus Christi*.
2. It is odd that eucharist receives little or no treatment in the otherwise valuable eschatologies of Küng, Hayes, von Balthasar, Ratzinger, Rahner and Boros referred to so often in this book. In happy contrast, as we shall see, are the works of Durrwell, Martelet, Teilhard de Chardin and Wainwright.
3. Hans Urs von Balthasar, *The Glory of the Lord: A Theological Aesthetics. I: Seeing the Form*, trans. E. Leiva-Merikakis, eds. J. Fessio and J. Riches, T. & T. Clark, Edinburgh, 1988, p.679.
4. Von Balthasar, *The Glory of the Lord*, pp.679f.
5. I use this phrase in the sense of David Tracy's, *The Analogical Imagination*, Seabury, New York, 1983.

6. Von Balthasar, *The Glory of the Lord*, pp.679f.
7. Here I am indebted to F.X. Durrwell, *L'Eucharistie, sacrement pascal*, Cerf, Paris, 1981. In what follows, I have relied especially on pp.77–113. Also of special value is G. Martelet, *The Risen Christ and the Eucharistic World*, tr. R.Hague, Seabury, New York, 1976, especially pp.160–197.
8. Though I have found Geoffrey Wainwright, *Eucharist and Eschatology*, Epworth, London, 1971, a rich resource for this chapter, he is surprisingly unsympathetic at this point:

> *It is fairly fashionable among Roman Catholic theologians to bring the consecration of the eucharistic bread and wine into relation with the notion of a transfigured creation; but they do so with only a vague awareness, if indeed they are conscious of it at all, of the problem that is thereby posed for them in connection with their* de fide *doctrine of transubstantiation... For many of them point to the consecrated elements as the first instance of the transformed creation. Now if one starts from the eucharistic consecration understood as transubstantiation of the bread and wine into the body and blood of Christ, then by a simple prolongation of the lines one arrives at a notion of the transfigured final creation as 'substantially' Christ, with the new heavens and the new earth as 'accidents'; but this is hard to distinguish from pantheism or from the total absorption of all things into the divine. On the other hand, if one starts with a vision of a transfigured creation on which Christ feeds his people at his own table on the abundant fruits of the new earth, then in coming to the eucharist one arrives at a view of Christ feeding his people at the holy table on (consecrated) bread and wine; but there is no transubstantiation of the bread and wine into his own body and blood...* (pp. 104f).

I suspect the ecumenical discussions of the last twenty years, and a more methodological distinction between theology and doctrine, to say nothing of a clearer investigation of what 'pantheism' might mean, would all serve to modify this judgment.
9. *The Roman Missal*, 'Eucharistic Prayer III'.

10. G. Wainwright, *Eucharist and Eschatology*, pp.110–118.
11. Tomas Tranströmer, 'The Half-Finished Heaven', *Collected Works*, trans. Robin Fulton, Bloodaxe Books, Newcastle upon Tyne, 1987, p.65.
12. Teilhard de Chardin, *The Divine Milieu*, Harper and Row, New York, 1960, pp.123–126. Note, however, G. Wainwright's lack of sympathy for this line of thought:
    > *The strong whiff of pantheism attaching to the writings of Teilhard de Chardin's eschatology is not unconnected with his penchant for using the doctrine of transubstantiation as a more general theological model.* (See G. Wainwright, *Eucharist and Eschatology...* p.192, n.396.)

    After quoting some passages, Wainwright concludes 'that there can be no thought of an easy escape by saying that there is merely an 'analogical' relation intended between the consecrated eucharistic elements and the final condition of creation.' (*ibid.*, p.192, n.327). The direction I have been pursuing here is, admittedly, the contrary. I have been maintaining that the analogical imagination does legitimately interconnect the mysteries of faith with considerable profit. I am sure that these seemingly contradictory positions could be ecumenically resolved. For the moment, I merely note that they are the outcome of differing theological stances: on the one hand, the Catholic analogical imagination; on the other, the more dialectical method of the classical Protestant tradition. *See* David Tracy, *The Analogical Imagination...*, pp.371–390. As a further reference on this theme: *See* Wainwright, *op.cit.*, pp.149f.
13. *See* Johann Baptist Metz, *The Emergent Church: The Future of Christianity in a Postbourgeois World*, tr. P. Mann, Crossroad, New York, 1981, pp.34–47; and G. Wainwright, *Eucharist and Eschatology*, pp.80–91; 150f. Paul Bernier, *Bread Broken and Shared: Broadening Our Vision of Eucharist*, Ave Maria Press: Notre Dame, Ind., 1981.
14. For a deeply challenging treatment of the eucharist as the sacrament of Christian community: *See* Francis Moloney, *A Body Broken for a Broken People*, Collins Dove, Melbourne, 1990. This book opens a way to re-instate the eucharist the sacrament of hope for those who, in the present determinations of Church law, are barred

from its full celebration.
15. *See* G. Wainwright, *Eucharist and Eschatology*, pp.148f.
16. For excellent reflections on the eucharist and the search for Christian unity: *See* G. Wainwright, *Eucharist and Eschatology*, pp.135–146.
17. G. Wainwright, *Eucharist and Eschatology*, pp.151–153.
18. *In Psalms Davidis Expositio, op. Omnia*, Parma 1873, vol.14, p.124.
19. *See* Geoffrey Wainwright, *Eucharist and Eschatology*, pp.78ff.

8 Purgatory: the Realism of Hope

After some years of comparative silence, theology is once more exploring the subject of purgatory.[1] No doubt, this recent reticence was caused by a number of factors. High on the list would have to be the more positive accent in the liturgy regarding the fate of the dead.[2] As white vestments replace the black in requiem masses, we have an emblem of a widespread effort to highlight the significance of resurrection in the context of Christian death. Then, in dealing with guilt, we have another indicator of this positive emphasis: 'going to confession' has become a 'celebration of the sacrament of reconciliation'. There have been other changes too; the somewhat unregulated Catholic industry, to say nothing of the economy, of having masses said for the Holy Souls is now moderated in the light of official discouragement of frequent votive masses for the dead. There has been a general pastoral and theological effort to dispense with any undue morbidity or calculation in matters eschatological: death is an encounter with the Risen Lord; and our lives in this world are not an anxious exile, but a pilgrimage into eternal life. Christian faith is not meant to shudder at the prospect of a capricious judge and an unpredictable judgment: it inspires a hopeful surrender to a boundless mercy. Compared to the past when purgatory was presented as a less terminal form of hell, today it has moved closer to heaven in our collective psyche.

Further, a rich variety of historical investigations

has thrown considerable light on the emergence of this doctrine in the hypothetical and passing remarks of Origen and Augustine. For example, Augustine was the first to consider I Cor. 3:10–15 as purgatorial. For him and other early theologians, purifying fire was always part of a larger activity of God, such as the trials of life and the final judgment.[3] Then, regarding the subsequent development of this theme along certain graphic lines, the authority of the *Dialogues* of Gregory the Great now appears to be questionable.[4] Historians, such as Jacques Le Goff, have deftly placed many of the stages and turns in the development of the Catholic doctrine of purgatory in their historical and cultural setting.[5] Then, too, as one would expect, the ecumenical context of modern theology has expanded the mystery of God's purifying and transforming love beyond the bounds of its distinctively Catholic formulation. The doctrine of purgatory has not been lost in these developments, but it has been set in a larger, more nuanced context.

How then might we have a new look at this eschatological symbol in a way that fits more surely with the basic account of Christian hope?

Church teaching

The formal Church teaching on this matter is quite restrained and modest, always being connected with the tradition of praying for the departed. A sense of purgatory has been present in Christianity in both the East and the West, at least from the third century. As a doctrine, it was defined only in the West, at the Second Council of Lyons (1274), the Council of Florence (1439) and the Council of Trent (1563). The first two instances arose out of discussion with the Eastern church. The third was a response to the Reformers.

These definitions are in fact quite minimal. They add up to three points: there is a state of purification;

in this state, temporal punishment still owing at the time of death is expiated and remitted as a prelude to admission to the beatific vision; those in purgatory can be helped by the prayers and good works of the faithful in this life. The Council of Trent affirms the existence of purgatory and underscores our solidarity with the fate of the dead through prayer and the celebration of the eucharist.[6] It warns against excessive theorising about what is necessarily beyond our experience: 'The difficult and subtle questions which do not make for edification and for the most part are not conducive to piety must be excluded from popular sermons...likewise anything belonging to the realm of superstition or smacking of dishonourable gain...'[7] Vatican II introduces purgatory in terms of the pilgrim nature of the Church, a communion spreading over time and reaching beyond the barrier of death: 'Some of his disciples are pilgrims on earth while others have died and are being purified and still others are glorified...we all in various ways...share in the same love of God and neighbour, and we all sing the same hymn to the glory of God.'[8]

Scriptural witness

Today's biblical scholarship does not permit any dogmatic proof of the existence or nature of purgatory. Its biblical foundation has to be sought more in the abundant scriptural reference to the holiness, justice and love of God purifying the individual and the community. The biblical data would be distorted if its witness to the whole mystery of God's purifying and liberating action was condensed into the particular Catholic theme of purgatory as it emerged within the tradition. The various classical references are there: 2 Maccabees 12:39–45 (the exhortation to pray for the dead who have fallen in battle and found to be wearing pagan amulets); I Cor. 15:29 (the mysterious practice of being baptised for the dead); Lk 12:59 (the necessity of making full reparation); I Cor. 3:10–15 (the 'fire' that tests the sort of work each one has done)—this latter has proved to be the most used text of all. The context of these and other texts certainly indicates the horizon in which the particular symbol of purgatory came to be expressed, even if we are a long way from dogmatic proof texts. The mood of the New Testament is that of celebrating the wonder of what God has done for us in Christ. The meaning of that salvation in various contexts of life and death, such as the postmortem fate of the Christian believer, was teased out in later tradition.[9]

Purgatory as symbol

In any present discussion, it is important to keep reminding ourselves that the only way 'the other side' can be expressed is through the use of symbols. Only in terms of what we know *here*, can we find a tentative language for expressing what happens *there*. There is no direct knowledge of the beyond. The symbols formed out of present Christian and human experience enable us to explore, in some dim approximation, the failure or fulfilment proper to that other dimension of which, as yet, we have no direct experience. Purgatory is, then, first of all a symbol.

But it is a symbol animated by a precise practice and fundamental experience: the practice of praying for the dead, and the experience of the communion of the saints. As such, it is not designed to offer information about the topography of the afterlife. It occurs, rather, as a focus of meaning within the rhetoric and imagination of the Christian community as the Church prays for the departed and expresses its hope for each one: 'Remember those who have died in the peace of Christ, and all the dead whose faith is known to you alone.'[10]

Some historical witnesses

A beautiful example of intercession for the dead is to be found in the Acts of the martyrdom of St Perpetua. As she awaits her execution in Carthage, in early March 203, she is inspired to pray for her young brother Dinocrates, who had probably died without being baptised. Her vision ends 'when I awoke and understood that he had been translated from his pains.'[11]

Another classic example is St Augustine's prayer on the death of his mother, Monica. Though he knows her to be a holy woman, he can acknowledge that she, too, was subject to human frailty and so could profit from prayers for the dead. He wrote in his grieving:

> *At last that wound of my heart was healed which might have seemed blameworthy for the earthliness of its affection, and I pour out unto thee, our God, on behalf of thy handmaid, a far different kind of tears, flowing from a spirit stricken by the remembrance of the dangers of every soul that 'dies in Adam'...Therefore, my praise and my life, God of my heart, as I lay aside her good deeds for which I rejoice and give thanks to thee, I now entreat thee for the sins of my mother...*[12]

And he does, thereby exemplifying the deep human need to deal with grief for the dead, the desire to be united with them, and the experience of the ambiguity inherent in every human life.

The original prayerful mood out of which this doctrine arose is classically expressed in the great intercession from the Liturgy of St John Chrysostom:

> *Let us pray also for the repose of the souls of the departed servants of God, and for the forgiveness of their every transgression, deliberate and indeliberate...The mercies of God, the Kingdom of Heaven, and the remission of their sins let us ask of Christ, our immortal King*

and our God...God of spirits and of all flesh, who has trampled on death and vanquished the devil, and given life to Your world, give rest, O Lord, to the souls of your departed servants in a place of light, in a place of refreshment, in a place of repose from which pain sorrow and sighing have fled. Because you are so good and love mankind, forgive their every offence, whether in word or deed or thought; for there is no one living and never will be, who does not sin: but You alone are without sin...[13]

'For there is no one living and never will be who does not sin.' Here we are close to the fundamental meaning which the symbol of purgatory conveys: a sober estimate of the human condition coupled with surrender to the transforming power of grace. There is no optimistic repression of our flawed humanity; no pretence to a perfection that would take us out of our pilgrim state. The realities of human imperfection in even the best of us invite hope to a further limit: a surrender to the purifying love of the crucified.

The communion of saints

As I have already indicated, the Christian practice of praying for dead draws its force from the reality of the communion of saints. The notion that the prayers of the living are an attempt to interfere in the personal destiny of the other arises out of a comparatively recent, highly individualised notion of personhood. The existential perversion that would understand personal existence as an enclosed monad owes more to the self-assertive individualism of late Capitalism than to any truly philosophical understanding. Indeed, the degree to which contemporary culture has interiorised such an unrelational notion of personal existence gives good grounds for understanding why purgatory is necessary! But that is to anticipate. What bears stressing now is that our actual individuation in the worlds of both nature and grace is a far more corporate matter than our cultural bias allows us to appreciate. To exist as a person is to be in relation to others: to exist from them (family), with them (society), through them (culture), for them (community). Admittedly, in the West, the practice of praying for the dead was often constricted to a rather legal or even penal form of imagination, as in the complexities of gaining indulgences. But that unfortunate caricature should not be allowed to obscure the reality of the intercessory bond joining us together in the communion of saints. And the Christian sense of our unity in the Spirit, in its turn, should not see itself other than as the redemption of the co-humanity of our history, the co-existence of our individualities, the pro-existence of our generative and affective lives. Every human person carries the grace and burden of the whole human community. So, just as the Spirit inspires praying for oneself, not to change the will of God, but in order to make one open to it, so we are inspired to pray for others in order that grace might touch and penetrate human freedom in its social reality. Intercessory prayer is an essential aspect of the love of neighbour, as it is inspired by the self-giving love of God, and mediates such grace to others. To that degree no human being comes before God save as related to membership in the body of Christ. The destiny of the whole community is at stake in the fate of each individual, just as the ultimate fate of each individual affects the life of the whole body. Hence praying for the dead is a recognition of such fundamental solidarity. If neither 'death...nor heights nor depths, nor things present nor things to come, can separate us from the love of God in Christ Jesus...' (Rom. 8:38f.), then neither do such powers separate us from one another, above all, those we love in Christ.

Understood in this way, it is immaterial whether our prayers are strictly contemporaneous with the death of the departed. What matters, in the eternity of God's love, is that we stand before God as one body, one communion in the Spirit. All the intercessions that have been made, or will be made, for the individual are of the Spirit's inspiration. They are all part of God's gift to this person in death. In the eternity of love, it is not as though future prayers work to make God's love more merciful. The opposite is the case: an index of God's predestining grace for this individual is the Spirit's continuing inspiration of such intercessions, so that the one concerned will come to salvation through the love of the whole communion of saints. Thus, all partake in the salvation of each one. Perhaps some applications of 'relativity theory' to matters eschatological might throw further light on the manner in which the human person exists in the different dimensions of eternal love, of the whole of historical time, and of an individual life-span.

Wherever such exploration might lead, it seems to me that two principles remain essential in appreciating the theology of interceding for the dead in the communion of saints. The first is this: 'all is grace'; all prayers, whether past, present or future in relation to the moment of death, are aspects of the Spirit's creation of this particular individual. The second is: each one dies and comes to salvation only in, and through, the communion of saints manifested in the prayerful compassion of the Church.

Purification

As a symbol of the Spirit's purifying love, purgatory provokes many possible ways of imagining and reflecting on its meaning. As a general symbol of purification after death, it bears a family resemblance to other ways of describing the stages of post-mortem purification necessary for the emergence of the true self. Here I refer to the typical Buddhist or Hindu accounts of the human condition, such as reincarnation, especially as they are being explored today in the extensive literature devoted to such themes.[14] It would be fascinating to compare the manner in which Christian hope and non-Christian hope use complementary languages in their respective concerns to deal realistically with the salvation or liberation of the true self. There may be a lot to be discovered here as Herbert Fingarette has indicated in his masterful work, *The Self in Transformation*.[15] In our psychic world we are condemned to an endless cycle of repetition if we do not break out of self-destructive compulsions and obsessions into the release of genuine self-transcendence. There is an often terrifying suffering involved in such growth as the self-transcending self struggles to go beyond the self to be transcended: the 'vital lie' of human character, with its compromises and self-absorption, does not easily give up its defences.[16] There are clearly whole ranges of questions here that Christian theology has barely begun to ponder. In past centuries limbo provided a convenient method for leaving 'on hold' all questions relating to the fate of those human individuals who seemingly never had a chance to live a history of freedom. In the decades to come as interfaith dialogue proceeds, and the exploration of the human psyche goes on, a lot of such questions that have been pending for centuries will certainly be discussed in a new context.

But for the moment, the wiser course, and perhaps the healthiest, is to live with the inherent vagueness and inconclusiveness of purgatory, by simply letting it be a symbol of both the terminal ambiguity of the human condition and the unconditional character of God's grace in Christ. For both as a symbol and as a doctrine, purgatory is meant to bring a certain realism into our hope; to make it a hope for the human beings we actually are. As a symbol, it is born of a practical hope, and exists to serve it, by inspiring intercession, solidarity, and conversion. Occurring as it does within the fundamental, practical thrust of hope, it does not primarily invite further speculation. It stands, rather, for a gracious communion with those who have gone before us to meet the Lord with the ambiguous resources of unfinished lives. And most of all, it expresses the conviction of hope that the patient humanity of God's love for all of us in our pilgrim condition will have its own way of bringing us to completion.

A precarious symbol?

But, of course, symbols can be degraded, as the history of lamentable abuses of 'selling indulgences' and the morbid industry of Masses for the Holy Souls sufficiently attests. The degradation consists in displacing purgatory as a symbol of hopeful solidarity with the dead into a sub-theological fantasy bent on manipulating or appeasing the judgment of God. Such a situation thrives on lurid information dealing with the fate of the dead. Too often, such an abuse has had its justification in an ungracious theology restricted to thinking of our relationship with God in terms of penal justice. In an authentic Christian tradition, this represented a peculiar amnesia. The universe of grace was subverted by petty, penal calculations arising out of thoroughly unredeemed systems of justice. Here is one example of a diseased theological imagination, taken from the translation of an influential French work of a hundred years ago:

> *Let us take a moderate estimate and suppose that you have committed about ten faults a day;[17] at the end of 365 days you will have a sum of 3,650 faults. Let us diminish, and facilitate the calculation[!], place it at 3,000 per year. At the end of ten years, this will amount to 30,000, and at the end twenty years, 60,000. Suppose that of these 60,000 faults you have expiated one half of these faults by penance and good works. There will still remain 30,000 to be atoned for.*[18]

In continuing his hypothesis, on the assumption that each fault will 'on an average' require one hour in purgatory, the author presents his tally of the time to be done: 'three years, three months, and fifteen days'. He allows that this is an extremely lenient calculation, given that there is no mention of expiating 'the debt resulting from mortal sins'. The dread possibilities inspire a Gallic transport, 'Years and centuries in torments! Oh! If we had only thought of it, with what care should we not avoid the least faults!'[19]

The problem here does not reside in being exhorted to avoid the least imperfection in Christian life. What is in question is the religious universe in which that perfection is sought. It appears overwhelmingly as a universe of miserable grace. To be entered into the biblical 'book of life' definitely means to meet up with a very meticulous divine bookkeeper who is definitely going to 'go by the book' at the moment of judgment.

Such an instance of degraded imagination with its odd calculations is a long way from, say, St Catherine of Genoa's classical *Treatise on purgatory* (1510). This little treatise, appearing in 1551, forty years after her death, had considerable influence in forming Christian sensibilities, especially as they were expressed in poetry.[20] For the extrinsic vindictive purgatory of the older writers, Catherine substituted a conception of 'an intrinsic, ameliorative purgatory into which the soul plunges by is own spontaneous impulse on the instant that the momentary vision of God enables it to realise its own turpitude.'[21] She writes:

> *I believe no happiness can be found worthy to be compared to the soul in purgatory except that of the saints in paradise. And, day by day, this happiness grows as God flows into these souls more and more, as the hindrance to his entrance is consumed. Sin's rust is the hindrance, and the fire burns the rust away, so that more and more the soul opens itself up to*

the divine inflowing. As the rust lessens and the soul is opened up to the divine ray, happiness grows, until the time be accomplished, the one wanes and the other waxes ... As for the will, never can the soul say these pains are pains, so contented are they with what God ordains with which, in pure charity, their will is united.[22]

Cardinal Newman, in *The Dream of Gerontius*, places himself in the tradition of 'an intrinsic, ameliorative purgatory' when he has his Angel say:

*...these two pains, so counter and so keen,
The longing for him, when thou seest Him not,
The same of self at thought of seeing Him
Will be thy veriest, sharpest purgatory.*[23]

The suffering of purgatory

If, on the other hand, purgatory is set within the horizon of God's grace precisely as an index of the divine compassion for the human condition, it is a different matter. For then such love is revealed as offering itself to the limited human beings that we are. Far from pretending that evil is good, that imperfection is fulfilment, that we have arrived at our best selves, redeeming love works for the reality of our total transformation. It goads us to the attainment of complete conversion, as it enables human freedom to integrate its scattered and stratified development into the purity of love, thus to be centred on the one thing necessary. In this light, purgatory symbolises our unfinished existence being possessed by the living flame of the Spirit. It is the final exorcism of the demons that have driven us, the ultimate undermining of all the idols that have structured our lives. The irruption of the reality of God and the eruption of true life cause radical disruption in the structure of the disordered self: that is purgatorial suffering:

> *Simply to look at people with any degree of realism at all is to grasp the necessity of such a [purifying] process. It does not replace grace by works, but allows the former to achieve its full victory precisely as grace. What actually saves is the full assent of faith. But in most of us that basic option is buried under a great deal of wood, hay and straw. Only with difficulty can it peer out from behind a lattice-work of an egoism we are powerless to pull down with our own hands. Man is the recipient of the divine mercy, but this does not exonerate him from the need to be transformed. Encounter with the Lord* is *this transformation. It is the fire that burns away our dross and reforms us to be vessels of eternal joy.*[24]

This approach, I believe, goes a long way towards meeting traditional Protestant objections to the doctrine of purgatory. The problem of abuses has been largely faced. More importantly, purgatory does not compromise the sheer graciousness of God as the Reformers thought, but is a consequence of that grace as it inspires human freedom to an unreserved conversion. In questioning the pre-theological status of purgatory, the Reformers were right: if it means taking away the all-sufficiency of the grace of Christ, purgatory can hardly figure in Christian orthodoxy. Further still, there is here no question of the 'dolorism'—salvation wrought by sheer suffering—as even Tillich had complained when he wrote, 'In Catholic doctrine, mere suffering does the purging...it is a theological mistake to derive transformation from pain alone instead of from grace which gives blessedness within pain.'[25] In response, we would say that there *is* suffering, but it is a suffering born out of love struggling into its authentic realisation as unreserved and complete surrender to the Spirit. The Reformers had rightly seen that any interpretation of God's love as either merited or appeased by suffering would send the Christian psyche reeling in hopeless contradictions. The God of such a purgatory would be hopelessly less than a human lover. If suffering established our worth in his eyes, an eternity with such a God is a fearful prospect.

Toward a theology of purgatory

After these various remarks, I would like to present a more comprehensive statement on the meaning of purgatory. It can be conveniently developed in eight points:

1. Purgatory pertains to the process of self-realisation

In the moment of death, or better, in the process of dying, the self is summoned into a final state of self-transcendence. The restless provisionality of our being-in-the-world now comes to a decisive moment of integration. The self that was in the making through the course of a lifetime is now crystallised into its full individuality. The true self, more or less dissipated in all the decisions, options, commitments, judgments of a lifetime, finally catches up with its destiny. For, in the action and passion of life, we are present to ourselves only in a stratified, distracted and usually ambiguous manner: the tumbling torrent of life keeps sweeping us along. In death, that restless mountain stream becomes a luminous deep pool. We catch up with the person that we are meant to be.[26] In life, our true identity was always ahead of us or behind us, or concealed deep within many layers of the ego, of role-playing and social conditioning—never completely or consciously possessed.

2. Purgatory implies a 'particular judgment'

In terms of Christian tradition, the moment of truth which death represents is not so much a judgment passed on us by God, but, rather, the realisation of the truth not only 'about' ourselves but incarnate in what we are. We enter into the possession of what we truly are, what we have decided to be, what we stand for; what, through the process of life, we have become. Death is the moment of personal truth. In dying, we come to judgment in a self now fully conscious of its basic form and orientation. We 'come to', as if waking from the semi-consciousness of a coma. The stream of personal life finally settles into a space which can fully contain it: freedom now knows its final shape.

3. Purgatory is a decisive encounter with Christ
In him, we are confronted with the ultimate form of human existence; indeed, he is met as the mystery fundamental to each one's unique identity. We become aware of ourselves as being made through him, for him, in him. In that encounter it becomes piercingly obvious that there is much in the make-up of our existence that is as yet outside him, not yet for him, not yet subjected to him. The tension between what we most love and want to be, and what in fact we are, is the beginning of understanding what the purifying suffering of purgatory consists in. In this sense, Christ is the judgment passed on our existence, and Christian humility is prepared to admit that most of us are found wanting:

> *Christ looks with utter love and complete graciousness on the one who comes to him. At the same time his gaze burns right into the innermost parts of that human existence. To encounter God in Christ's eyes of fire is the highest fulfilment of our capacity for love and also the most fearful suffering our nature ever has to bear...the encounter with Christ would be our purgatory.*[27]

4. Purgatory is conformity to the Crucified
If this moment of truth reveals the anti-Christ or the counter-Christ within us, it is also a final entry into the dying of Christ himself. For meeting Christ in death reveals in fact that we are still refusing to die:

the residue of selfishness and lovelessness appears as our way of clinging to an existence resistant to the reign of God. But in the depths of our selfhood, Christ now appears as 'the way'. In his descent into the hell of all our separation from God, he now summons us to the death of a final self-surrender. We are drawn to participate fully in the mystery of his death, his self-emptying for the life of the world. He who has died for us, now dies in us, to make of each individual existence a passion for God. Thus we meet the Crucified as the subversion of all our clinging to spurious forms of life. And purgatory becomes pure faith—the loving, but dreaded letting go of anything less than a totally 'Christened' existence.

In this context, the eminent Anglican theologian, John Macquarrie remarks:

> *The kind of suffering envisaged in purgatory is not an external penalty that has to be paid, but it is our suffering with Christ, our being crucified with him as we are conformed to him, the painful surrender of the ego-centred self that the God-centred self of love may take its place.*[28]

5. Purgatory is a suffering born out of love

To reflect on any experience of love, in whatever form it might occur—in marriage, family, friendship, community—is to become aware that fundamental to such experience of loving and being loved is an uncanny sense of gift. For something new has entered into the foundations of our being. It touches the depths of who we are and calls forth wondrous other-directed energies while, at the same time, giving us back to ourselves, as selves renewed, illumined, affirmed.

Precisely because love is such a gift, it brings its own kind of suffering. To the degree that any great love possesses us, it makes us aware of ourselves, at some level of our consciousness, as failed lovers, as incapable or unresponsive in regard to what has been given. For love unmasks our selfishness, threatens our independence, demands too much, subverts the comfortable, enclosed organisation of our lives. Though it might be the most bracing liberation of what and who we are, it is also inherently a burden and a demand. Here, love brings its own kind of suffering, not as something inflicted by the beloved other, but as a pain somehow inherent in the loving response we would wish to make. For, as love inspires and summons forth our best selves, it also brings into our awareness resistance to it: possessiveness, self-absorption, violence, manipulation, limitation and fear. In such a sense, we become aware of our unworthiness in the face of such a gift. 'Show me a lover and he will understand' (St Augustine) is applicable here. Only the lover understands the pain of not being fully accessible to the other, of not having enough freedom to be completely for the beloved.

In many ways, it is a curious aspect of human experience to fear being loved, to feel the temptation to cling defensively and destructively to the security of an isolated self. Hidden somewhere in the joy of new loves or old, there is an intimation of a special kind of death: the need to die out of an isolated pattern of life into a life of relationship. The authentic self that love summons one to can only be realised through a continual process of self-surrender, in a new world, a more real world—but a profoundly upsetting state of affairs.

The searching intimacy of marriage and family, the delicate negotiations of friends, the continual discipline of communication for any group, all the agenda of all the meetings required in the promotion of a worthwhile cause, are all instances of the suffering that love can cause. As such they tell us a lot about purgatory: the lucid but burning awareness of an ultimate love exposing all our residual unworthiness and unwillingness in its regard. Purgatory, from this point of view, is the moment when the fundamental love of one's lifetime finally comes to terms with itself.

6. Purgatory is the entry into a truly compassionate existence

Here, we stress the social reference of purgatory. Though it is an individual moment of truth, the truth concerned bears on the quality of our relationships with others. The final dying into the self-offering of Christ, must also be understood as a realisation of his self-giving to the world. Hence, inherent in any understanding of the process of purification is our self-expansion in compassion for the sufferings of the whole body of Christ, to which we have undoubtedly contributed. Our sinfulness has in fact held us back from a fully creative immersion in human history, just our lack of love has left others unloved, ignored, forgotten, rejected. It is not improbable, then, that the suffering of purgatory may well be the process of one's becoming a truly compassionate presence in the emergence of the human race. Such suffering is not the kind of pain that isolates us from the rest of the world, but a suffering related to belonging more deeply to crises and struggles that had left us indifferent and unconcerned. As I have already mentioned, this may be the point that Christians have most to learn from the myths of reincarnation. Though one is reluctant to put too much credence in reports of 'souls being sent back to earth to undo the harm they have done' and so forth,[29] there may be a deep theological point hidden in such necessarily naive expressions: through the creativity of compassion and intercession, purgatorial suffering is a process of growth into a selflessly loving relationship to the world which, in some way, has suffered from the distortion of our own particular history. Each human life has, at least to some degree, left a polluting vapor trail in the atmosphere of life: we may have loved humanity, but the actual human beings who formed the community of our lives were the problem, whether this was manifested in a routine lack of helpfulness, failures to forgive, tolerance with what was destructive, manipulation of the liberty of others—all the ways any of us simply did not really engage the real people, the neighbour, the friend, the stranger, the enemy, who were *there*.

So, purgatory can be helpfully thought of as the process in which our resistant individuality is opened to be truly inclusive of the other. It is a transformation of our individuality into the truly personal as the substance of our lives becomes completely relational (here an analogy with the divine persons as 'subsisting relationships' would be instructive!). In such a suffering transformation we become pure grace for others, to affirm their being and value where before in a thousand ways we may have denied it. Love burns residual selfishness out of us to make us creative, redemptive agents in the lives that were especially given into our care. Such a growth in love, to that greatest love in which we would lay down our lives for our friends, marks our existence with the compassion of Christ (Jn 15:13).

7. The fire of purgatory is the flame of the Holy Spirit

All these aspects of the purifying fires of purgatory can be brought together *in a new appreciation of the flame of the Holy Spirit* (cf. Lk 3:16; 12:49; Acts 2:3f.; I Thes. 5:19). This, above all, is the 'fire of purgatory', as the flame of the Spirit possesses and transforms our existence. True, the action of the Spirit must be set in the larger context of the Christian vocation. Through every stage of this, the Spirit of love creates, redeems, reconciles, liberates, and purifies,[30] to open every stage of existence to a further fulfilment. Such a Spirit indwells the human spirit as the Spirit of the ever greater God, and of our ever greater selves in Christ. The Spirit is the ultimate life-energy causing our birth to the fullness of life, bringing us to full term in the new creation. In this present life, the Spirit works against any clinging to the past or to lesser versions of ourselves, to lead us on to what was still to be realised, to the eschatologically new. It is the Spirit of unity breaking open the bias of individualistic self-enclosure in the interests of a larger belonging to the community of others, in love and service. The work of the Spirit is always to conform us to the crucified Christ that we might rise with him. As the Spirit of the creative love, it cannot rest content with anything less than our whole, free selves in a transformed universe.

But each transformation implies a death: the suffering of dying out of lesser versions of the self, and in dying into the ultimate dimensions of life. The great mystics witness to the Spirit's transforming action. They speak of the 'dark night' of suffering as all the glaring objects of secure little worlds become dark in the radiance of ultimate light. As Yves Congar noted, 'in purgatory, we will all be mystics'.[31] Take these words from St John of the Cross as one example:

> *The dark night is the inflow of God into the soul, which purges it of its habitual ignorance and imperfections, natural and spiritual...Through this contemplation, God teaches the soul secretly, and instructs it on the perfection of love without its doing anything, nor understanding how this happens ... There are two reasons why this divine wisdom is not only night and darkness, but also affliction and torment. First because of the height of the divine Wisdom as it exceeds the capacity of the soul. Secondly, because of the soul's baseness and impurity; and on this account, it is painful, afflictive and also dark for the soul.*[32]

In this sense, the fire of purgatory is the Holy Spirit, penetrating, possessing, and finally transforming all that we are.

8. Purgatory and time

How long does purgatory last? In the light of a more theological understanding of purgatory, the calculations of Père Schouppe (*See* page 163) *more usefully yield to two possible types of language*—granting that we cannot escape from thinking in terms of the temporal duration of our present existence. In so far as purgatory is an encounter with the risen Lord, in as much as it is a definitive entry into the death of Jesus, the language of a *moment* of purification and perfect contrition seems appropriate. From such a point of view, temporal duration makes little sense. On the other hand, if we conceive of purgatory as a new, compassionate relationship with the history of the world adversely affected by our failures in love, then we can speak of it in terms of *historical duration*. We cannot be completely 'in heaven' as long as our sin-affected history continues.

Leaving the matter there confronts us with many paradoxes.[33] Perhaps these can only be resolved by yielding to a larger mystery still—the manner in which Christ himself suffers the incompletion and imperfection of his Body. The great Origen wrote:

> *You will have joy when you depart from this life if you are a saint. But your joy will be complete only when no member of your body is lacking to you. For you too will wait, just as you are awaited. But if you who are a member do not have perfect joy as long as a member is missing, how much more must our Lord and saviour who is the head and origin of this body consider it an incomplete joy if he is still lacking certain of his members?... Thus he does not want to receive his perfect glory without you: that is not without his people which is 'his body' and 'his members'.*[34]

This passage is not, of course, speaking about purgatory, and certainly not about Christ's sufferings in any purgatorial sense. On the other hand, it might suggest an understanding of purgatory as a moment of purification, and as an ongoing relationship with history. The way the head of the body awaits his complete joy, the way the members of the Body who are in glory await their complete joy, must have some parallel in the way those 'in purgatory' await their complete joy. Suffering the incompleteness of history is realised in different but related ways—all aspects of how the eternal mystery of love has time for our full growth to humanity.

Admittedly, all thinking about purgatory is a stab in the dark. But there is a centre of light, the fundamental meaning of this symbol and this doctrine. It is the mystery of God's love finally penetrating all the resistant dimensions of our being, to conform us to itself, and to lead to the 'perfect love [which] casts out all fear' (I Jn 4:18). So, in the end, purgatory is not a state of dread torment, but of love's overcoming our basic fears: the fear of God as a threat; the fear of the other as a rival; the fear of dying as extinction; the fear of self-surrender as a loss; the fear of loving as a demand too great to bear.

1. An earlier version of this chapter has appeared in: Tony Kelly, *The Range of Faith: Basic Questions For A Living Theology*, St Paul Publications, Homebush, NSW, 1986, pp.173–181.
2. See Robert Schreiter, 'Purgatory: In quest of an image', *Chicago Studies* 24/2, August 1985, pp.167–179.
3. Jaroslav Pelikan, *The Emergence of the Catholic Tradition (100–600)*, University of Chicago, Chicago, 1971, pp.355f.; *The Spirit of Eastern Christendom (600–1700)*, University of Chicago Press, Chicago, 1974, pp.279.
4. See Peter McEniery, 'Pseudo-Gregory and Purgatory', *Pacifica* 1, January 1988, pp.328–334; F. Clark, *The Pseudo-Gregorian Dialogues, I–II*, E. J. Brill, Leiden, 1987.
5. Jacques Le Goff, *The Birth of Purgatory*, tr. A. Goldhammer, The University of Chicago Press, Chicago, 1984.
6. Peter Beer, 'Purgatory, Trent and Today', *Australasian Catholic Record* LXI:4, October 1984, pp.369–384.
7. J. Neuner and J. Dupuis, eds., *The Christian Faith in the Doctrinal Documents of the Catholic Church*, Collins, London, 1982, n. 2310.

8. *See Lumen Gentium* par. 49f.
9. Josef Ratzinger, *Eschatology*..., pp.218–228.
10. *The Roman Missal*, Eucharistic Prayer IV.
11. *See The Passion of SS. Perpetua and Felicity*, tr. and ed. W.H. Shewring, Sheed and Ward, London, 1931.
12. St Augustine, *Confessions* 9, 13, 34–37.
13. Quoted from George Maloney, *The Everlasting Now*, Ave Maria Press, Notre Dame, Ind., 1980, p.64.
14. See André Couture, 'Réincarnation ou résurrection? Revue d'un débat et amorce d'une recherche I and II, *Science et Esprit* XXXVI/3, 1984, pp.351–374; and XXXVII/3, pp.75–96. For Karl Rahner's position: *See* Peter Phan, *Eternity in Time*..., pp.128–131; 133f.
15. Herbert Fingarette, *The Self in Transformation. Psychoanalysis, Philosophy and the Life of the Spirit*, Harper Torchbooks, New York, 1963, pp.216–237.
16. *See* the treatment of Becker's *Denial of Death* in chapter four.
17. Note that the author is being pessimistic even here: he has been reflecting on the biblical statement, 'The just man falls seven times a day'. He could have been aware of the rather open-ended significance of the biblical 'seven', but I doubt it. That might have justified him in increasing his 'moderate estimate' to a much larger number!
18. F.X. Schouppe, *Purgatory. Illustrated by the Lives and Legends of the Saints*, tr. J.J.S., Burns and Oates, London, 1893, pp.69f.
19. *ibid.*, p.70.
20. Herbert Thurston, *The Memory of Our Dead*, Burns and Oates, London, 1918, pp.195–200.
21. *ibid.*, p.194.
22. St Catherine of Genoa, *On Purgatory*, trans. Charlotte Balfour and Helen Irvine, Sheed and Ward, New York, 1946, pp.18f.
23. As quoted in Thurston, *The Memory*..., p.195.
24. J. Ratzinger, *Eschatology*, p.231.
25. Paul Tillich, *Systematic Theology* III, University of Chicago Press, Chicago, 1951, p.417.
26. *See* Boros, *The Moment of Truth*..., Burns & Oates, London. pp.86–98.

27. *ibid.*, pp.138f.
28. John Macquarrie, *Principles of Christian Theology*, SCM, London, 1970, p.329.
29. F. Schouppe, *Purgatory*, pp.113–123. Compare this with the approach of David Hay, *Exploring Inner Space: Is God still possible in the twentieth century?* Mowbray, London, 1987, pp.145, 163.
30. For the tradition of 'the cleansing fire', R.B. Eno, 'The Fathers and the Cleansing Fire' *Irish Theological Quarterly* 1987:3, pp.184–202.
31. Quoted in G.L. Mueller, 'Purgatory', *Theology Digest* 34:1 Spring, 1987, pp.31–36.
32. John of the Cross, *The Living Flame of Love*, stanza 1.
33. For some teasing remarks on this whole matter, see S. Tugwell, *Human Immortality...*, pp.169–174.
34. *In Leviticum homiliae* VII, 1–2. See J. Ratzinger, *Eschatology*, p.185 for full text.

9 Hell: the Limit of Hope?

In a sense, all that can be said about hell as a possible terminal point in human destiny has been said in previous chapters. The saving mystery of Christ's descent into hell presupposes unimaginable depths from which we need deliverance. One is tempted to leave well enough alone at this point. There is a place for reserve; and surely it is here.

Evasiveness?

But reserve is one thing, and evasiveness is another, and not very bracing, quality in any account of hope. One senses that something more explicit needs to be said. Admittedly, the things we most fear are seldom immediately attractive, but keeping silent on the fundamental and tragic possibility of hell solves no problem. Excluded from discussion, hell can continue as a subterranean fantasy twining itself into religious sensibilities, perhaps to surface in odd and destructive ways—in nameless fears or religious vendettas; perhaps in a nausea felt in any talk about the goodness of God; most of all, in a despair over the evils of the world, so routine that it passes unnoticed. Repression of either death, or of what the Bible has called 'the second death', does not make for spiritual health.

Certainly, theology would make itself ridiculous if it pretended to offer another guided tour of the afterlife, or found itself pronouncing on the ultimate destiny of particular human individuals or groups. On the other hand, it would be just as fatuous if it lost its nerve here; and became only an expurgated version of Christianity's account of the human drama. For the symbol of hell is inextricably part of any world-view that pretends to be Christian. For that reason, any account of hope that refuses to name it, is thin, bland and embarrassed. No longer a hope against hope, it cannot speak to the heart of the world's darkness.

Reasons for reserve

Certainly, as von Balthasar points out,[1] hell has been something of a literary topic. Sartre's oft-quoted, 'Hell is other people' is accompanied in French literature by other quotable pronouncements: 'Each day we take a step into hell.' (Baudelaire); 'I believe in hell. I exist there as well.' (Rimbaud). *Une saison en enfer*, 'a time in hell', is an experience recommended to the aspiring poet. The aesthetic rebel derives a peculiar energy from exploring this theme. Indeed, infernal imagery has a large place in a number of classic expressions of the drama and heroism of human freedom, as instanced in Milton's Satan, Byron's plea on behalf of Lucifer, and in the Faust of Lessing and Goethe. Full aesthetic enlightenment apparently has need of the flames of hell! Authentic self-knowledge, it seems, comes only out of this abyss: 'I can by myself raise up a kingdom against God over which God has no power; that is hell' (Marcel Jouhandeau); and 'If a man does not understand hell this means that he has not understood his own heart'.[2]

When literary genius glorified the infernal as the locus of untrammelled human freedom, stolid theological thought, dispossessed of its most dread symbol, was shocked into hesitation. The prevailing wisdom was inclined to let matters run their course, even if this would have its predictable outcome in the acute solipsism of the Me Generation.

But that is not the only problem. There are complex

psychological issues inducing further hesitation. Both the promotion and the avoidance of this theme of Christian doctrine reveal a lot about our psyches. A fundamentalist fixation on hell may well mask baleful hatred of one's world and one's culture. It may indicate a radical loss of hope. By projecting its dissatisfaction on the universe, an embittered and isolated psyche cherishes hell as its own spiteful certainty, to find itself in a world in which the God of grace is ultimately defeated. A remark of Bernard Lonergan is pertinent here:

> *Unless religion is totally directed to what is good, to genuine love of one's neighbour and to a self-denial that is subordinated to a fuller goodness in oneself, then the cult of a God that is terrifying can slip over into the demonic, into an exultant destructiveness of oneself and of others.*[3]

At the other extreme, simply being 'against hell' may just as simply be the result of a fundamentally frivolous tolerance which takes seriously neither human freedom nor its demonic capacities.

Still, invoking hell as the ultimate sanction, can be a powerful form of mind control. When popular evangelists, uncertain of the persuasive power of either love or intelligence, bully conscience with the threat of hell-fire, they secure their authority as the dispenser of eschatological threats. Manipulating others by terror is a temptation to anyone experiencing the conflicts and rejection that are the inescapable lot of the communicator of transcendent meanings. At the other extreme, when even threats do not seem to work, and the hell-fire preacher becomes a figure of fun, the religious communicator can soothingly reassure everyone that all is well, perhaps quoting both ancient mystic and modern poet to the effect 'that all manner of thing shall be well'.[4] But once more there is something suspect: another effort of manipulation? Another cry for acceptance by slanting religious doctrine to ensure that its representative is to be numbered among the 'good guys'? But here again, there is no real effort to understand, no real hope, no genuine engagement with that world of conflict which the Gospel takes for granted and our own times tragically exemplify.

Any theology critical of the simplifications of such popular communication will understandably opt for a certain reserve. But there is, I think, a deeper, sadder reason for such discretion. We are all too familiar with evil. The death, torture, repression, violence and manifold human degradation of our terrible century leave the human imagination appalled: hell has become too obvious. A general low self-esteem, culturally engendered by centuries of materialist reductionism, makes even the most cautious exploration of this dark limit a most delicate communication, if great damage is to be avoided. One can feel that the only issue worth discussing is hope. To urge the possibilities of ultimate damnation when the historical mood is bereft of any intimations of salvation appears tragically misplaced.

Neglecting hell: the consequences

And yet, what happens when hell ceases to be a theological topic? I alluded above to the possible psychological consequences. Allied to such, there is a larger political consideration in dealing with the secularisation of the symbol of hell.

As the notions of God, immortality, salvation, and heaven are displaced into some secular substitute, so too is hell. Hell, like God, is now located within this world, merely as a symbol of human experience. This point is well introduced in the following observation:

> ...*whenever hell is neglected, it returns under another form. The tradition of Aquinas is that all evil will be punished ultimately, that all human evil is precisely chosen. But it need not*

> *be the function of politics to punish all evils or to correct all evil choices...the effort to create a perfect, self-conceived society on earth invariably seems to result in a kind of incarnate hell...*[5]

Hell comes to be identified as an 'evil empire' deserving of utter reprobation. Its masters, its servants, its members are among the collective of the damned. The blocs of the historically saved, of the ideologically justified can make no peace with the damned and the intrinsically evil. 'In the modern era, evil and hell have become objects and movements to be overcome rather than mysteries lying deeply at the heart of human choice...'[6] This displacement of hell, from a religious to a secular symbol, from an objective eschatological possibility to the focus of historical hatred, has consequences. It caused Hannah Arendt to ponder:

> *The most significant consequence of the secularisation of the modern age may well be the elimination from public life, along with religion, of the only political element in traditional religion, the fear of hell.*[7]

The result is that there is no room for both the inconclusiveness and the possibilities of change that are the mark of human history. For the infernal is already here, and the devil is one of us! By dragging ultimate destruction into the time and space of history, human freedom can congeal into a terrible rigidity, and so freeze the hopeful imagination. Now history, instead of being the ever inconclusive play of the human drama, is weighed down with its own kind of eschatological responsibility. We are locked into the terrible pretence of being Utopia. Nothing can be left to an ultimate, transcendent judgment. Anyone who is part of the evil system, whether this be identified as capitalism, communism, fascism, racism, sexism or any other ideology, falls under a kind of ultimate historical judgment. The ferocity of such merciless moralism can imagine no response save that of elimination of the enemy. But the real hell 'frees politics from an impossible worldly burden inasmuch as it enforces a contingent, imperfect civil order in such a way that the same civil order is not required to exercise absolute justice and punishment'.[8]

History is thus made to contain its ultimate judgment, to be pronounced by some group of the enlightened. By locating hell in our midst, we begin to have a strange familiarity with the demons that infest it.[9]

The hell of Christian eschatology

There is something to be said, then, for a sober theological statement. Here, hell is a symbol of ultimate eschatological judgment on the sinner: it results from evil irrevocably chosen. Whether or not such an ultimate fixation in evil occurs, we simply do not know. What we do know, with all the force of Gospel, is that such a judgment is reserved only to God. Any rush to judgment is arrested by the biblical injunction: 'Judge not and you shall not be judged ' (Lk 6:37f.). In Christian communication, hell may not occur as a curse on those whose conduct we may rightly deplore. Indeed, the undeniable serious rhetoric of Christian faith dealing with the sinner always stops short of anything approaching ultimate reprobation. Saints are solemnly declared to be in heaven, but no one is declared to be in hell. Anyone tempted to go beyond this limit and indulge in exercises of eschatological damnation, might be persuaded to a more genuine Christianity by suggesting the surest way of going to hell is to arrogate to oneself God's final judgment on the personal worth of others. This would amount to replacing the inexhaustible possibilities of ultimate mercy with a spurious eschatology of one's own last judgment. The cross shines into all darkness; it forbids human judgment to pursue any doer of evil into eternal life.

The data

What, then, of the Christian doctrine of hell? The biblical data on hell have been frequently summarised.[10] As Israel's sages and prophets contemplated the scope of God's action, gradually, a more differentiated notion of hell, *Sheol, Gehenna*, emerges. From being a rather neutral, shadowy existence, hell becomes the place of darkness and wrath: for God's judgment on both the good and the bad is not exhausted merely in terms of this life. There is a final dimension of exclusion from the God of life, which the apocalyptic imagination began to fill with the fire, worms, chains and so forth. These lurid descriptions passed over into the received language of the New Testament writers themselves (Mt 3:12; 5:22, 29ff.; 10:28; 13:42,50; 18:9; II Pt 2:17; Jude 1:6f.; Rev. 21:8).[11]

The essential point implicit in such varied expressions is that the New Testament's record of the ministry of Jesus is scarcely intelligible without a sense of some ultimate and irrevocable judgment. Jesus conducts his whole life in the light of such a crucial reality. Indeed:

> *The interpenetration of the themes of judgment and deliverance is inescapable. One cannot grasp, or even begin to grasp, the sense of the latter apart from the former. It is in the ministry of Jesus that the arraignment with which Paul confronts his readers at the outset of his letter to the Romans receives concrete interpretation, and the redemption which the apostle in triumphant ecstasy acclaims in Rom. 8:31ff. is one that has measured the depths of that from which men and women must be delivered.*[12]

An attempt to give expression to these depths from which we must be delivered is made in the various creeds and councils though the ages.[13] Anyone fixed in evil suffers the reality of hell immediately after death.[14] Its essential pain is the loss of God, to which is joined certain particular punishments due to particular sinfulness.[15] Further, hell is everlasting:[16] there is no final reconciliation of sinners as Origen had suggested.[17] Though no individual human person is declared to be in hell, though no limit is placed on Christian hope, the doctrine is sober, definite and clear. And as such it been reiterated in recent times.[18]

Hope and hell

How then can this doctrine of hell be worked into the account of hope? I suggest five main points:

1. Healthy Fear

First, a candid admission. Hell figures in Christian discourse as the language of fear and threat. I have already sufficiently stressed how such language can be abused. But need this always be the case? Must the motive of fear be restricted to the language of manipulation? Obviously not. Fear can have its part in motivating genuine human achievement, even though one does not need to be a developmental psychologist to admit that it is not the most mature motive.[19] Conscience is quite properly energised to the true good by fear of failure, self-destruction, disgrace. The therapeutic reconditioning of the addicted, to say nothing of the legal system itself with its variety of penalties, assumes this fundamental human fact. We should note, too, that the fear of hell is a dominant feature of any genuinely popular religion: when all are involved, whatever their social position, in a dreadful possibility, a certain levelling of human pretensions occurs. Human society is most truly a democracy of the spirit in its awareness of a transcendent and universal judgment by which evil and evil-doers will be contained and unmasked.

To the degree that the symbol of hell is a carrier of wholesome fear, it objectifies the opposite to self-transcendence, the possibility of self-destruction. As such it is meant to shock the imagination into the creation of an authentic life-project, to work and hope for true self-realisation.

So, to place this fear where it belongs, not in some collective recrimination but in our common experience of the enigma of human liberty, can be no bad thing. This is an implicit recognition that the universe is one in which human liberty is taken seriously; and indeed one in which our choices will be revealed for what they are. The quality of such fear is not servile. It is not meant to cripple the psyche with terror. The mature fear we speak of is one born out of personal and historical experience. It knows the precariousness of human freedom, and recognises that the universe, if freedom is to expand to its full development, is not a giant automatic salvation machine. Even though the manner in which such a wholesome fear is to be communicated is problematical today, associating it with the possibilities of self-destruction is surely the right emphasis. The threat of hell is simply the acknowledgment that human beings can choose an ultimate self-enclosed lovelessness as their final state.

2. Divine and Human Justice

This brings me to a second point in dealing with the language of absolute condemnation. The problem is how to speak *theologically*, in a language and categories appropriate to the Christian mystery of salvation. Discourse on hell has too often been infected by metaphors drawn from an unredeemed experience of the world. Too rarely has the fundamental reference point been the universe of superabundant grace. Today, when more enlightened societies typically struggle to get beyond the inhumanity of their own legal systems by abolishing the death penalty, by declaring periods of amnesty, and by exploring the possibilities of rehabilitation, there must be some proportionate self-criticism on the part of Christian theology if it is to share David Hume's sentiment: 'The damnation of one man is an infinitely greater evil in the universe than the subversion of a thousand millions of kingdoms.'[20] For so much traditional talk on the subject of hell has been in terms of penal justice. The criminal offence must be punished in accord with the principles of equity and deterrence. But is such human justice the basic model of ultimate reality? Is it the one essential value fundamental to the universe of grace? To act as if it were, places us very much this side of a redeemed creation. When the Gospel becomes law, a just law requires sanctions; and sanctions must be applied if justice is to be done: God is thus essentially a judge acting according to the laws of a world of scant redemption. Oddly, the Gospel is made to conform to the world rather than challenging the world to re-imagine itself in the light of grace. In short, there has been all too little evidence of negative theology to purify analogies drawn from human experience. And that human experience may be so distorted as to prevent us from imagining how the God of grace works to transform our world.

But authentic hope lives within a universe of grace. Already anticipating that world transformed beyond any conception of human justice, such hope can ask with Paul, 'Who shall separate us from the love of Christ?' (Rom. 8:35), to find an invincible comfort in his answer:

> *I am sure that neither death nor life...nor things present nor things to come...nor anything in all creation can separate us from the love of God in Christ Jesus...'* (Rom. 8:38f.).

The Pauline vision looks to a final state when all things are made subject to Christ, that God may be everything to everyone (I Cor. 15:27f.). It awaits a 'fullness of time' when the mystery of God's saving purpose will be realised, 'to unite all things in him, things in heaven and things on earth' (Eph. 1:9f.; cf.

Phil. 2:10; Col. 1:20). If Paul gives classic expression to the cosmic vision of Christian hope, John evokes the depth of its feeling:

> *that there is no fear in love, but perfect love casts out fear. For fear has to do with punishment, and he who fears is not perfected in love'* (I Jn 4:18f.).

Throughout the New Testament, hope bases itself on the possibilities of God, as they surpass and surprise all human calculation (cf. Mt 19:26; Mk 10:27; Lk 18:27).

Though such passages can hardly be presented as proof texts for the universality of salvation, each in its own context invites hope not only to go beyond the cultural and social structures of an imperfect and often inhuman penal justice, but also to go to that point where it can never find a reason to limit the possibilities of divine grace and mercy. In such possibilities, heaven and hell are not simple alternatives, however much a spirituality or a theology, more intent on the balance of symmetry or system than on the mystery of how God has acted in Christ, might so present them. Karl Rahner represents a larger wisdom when he writes:

> *For since we live in the eschaton of Jesus Christ...we know in our Christian faith and our unshakeable hope that, in spite of the drama and freedom of individual persons, the history of salvation as a whole will reach a positive conclusion for the human race through God's own powerful grace. But we neither can nor must say anything about the end of an individual who suffers final loss except that a person who is still in human history and who is just now exercising his freedom must reckon with this possibility seriously. He may not abolish indiscriminately the ambiguity of his own individual history of salvation by an-*

ticipation, holding a positive theoretical doctrine about apocatastasis, that is the salvation of absolutely everyone. But...we are not obliged to declare that we know with certainty that in fact the history of salvation is going to end for certain people with absolute loss. As Christians then we do not have to regard the statements about heaven and hell as parallel statements of Christian eschatology.[21]

3. Hope for Judgment

Thirdly, within such a context, hell can figure in the vocabulary of hope itself. Paradoxical as this may seem, it is an expression of hope to anticipate a state in which evil will be revealed for what it is and be brought to nothing. The theme of hell, for all the reserve with which we must use it, and however much we must continue to abstain from passing ultimate judgment on anyone, is a theological reality. It represents God's ultimate judgment on evil, on the evil perpetrated by human agents within human history. Hell figures as the divinely imposed limit to evil's destructive capacities; 'in hell', there is no further room for the perverse creativity of evil. Thus, hell has its place in the language of hope as our reprobation of the actual evil-doing we experience in ourselves or others. It forbids any representation of God's love as tolerance of evil or compromise with it. The symbol of hell stands for that point where evil is contained and rendered impotent, and made to serve the higher purposes of a good creation, where the anti-Christ is vanquished, and when evil has to face itself for what it is in the light of God. In that radiance there will be no pretence, no evasion, no compromise, no further subversion of the good.

A few years age, the noted Neo-Marxist sociologist Max Horkheimer expressed his hope in an interview entitled, 'A Yearning for the Wholly Other'. He had this to say:

> *Theology is the awareness that the world is an appearance, that it is not the absolute truth, that it is not the absolute reality...it is the hope that the injustice by which the world is characterised will not persist, that injustice cannot be the last word...*[it is] *the expression of a longing that the murderer will not triumph over the innocent victim.*[22]

By citing such a passage, we are not, of course, legitimating a sort of positive hope that individual evil-doers will be condemned to hell. Nonetheless, it seems essential to authentic hope to positively desire an absolute judgment that will not be a compromise; and that what we have found to be hateful and worthy of utter reprobation will have no part in the new creation.[23]

This purposely abstract way of expressing the point is not meant to obscure the fact that evil does not exist without evil-doers. Admittedly today, we can speak of social structures of evil, and, surely, hell, under one aspect, means their inglorious collapse. But the evil-doers that planned, consented to and maintained such destructive forces to the end, what of them? How is hell not only the divine condemnation of evil, but a dread possibility for evil-doers?

4. A Universe of Freedom?

That question takes us to the fourth remark, where one can only reflect on the enigma of human freedom. The mystery of creation implies that God really does create the world to exist in its proper independence. And creation is never more creation than in the case of the free human creature. To be free, really means to be free, not as an independence merely permitted or tolerated by God, but as the quality of being, initiated, willed and sustained by the creator. No recognition of this freedom is realistic if it does not allow freedom to be truly free. Here resides the possibility of eschatological tragedy: free human agents can opt for themselves, against God, and do so definitively; not as an accident but as an irrevocable choice into which they have put the whole deliberate weight of their lives. Not to allow for this possibility of ultimate self-enclosure is to suffer a diminishment of hope: God is the manipulator of a fundamentally illusory freedom. If salvation were automatic, the new creation would, in the end, be populated by automata.

The nature of the this tragedy has been unforgettably evoked in Dostoievsky's *The Brothers Karamazov*,: 'What is hell? It is the suffering that comes from being unable to love.'[24] In contrast to the tragic drama that Father Zossima describes is C.S. Lewis' memorable passage, as it suggests more indirectly the utterly banal character of ultimate selfishness:

> *To love at all is to be vulnerable. Love anything, and your heart will certainly be wrung and possibly broken. If you want to make sure of keeping it intact, you must give your heart to no one, not even to an animal. Wrap it carefully around with hobbies and little luxuries. Avoid all entanglements: lock it up in the safe casket or coffin of your selfishness. But in that casket—safe, dark, motionless, airless—it will change. It will not be broken. It will become unbreakable, impenetrable, irredeemable. The alternative to tragedy, or at least the risk of tragedy, is damnation. The only place outside of heaven where you can be perfectly safe from the dangers and perturbations of love is hell.*[25]

Hell is the human possibility of ending up alienated in a universe whose life-breath is love, with a heart 'unbreakable, impenetrable, irredeemable'. Does the imagination of hope come to a dead end in its vision of the capacities of the human heart to choose an ultimate selfishness? Is that the last word on hell?

5. Hope against hope

I do not think theology can rest there. For theologians also know in their own way 'the dangers and perturbations of love'. So here, our reflection must be refocused on the mystery of Christ. In the paschal mystery of the death, burial and resurrection of Jesus, God has already gone beyond our most dreadful presentiments to touch realities we can barely imagine. The symbol of Holy Saturday, as was mentioned before, communicates this all but inexpressible outer limit of hope.

The all-enfolding mystery of God's love reaches into the infernal isolation of human freedom. God, in creating the world, has already accepted this point of darkness in creation. The self-giving love of the Trinity, in calling the world into being, comprehends its every moment, its every possibility, its every dimension. So, as we have stressed before, the paschal mystery represents Jesus descending, in loving solidarity even with the definitively lost, into their hell. In this way, the redeemer is present within the space furthest from God:

> ...exactly in this way, he disturbs the absolute loneliness striven for by the sinner: the sinner who wants to be 'damned' apart from God, finds God again in his loneliness, but God in the absolute weakness of love who unfathomably in the period of non-time, enters into solidarity with those damning themselves.[26]

Von Balthasar's trinitarian imagination of the whole mystery of human redemption is in the end an extraordinary statement of hope. While respecting human freedom, it does not absolutise it as the 'last thing' in creation. The ultimate *eschaton* is Christ:

> *The freedom of the creature is respected, but it is retrieved by God at the end of the passion, and seized again in its very foundations. Only in absolute weakness does God will to mediate to the freedom created by him the gift of love that breaks from every prison and every constraint: in his solidarity with those who reject all solidarity.*[27]

In expressing this kind of loving 'subterfuge'—is there a better word?—on the part of God who refuses to be anything else but love, the language of hope can probably go no further. The rest is the silence of hope itself.

Yet in that inarticulate silence, hell is the outermost limit, touched in a special way only by the compassion of the saints in their intercessions. It seems to me that we do not often question our hearts when, perhaps all too easily, we abolish hell in the name of a tolerance that accepts everything and expects little from human freedom. For the true abolition of hell is a harsh demand: to share the future of God with those we have most feared, most despised, most condemned, and have found most unforgivable. Emptying hell means populating our heaven with those we may well have found, either in the intimate or public conduct of our lives, most hateful. It is at this point where the holy ones, all who pass over completely in the compassion of God to leave behind all self-regarding notions of happiness, really work for the abolition of hell:

> *Hell is not so much a threat to be hurled at other people, but a challenge to oneself. It is a challenge to suffer in the dark night of faith, to experience communion with Christ in solidarity with his descent into the night. One draws near to the Lord's radiance by sharing his darkness. One serves the salvation of the world by leaving one's own salvation behind for the sake of others.*[28]

In the end, the possibility of hell must find its place only within the actuality of a larger mystery: 'God was in Christ reconciling the world to himself' (II Cor. 5:19). As a modern poet prayed:

> *Thus it may be: and worse.*
> *And may we know Thy perfect darkness.*
> *And may we into Hell descend with Thee.*[29]

1. Hans Urs von Balthasar, *The God Question and Modern Man*, tr. Hilda Graef, Seabury, New York, 1967.
2. *ibid.*, p.123.
3. B. Lonergan, *Method in Theology*, p.111.
4. I refer, of course, to Dame Julian of Norwich and T.S. Eliot.
5. James V. Schall, 'Displacing Damnation: The Neglect of Hell in Political Theory', *The Thomist* 44/1, January 1983, p.43.
6. *ibid.*, p.44.
7. Hannah Arendt, *Between Past and Future*, Viking, New York, 1968, p.133.
8. Schall, 'Displacing Damnation...', p.33.
9. Lest my remarks be taken as an attack on liberation theology, I should add that the best of such prophetic theology while it summons to solidarity with the poor and oppressed, while its provokes resistance to the oppressive structures of evil, always remains a Christian theology including all the themes of grace, reconciliation and ultimate hope. An inspiring example is Gustavo Gutierrez, *We Drink from our own Wells*, tr. M. J. O'Connell, Orbis, New York, 1987.
10. Zachary Hayes, 'Hell', *The New Dictionary of Theology*, Wilmington, Del., Glazier, pp.457–459.
11. On the other hand, Paul, in less figurative language, speaks of the banishment and destruction of those who do evil (II Thes. 1:9; Rom. 2:9; 9:22; Phil. 3:19); and John is even more removed from such imagery in his language of darkness, death, judgment (Jn 2:19; 8:24; 10:28).
12. Donald M. McKinnon, 'Eternal Loss', *New Blackfriars*, 69/921, November 1988, pp.473f.
13. *See* Z.Hayes, 'Hell', *The New Dictionary of Theology*, pp.457f.
14. *Benedictus Deus*, DS 1000f.
15. DS 780.
16. DS 801; 856ff; 1306; 1539; 1575.
17. See the Synod of Constantinople (543), (DS 411). Let me emphasise again that Origen's teaching on a final restoration was condemned as a matter of fact, not as an object of humble hope.
18. *See* the document of the Sacred Congregation for the

Doctrine of the Faith, *A Letter on Certain Questions concerning Eschatology*, May 17, 1979, par. 7.
19. See Walter E.Conn, *Christian Conversion: A Developmental Interpretation of Autonomy and Surrender*, The Paulist Press, New York, 1986, pp.33–68; Donald Evans, *Struggle and Fulfilment: The Inner Dynamics of Religion and Morality*, The Fortress Press, Philadelphia, 1981. Admittedly the 'life-cycle' model of human development is a very optimistic one; perhaps it is best understood fundamentally as a psychology of hope. No doubt, it needs rounding out in reference to the variety of fears appropriate to the various stages of development.
20. Quoted by John Orme Mills, O.P. 'Preface', *New Blackfriars* 69, November 1988, p.469.
21. Karl Rahner, *Foundations of Christian Faith*, tr. W.D. Dych, The Seabury Press, New York, 1978, p.435.
22. Quoted in Hans Küng, *Eternal Life?*, Doubleday, New York, 1984, p.198.
23. Walter Wink in his *Unmasking the Powers: The Invisible Forces That Determine Human Existence*, Fortress Press, Philadelphia, 1987, pp.39f., interprets this point in an interesting psychological way, perhaps more pertinent to the theme of purgatory than hell.
24. *The Brothers Karamasov*, Bk.6, ch.3.
25. C.S. Lewis, *The Four Loves*, Bless, London, 1960, pp.138f.
26. *The von Balthasar Reader*, p.153.
27. *ibid.*, p.153.
28. J. Ratzinger, *Eschatology*, pp.217f.
29. David Gascoyne, 'Tenebrae', in *Collected Poems 1988* 1988 by permission of Oxford University Press.

10 Heaven: the Fulfilment of Hope

In speaking of this desire for a far-off country, which we find in ourselves even now, I feel a certain shyness. I am almost committing an indecency. I am trying to rip open the inconsolable secret in each one of you—the secret which hurts so much that you take your revenge on it by calling it names like Nostalgia and Romanticism and Adolescence; the secret which also pierces with such sweetness that when, in very intimate conversation, the mention of it becomes imminent, we grow awkward and affect to laugh at ourselves; the secret we cannot hide and cannot tell, though we desire to do both. We cannot tell it because it is a desire for something which has never actually appeared in our experience. We cannot hide from it because our experience is constantly suggesting it, and we betray ourselves like lovers at the mention of a name.[1]

The memorable words of a great modern Christian writer introduce our final theme.[2] Heaven has been implicit in almost everything we have treated so far. The prospect of fulfilment in a final union with God tugs like an undertow in the depths of human consciousness, the 'secret we cannot hide and cannot tell': a fulfilment not only explicitly promised in the scriptures and traditions of our faith, but intimated in all our searchings, all our loves, all our hopes. The self-transcending thrust of our being is a promise yet to be kept.[3] There is a homing instinct at the heart of our selfhood, life longing for its fullness.

The unknowing of heaven

As such it cannot be hidden; and yet cannot be told. It is one thing to have a hope opening the heart in anticipation of an ultimate fulfilment. It is another matter to fill that expectation with definite objects of shape and colour by using the words and images of a provisional world. Very interestingly, for all the explicitness of their promise of eternal life, for all the variety of images they employ, the scriptures themselves exhibit a marked reserve in describing the absolute future. The biblical word of God is familiar with the double silence in the narrative of its hope: that of the Lord's death and resurrection—the dark silence where the human voice is stilled; the luminous silence in which faith trembles in the presence of the new creation. Though, as we have pointed out, the paschal mystery remains, the basic parable of Christian existence, it takes none of the waiting or wonder out of our hope: 'Eye has not seen nor ear heard nor the heart of man conceived what God has prepared for those who love him' (I Cor. 2:9).

The horizon of hope is itself, to borrow the title of a great mystical classic, a cloud of unknowing. Compared to our human judgments, the ways of God are inscrutable, just as his judgments are unsearchable (Rom. 11:33). Eschatology has to learn the discretion of a *theologia negativa*, the way of negation, if it is to serve as an authentic expression of hope. We may not settle on any provisional version of humanity, however advanced that might be, for 'it has not yet appeared what we shall be' (I Jn 3:2). We cannot turn history into a human plan, since it is not given to us to know the conditions of the times and the seasons of God's initiative (Acts 1:7). Hope prepares us to meet the future, rather than to foretell it.

Even as hope moves with all its positive passion toward God's future, our understanding can only back into it, or see it in a rear-vision mirror: what is 'perishable...dishonourable...weak...physical' will become, through the creative power of the Spirit, imperishable, glorious, powerful, spiritual (I Cor. 15:42–44). Christian hope goes beyond its capacity to understand, to await a fulfilment in him who, 'by the power at work within us is able to do far more abundantly than all we ask or think' (Eph. 3:20). It does not allow our fulfilment in God to be reduced to any category within the present sphere of our experience: '...hope that is seen is not hope' (Rom. 8:24).

Thus, the scriptures provide a wholesome lesson. Hope expands into its proper proportions only within the cloud of unknowing. The presence of the Holy Spirit is the fundamental expectant energy within our hearts, 'for we do not know how to pray as we ought, but the Spirit himself intercedes for us with sighs too deep for words' (Rom. 8:26). John's gospel will even present Jesus as saying that it is to 'your advantage that I go away'—evidently to make room for a Spirit-guided history—'...otherwise the Paraclete will not come to you. But if I go, I will send him to you' (Jn 16:7). As present to the disciples, this Spirit will declare 'the things that are to come' (Jn 16:13).

Failure to absorb this scriptural way of thinking has resulted in a trivialising of the mystery of Heaven. Instead of being understood as the world's surpassing fulfilment evoked through the interplay of various images drawn either from nature (the garden of paradise), of culture (the city of God), of personal union (the wedding feast), of conviviality (the great banquet), of enlightenment (the beatific vision), heaven becomes a neatly located object within the world of our experience. There it congeals in one or other particular image. The relativity, the multiplicity, the interplay of the scriptural images, and, above all, the biblical reserve in using them, are forgotten. Not surprisingly, a certain distaste or repugnance regarding the subject of heaven results. It begins to look like either a cloyingly ethereal state designed for the consolation of the devout, or something like an unending binge for a consumer society!

The heaven of liberation

Allied to this scriptural displacement of heaven into the cloud of unknowing, there is another form of displacement of heaven in the consciousness of the Church today. For the final fulfilment of life is being imagined from within a vigorous social engagement. Such is the result of the Church's deliberate missionary option for the poor and oppressed. Theology, responding to the signs of the times, becomes one of liberation. Instead of interpreting the world in reference to a devoutly imagined heaven, theology is more inclined to understand heaven in terms of a passionately imagined world. The more Christian hope immerses itself in the struggles of the world, the more realistic is its tone in speaking of a transcendent abundance of life. The world is seen less as a troubled place of exile, less as a languid antechamber to the halls of celestial bliss: it is the theatre of life-in-the-making, of eternal life already begun in the works of love and justice and mercy. To adapt the Johannine expression, loving our neighbour who we can see is the best preparation for meeting the God of love whom we cannot see (I Jn 4:20).

Contemporary Christian conscience recoils from any presentation of heaven that could distract from commitment to the struggles of this world by justifying a religious escape from the challenges posed by our times. Radical hope lives by the conviction that life to the full must be realistically anticipated by contesting the oppressive limitations of life in the present. As such hope promotes and defends the life of our shared humanity in practical compassion, it becomes a world-shaping force. This change of emphasis is strikingly, perhaps extremely, expressed in the words of a modern martyr, Archbishop Oscar Romero of El Salvador as he uttered them a few weeks before his murder:

> *My life has been threatened many times. I must confess, that, as a Christian, I don't believe in death without the resurrection. If they kill me, I will rise again in the Salvadoran people. I'm not boasting or saying this out of pride, but rather as humbly as I can...*[4]

In this connection, the less dramatic words of Vatican II come to mind:

> *As the form of this world, distorted by sin, is passing away, we are taught that God is preparing a new dwelling and a new earth as the abode of justice. Its joy will fulfil and surpass all that the human heart has longed for: with death conquered, the sons and daughters of God will be raised in Christ; and what is sown in weakness and dishonour will put on the imperishable. Charity and its works will remain, and all creation, which God made for humankind, will be freed from its bondage to decay.*[5]

Both the witness of the martyrs and the prophetic teaching of the Church challenge hope to imagine heaven out of a passion for humanity: 'charity and its works will remain'. A few months before his death in Africa, a great contemporary figure, Dag Hammarskjöld, the then Secretary-General of the United Nations, wrote in his celebrated *Markings*:

> *I don't know Who—or what—put the question. I don't know when it was put. I don't even remember answering. But, at some moment, I did say Yes to Someone—or Something—and from that hour I was certain that existence is*

meaningful and that, therefore, my life, in self-surrender, had a goal.[6]

Hammarskjöld's self-committing 'Yes', and the assurance that resulted of being directed onward, well describes the experience of hope. The often obscure and struggling 'Yes' of life is looking to eternal affirmation. The eternity of heaven is made out of those decisions for love and justice through which we commit ourselves to time-defying truth and value. Heaven in such a perspective becomes a symbol of our ultimate love for life. It is the expression of a splendid defiant hope: what we value most will not be at the mercy of what we value least. If what we value least—hatred, violence, brute power—are accepted as the basic world-forming realities, then risking one's life for the sake of what we value most, be it a commitment to truth or service of our neighbour, must appear as a risk too great for our present securities, given the doomed precariousness of what we understand life to be. But if 'charity and its works' do remain, if authentic life will be vindicated in glory, if eternal life is already in the making through the decisions of our present history, the question for hope is: Why not live now? When the reality of death collides with the radiant goodness of the martyrs, it is the meaning of death that changes. It becomes the door opening to eternity, that realm of ultimate life which contains within it the affirmation, the vindication, the homecoming of our true selfhood. To die in the Lord is to be glorified in what our loves have made us.

While I have been attempting in the above paragraphs to evoke a sense of heaven related to an energetic and even heroic social commitment, I realise that it could sound all too much like the heaven of the young. Such a heaven of life's promise and energy contrasts with what can be termed the heaven of the old—a heaven imagined at the limits of life's weariness, failure, exhaustion, defeat, isolation, and inevitable dying. But there are surely times when the proper accent of hope is simply that of transcendent promise. And, if the symbol of heaven truly belongs to the language of the affirmation of life, then it must affirm all life, in all its moods and phases. Emphasising the witness of the martyrs provokes a rethinking of heaven as an ultimate mode of existence formed by life's commitments. But this need not deny that it is a liberation from life's miseries: old-age, illness, hopeless poverty. There are times when heaven is all that Christian hope has to offer; when it is the only thing that counts; the only hope that remains. Then, hope for heaven is both the affirmation of the eternal value of the personal and a protest against all forces threatening to degrade or destroy human dignity.

Christ as heaven

So, whatever the different accents in which heaven can be presented, and whatever the extraordinary diversity of images used in evoking its meaning, we must now emphasise the precisely Christian form of heaven. For the heaven of Christian hope contrasts with the numerous religious, philosophical, and cultural ways of imagining human fulfilment.[7] Indeed, there is something more basic at stake. It has often been remarked in recent times that Christ hardly figures in standard Christian accounts of heaven.[8] The blessed, after a life of seeing 'in a mirror dimly', in heaven see God 'face to face' (I Cor. 13:12). But, if a lot of theology is to be believed, in that moment of supreme bliss, the saints appear to forget their Christian identity! All too often the impression has been given that the reality of Christ is somehow a packaging of the mystery of God that in the end will be torn off to reveal the hidden content. Or, to change the metaphor, the crucified and risen humanity of Jesus pertains simply to the *way* rather than to the *goal* of Christian existence.

Such a de-christifying of heaven undermines the

very foundation of Christian hope. Given our already rather extended treatment of the christological meaning in the chapters dealing with the paschal mystery and the eucharist, I will emphasise a few particular points.

God has not only revealed himself in Christ, but radically given himself to us in a personal, unconditional manner in the incarnation, death and resurrection of the Son. Jesus Christ is God's personal engagement in our humanity, and his identification with it. God is thus self-defined as the Father of our Lord Jesus Christ. The *Logos* incarnate in Jesus is the *Logos* of eschatology, the meaning and goal of Christian hope. Hence to detach the vision of God from union with Christ would mean a severe distortion: God himself is never detached from Christ; for him, the divine mystery has irreversibly defined itself as our God: 'he who has seen me, has seen the Father' (Jn 14:9).

No doubt the reason for a strangely Christ-less heaven was the necessity theology was under of maintaining the theological aspect of heaven's promise: it was a beatific vision in which God was seen 'face to face'. From the fourteenth century, it has been official Church teaching that the blessed 'see God immediately', without any finite intermediary.[9] The interposition of any created reality would essentially distort and restrict the infinite mystery. In such a context, any mediation of the humanity of Jesus in the vision of God would seem to be precluded.

On the other hand, the finite mediation that is here disallowed clearly has to do with anything that comes between God and the blessed: that is, anything restrictive, provisional, imperfect—all the limitations of thought and word and sign which belong to 'seeing in a mirror dimly', and not 'face to face'.

But there is clearly another kind of mediation possible. This would not place a limitation on God's complete self-communication, but would be, rather, an aspect of its perfection. Here Christ is the mediator of our encounter with the infinite mystery of God as self-giving love. For he is the unsurpassable event of God's self-giving to creation. The incarnation has eternal significance.[10] Jesus reveals God as the one who gives himself in solidarity with us in the incarnation, in the compassion of the cross, in the victory of the resurrection. Heaven, as union with Christ, is possession of God precisely as the Father of our Lord Jesus Christ, precisely as the mystery incarnate in him, precisely in the gift of the Spirit breathed by him. To see God 'face to face' means seeing God in the face of Christ: 'For it is the God who said "Let light shine out of darkness" who has shone in our hearts to give the light of the knowledge of the glory of God in the face of Christ' (II Cor. 4:6). To see no eschatological significance in Paul's words here, is surely to distort them. Far from making Christ disappear into the shadows, the radiance of the divine light is ever focused in the reality of Christ. Though heaven is the vision of God, the divine mystery remains ever defined by what has been given in the beloved Son.

Though the theological tradition emphasised heaven as seeing God without any finite intermediary, it has left comparatively unexplored other aspects of perceiving the divine reality. Seeing has indeed been the dominant model of knowing for most Western thought; the visual, especially with the advent of printing, has been the privileged mode of perceiving. But there are other spiritual senses. It is possible to imagine the perfect knowing of God as a perfect hearing of the divine Word, as touching and holding the divine reality, as tasting the divine sweetness, as inhaling the divine Spirit, as drawing close, and plunging into its mystery.

As we enlarge our notions of the spiritual senses, it is easier to imagine the humanity of Christ as the medium through which we share in the divine life. The divine Word is heard in his voice; in him, the divine Spirit is breathed forth as the living atmosphere of the new creation; through him, the blessed taste the sweetness of Lord. Christ is the milieu, the God-given relational space in which the life of true communion is lived. As he comes forth from and returns to the Father, the blessed share in his intimacy with God, as 'sons and daughters in the Son'. In his presence to the whole communion of saints, they are given to one another as brothers and sisters in the one mystery of divine life. Through the mutation of the universe that has occurred in him, they enter a transfigured world.

As Josef Ratzinger writes:

> *Heaven therefore, must first and foremost be determined christologically. It is not an extra-historical place into which one goes. Heaven's existence depends on the fact that Jesus Christ, as God, is man, and makes space for human existence in the existence of God himself. Heaven is thus primarily a personal reality, and one that remains forever shaped by its historical origin in the paschal mystery of death and resurrection. From this christological centre all the other elements which belong to the tradition's concept of heaven can be inferred.*[11]

All this is to say that to de-christify heaven, however unwittingly, is to place heaven in a transcendent nowhere. Detached from the personal, concrete 'living one' (Rev. 1:18), the theology of heaven is at the mercy of an uncontrolled imagination. Such fantasies may say more about the dynamics of wish-fulfilment than about the movement of Christian hope towards its goal to be with Christ: 'For life is to be with Christ; where he is, there is life, there is the kingdom.'[12]

The heaven of God

To envisage a heaven in which Christ is the medium through which the blessed see God face to face points to an even more radical point. Heaven is the moment in which God's self-communication to the creature is achieved.[13] Once more, I am merely emphasising what was said previously. We must leave aside any image of God as an infinite, but inert form, somehow filling the vacuum in human existence that death has caused. For our notions of God and heaven must never be considered apart from the most intense affirmation of Christian faith: 'God is love' (I Jn 4:8,16). John reminds the believer that it is not as though we first loved God, but that he has first loved us (I Jn 4:10). This remains the determining feature of heaven as well. The creature's coming to be in God always lives from God's self-giving, the divine coming to be in creation.

In such a perspective, heaven is the point when all the graces of life (and death) reach a culminating moment. The Trinity, giving itself to creation as self-communicating love, is an open circle of a divine communion. The divine three draw each and all into their own 'love-life'. The dynamism of this divine communication reaches an irreversible moment of success in the destiny of each of the blessed. For in each of the saints, the divine mystery realises its self-giving. Each of the blessed enters the joy of the Lord, because the Lord has entered into his own joy, in the actualisation of the God-self in each one.

Heaven is, then, an essentially theological mystery. The fulfilment of the divine joy of self-giving is fundamental to the joy of human fulfilment. An excessively anthropological, let alone anthropocentric, version of heaven, has been inclined to think of heaven as a reward for a life well-lived; or, more philosophically, the moment of final self-transcendence into God. What both such notions obscure, and, indeed, what both rely on, is the mystery of divine love communicating itself in the energy of the Spirit, as the light of the Word, as the absolute origin and goal in the Father. Only in such grace is the movement of human self-transcendence possible. The supreme attainment of such self-transcendence presupposes the self-communication of God. Hence, heaven is primarily a divine moment of success in God's self-communication to creation. It is primarily the mystery of God coming into its own. *...ipse [Deus] post istam vitam est locus noster:* '...after this life, God himself is our place'.[14]

Heaven as the fullness of life

Now, this fundamental dynamic of divine self-communication would be literally without flesh and blood unless it is related to the human longing for the 'life to the full' that Jesus came to give (Jn 10:10).

Since the fulfilment of heaven must be as large as life, there are innumerable ways of imagining it. In what follows, I will dwell on three of the ways in which hope can imagine life's fulfilment: first, heaven as the resurrection of the body; secondly, heaven as the fulfilment of love and relationships; thirdly, heaven as the vision of God.

(i) The Resurrection of the Body

Christian hope for life to the full necessarily expresses itself as belief in the resurrection of the body. Without some form of embodiment, the human person can scarcely be said to exist.[15] For to be human is to be, from different points of view, both an animated body, and an embodied soul.[16] In terms of what we have already mentioned in chapter two, the spiritual self-actualisation of the human person is a progressive embodiment in a great cosmic process.[17] Our bodies are not an exclusive possession of a part of the world. More fundamentally, they express our distinctive relationship to the totality of the world. Through the body, we are immersed in an unfolding cosmic dynamism, and are possessed by it. For human, personal existence both incorporates a world, and, at the same time, is incorporated into the larger corporate process of interconnected cosmic realities.

To that degree, the body is far less definable than common sense would think. Because I can imagine my own corpse, I may think of my true self as oddly external to the 'somebody' I am. I can refer to it as one thing among other things in the cosmos. More deeply, through the body, I am in relationship to everything, in an inter-connected dynamic world. My body is an element in a continuing process, a continuing incorporation of the human self in the emerging universe. Thus, it is my participation in a cosmic generation, as the earth brings forth all its generations of living things: through our bodies we are generated into life, to become ourselves generative agents in the increase, the expansion, the unfolding of life.

When hope imagines its future from within such cosmic embodiment, it envisages its fulfilment as the resurrection of the body in a transfigured universe. Let me indicate some dimensions of our contemporary experience of the world as they bear on the cosmic, embodied nature of heaven.

For today we are able to conceive of our embodiment in the cosmos in dimensions of space and time which would have been incredible to our forbears. From time immemorial, the human eye could see 'The heavens declare the glory of God' (Ps. 19:1) in the light of the sun and moon, in the twinkling stars and the steady glow of the planets, in the shimmering beauty of the Milky Way. But today that vision of that eye has been so extended that it can discern or at least decipher, through its technological extensions, more mysterious realities: the rings encircling Saturn, the Trifid Nebula, Neptune's moons, the mountains of Mars, the enchanting blue of the earth as it was photographed from the moon, our galaxy of three hundred billion suns, the pulsing energy of the quasars, enormous, explosive supernovas, enigmatic black holes. The light that radiates through the cosmos, at one hundred and eighty-six thousand miles a second, to reach our eyes takes one hundred thousand years to span just our particular galaxy. From the quark, with its eighteen variations, to the quasar, it is a universe of incredible proportions.

Our hope now has also to include the memory of hitherto unimaginable expanses of time. And, within this new awareness of the billions of years that have gone into our making, our hope for the future has to set itself within the evolutionary dynamics that have produced this human world. Human consciousness, trembling before the extent of the eleven-billion-year history of this universe, comes to realise that these thousands of millions of years are, quite literally, *our* past. In an uncanny sense, the universe, from its beginnings, 'knew we were coming'. As one philosopher of science puts it, 'if the universe were in fact different in any significant way from the way it is, we wouldn't be here to wonder why it is the way it is'.[18]

For, in the first few seconds of this eleven-billion-year-old universe, there appeared all the fundamental particles and constants without which life on this, seemingly insignificant, little planet would have been impossible. The velocity of light, the charge on the electron, the mass of the proton, the constant emissions of energy, the pull of gravity, the velocity of light are exactly what they should have been if life were to teem in all its forms on earth. A slight difference then would have meant no life now. The universe as we know it, would never have come to be. All those millions of hydrogen atoms formed twenty billion years ago, which today in various combinations make up the composition of the human body, would have turned into the inert gas, helium. There would have been no water, no life, no you reading, nor me writing, in this instant.[19]

And yet, here we are, in this moment of consciousness, alive on this planet, participating in this universe which has brought us forth. In body, mind and heart we are part of an awakening cosmic mystery. Paul described the whole of creation as groaning in one great act of giving birth. He saw us human beings as groaning too, for the fulfilment that is not yet. More mysteriously, he saw the creative Spirit of God groaning within us to inspire hopes worthy of the mystery at work (Rom. 8:18–28).

Such a vision is not far removed from that of a respected American scientist, Eric Chaisson of Harvard:

> *We are not independent entities, alien to the earth. The earth in its turn is not adrift in a vacuum unrelated to the cosmos. The cosmos itself is no longer cold and hostile—because it is our universe. It brought us forth and maintains our being. We are, in a literal sense, 'children of the universe'.*[20]

A contemporary sense of the mystery of creation can bring together an appreciation of how we human beings are from God—'children of God' in the biblical sense—and 'children of the universe', born of the earth. We are made in the image of God, and yet we are earthlings: we live only in a genetic solidarity with a myriad others forms of life on this planet. For we human beings are related in a web of life with some ten million other species, be they whales or wombats, orchids or orang-outangs, pine-trees or pythons . In the one web of life, they are all our relatives in a wondrous cosmic solidarity. Indeed, elements of the stars are in the phosphorous of our bones; and the same hydrogen which makes the stars blaze, energises our bodies and powers our imagination.

To exist as a human being, even in what is most spiritual about us, means to be embodied in the matter of the world. The human spirit exists and functions in what is other than itself. It becomes embodied in that ensemble of relationships, dynamics, conditions we understand as our world. To have a body means to have a world, to be intrinsically part of a larger whole, in all its emergence through decay and death to an increasingly complex and unified sphere of life.

If then Christian hope expresses itself in terms of the resurrection of the body, it is not longing for a resuscitation in this little bit of exchangeable matter. It is envisaging a complete embodiment in that world which, though always radically God's creation, embraces us and bears us on in its cosmic unfolding. Such a hope does not want to escape from its material world, but to become a creative presence within the emerging whole.

For, embodied in such a world, the human spirit has been sustained and expanded to its proper creativity. In such a world, we human beings have found beauty and felt the breadth of our universal belonging. Within it, we have adored the creative mystery of everything that is and will be. In the evolutionary history of such a world, we have sought for and met the Christ: as the old Advent antiphon sang, *aperiatur terra et germinet salvatorem*, 'Let the earth be opened and bud forth the saviour'. And into such a world, generation after generation of living things have been born and have died, to make the earth fruitful and hallowed for the generations to come.

In the minds of our great thinkers, the world has become a universe present to itself as an immeasurable wonder. To the inspiration of our artists, it offers its shapes and colours, its sounds and movements, to burst forth into ever new forms. In our mystics, it is a world come home to itself as something holy, a vast sacrament bearing within itself the presence of all-creative mystery. In human science and craft, it yields itself to human use, no longer as a blind force threatening human kind, but as the earth nurturing the emergence of a global humanity. The mystery of the cosmos has smiled on us in the wonder of a human face, and given birth to each of us from the womb of a woman.[21] It has given man and woman to each other in the life-giving intimacy and shared joy of sexual love. This material universe has become, as it were, the shared body of the human spirit. To hope, then, for the resurrection of the body implies a cosmic hope, that we are saved with and in our world.

In such a vision, the human spirit becomes a self through its immersion in an ever-emerging world. If the human spirit has been embodied in a material world, that world of matter has been taken up into new levels of being through the activity of the human mind and heart and hand. Indeed, in the incarnation of the Word, the material world has been occupied and possessed by the divine mystery as its own. In the resurrection of Christ, it has become the beginning of a new creation. Neither for the New Adam nor for us who believe in him, can heaven mean leaving this world behind: this world, and ourselves within it, are destined, through death and resurrection, for a final transformation. All the groaning of the cosmos will yield to the 'Alleluia' of a creation finally at home with its creator.

Where an older theology was content with the treasured axiom of grace perfecting nature, the analogical imagination of today unfolds into an ever-expanding horizon.

For a gravitational bond unites all the galaxies; electromagnetic forces bind molecules into progressively more complex forms; genetic codes connect all the generations of living things in the one great tree of life. The tree of life has blossomed into human consciousness, and borne fruit in human meaning and human value. The world has become thereby a universe to be progressively explored as an awesome mystery, the blessed ground of our co-existence. As the meanings and values that live in the human mind and heart are shared, the many cultures of the world come together. New forms of interdependence and collaboration anticipate the realisation of one human history.

Then, in the fullness of time, human consciousness came to be illumined by the presence of incarnate mystery. From then on, it is summoned to surrender to Christ's Spirit as it animates all creation, as a limitless field of self-transcending energy. This Spirit moves, connects and, in the end, transforms all reality into the Cosmic Christ, the Lord of the universe of grace. Ambrose of Milan sums up the cosmic sweep of the mystery of Christ: 'In Christ's resurrection the world arose. In Christ's resurrection, the heavens arose, in Christ's resurrection the earth itself arose.'[22]

It is here that the Catholic doctrine of Mary 'assumed body and soul into heaven', has special significance. For the Assumption of Mary is a concrete symbol of the creativity of our God-charged world.

Early patristic theology thought of Mary as the New Eve, formed from the New Adam (cf. Gen. 2:21–23), as the 'mother of all the living'. In such a context, the Assumption is not one more unique Marian privilege. As now assumed into the glory of Christ, she is the anticipation of the heaven of a transfigured creation.[23] She is the paradigm instance of creation open to, collaborating with, the creative mystery of God in Christ. As the Mother of Christ, she symbolises the generativity of creation as it is penetrated by the Spirit: in her the earth has been opened to bud forth the saviour. Her Assumption nourishes hope with an assurance that our nature and our history have already, in her, reached their term. She embodies the reality of our world as having received into itself the mystery that is to transform the universe in its entirety. In her assumption into glory our world has already become heaven.

Hence, she is invoked as 'Holy Mary', the creature uniquely surrendered to the self-giving of God. As 'Mother of God', as God-bearer, *Theotokos*, she is the one in whom the great cosmic act of giving birth (cf. Rom. 8:22) has been achieved. For in her the genesis of God within this world has effected the genesis of humankind within the mystery of God. To the still-groaning creation, in all the fear of living and dying that we know, Mary assumed into heaven is a symbol for hope. Transforming grace has achieved its success: one of our number has been wholly transformed by the Spirit of Christ. As such, she is present in the communion of saints, as the Mother of the Church, interceding for all on the pilgrimage of hope: 'Holy Mary, Mother of God, pray for us sinners, now, and at the hour of our death.'

Hope might find in the Assumption of Mary an even richer context in a sponsal relationship between God and creation. This looks to the consummation of a cosmic marriage (cf. Rev. 12:1–4). In Mary, the Spirit has brought forth the particular beauty of creation in the sight of God. In her, our history has come to its maturity, its age of consent, to surrender to the transcendent love for which it was destined. Out of such a union, the whole Christ of a transfigured creation is born.

Thus, while the clear focus of Christian hope is the paschal mystery of Christ, there is a subsidiary focal point in the manner in which the gift of transforming grace has already been received and assimilated by the human world. In such a context, the many-faceted Marian symbolism has a special role to play. In the contemplation of such mysteries as the Assumption of Mary, the creative imagination of hope is stirred to envisage the destiny of the created world and the history of its freedom as a collaboration with the divine in bringing forth our new humanity in Christ. Though the mystery of the future comes *from* God as a transcendent gift, it comes *to* human freedom in a slow growth through history to the maturity of its full collaboration with God.

(ii) **Heaven as Love**

Because heaven is the complete embodiment of our existence in Christ, because it is our entry into the love-life of the Trinity, we can conceive of eternal life as an ultimate state of being-in-love. Heavenly fulfilment is pre-eminently the homing of the heart.

However we might define the essence of our earthly lives, the fundamental tone and passion of our existence is surely revealed in our loves: 'Where your treasure is, there is your heart also' (Mt 6:21). What we spontaneously call our real life is essentially to be found in our loves, our relationships—everything and everyone we have conscientiously given ourselves to. In such loving, we have experienced what most makes up the fundamental joy and suffering of our being. To love is to be taken out of an isolated individuality into a new sense of the world. We lose ourselves only to find ourselves in a world more or less radically transformed.[24] To one who is in love, not only the beloved other, but other persons, formerly ordinary words, places, gestures, the body itself, are transformed. Everything is suffused with a new energy and enchantment. The Canticle of Canticles, 'the greatest song', remains the classical biblical affirmation of this fundamental ecstatic feature of human existence: 'I am my beloved's, and his desire is for me' (Cant. 7:10).[25] To the lover, the world is a new creation. Life is revitalised to such a degree that, in the memory of lovers, they seemed hardly to exist before. As an astute psychologist remarked:

> *It is a very common experience. Everyone who has truly fallen in love has had it, and sex, in the narrow sense, is not the important thing. It is the recognition of 'our native country' through love of another. We glimpse his or her eternal destiny and so also our own—we know, in that moment, that we have the freedom of that country forever.*[26]

In the loving self discovered in such an ecstasy, in the beloved other, 'glimpsed in his or her eternal destiny', as well in the 'native country' to which one comes home, we find the most evocative, and perhaps the most neglected, anticipations of the life of heaven.

No doubt, especially because of the demonic eroticism of contemporary Western culture, such an experience is frequently associated with pain and the possibilities of self-destruction. And, indeed, because of an excessive moralising in matters of sexual morality, this most precious intimation of the existence of heaven is too often compromised by darker forebodings.

In this context, it would be instructive to ponder anew the eschatological meaning of marriage precisely as a sacrament. In the celebration of Christian hope, the sexual union of man and woman is a 'visible sign of invisible grace'. This Christian conviction suggests that the invisible grace of heaven is, indeed, a life of self-giving ecstatic love. There is a deeper sense of the old saw, 'marriages are made in heaven'. In marriage, whether in human judgment it succeeds or fails, hope is inspired to imagine heaven in terms of the many-splendoured experience of being-in-love. No less a thinker than Bernard Lonergan pointed to this familiar experience as the apex of human development:

Once it has blossomed forth and as long as it lasts, it takes over. It is the first principle. From it flow one's desires and fears, one's joys and sorrows, one's discernment of values, one's decisions, one's deeds.[27]

He acknowledged, naturally, that such being in love is 'of different kinds',[28] for besides the love of intimacy, there is the love of community, of society, of the world, of God himself. But the point to make here is that not only the world's mystics, not only its martyrs, but also its lovers must be permitted a say in what life to the full will finally mean. It is unwise for any theology of hope to demean as an occasion of sin what for most people, for most of their lives, is *the* experience of self-transcendence, of transfigured existence, of relationship. Ultimate being-in-love, as we participate in the limitlessness and self-giving of trinitarian love in the unity of the Holy Spirit, will of course mean more than the fragility and incompleteness of earthly love; but it does not mean less. For that transforming love subsumes and brings to completion everything that our present experience of love has found to be real life.

Hence, it is entirely in accord with the imagination of Christian hope to envisage heaven as the fulfilment of the passion of our existence to be for others. Heaven is the world transformed as a sphere of love, in a communion of unreserved giving and receiving. All earthly loves are the most vivid and the most familiar anticipation of what we shall be. They are not excluded from the great Pauline affirmation: 'Love remains' (I Cor. 13:8).

The following words, taken from a notebook of Dostoievsky, provide a convenient and inspiring conclusion to this brief reflection on heaven as love. They express both the limitation of earthly love and the fulfilment it looks to in Christ:

> *To love somebody else as one loves oneself, which Christ told us to do—that is impossible. We are bound by the force of earthly personality: the 'me' stands in the way. Christ, and Christ alone, did it; but he was the eternal ideal, the ideal of the ages, to which one aspires and must aspire, impelled by nature.*
>
> *Nevertheless, since Christ came to earth as the human ideal in the flesh, it has become clear as daylight what the last and highest stage of the evolution of the personality must be. It is this: when our evolving is finished, at the very point where the end is reached, one will find out...with all the force of our nature that the highest use one can make of one's personality, of the full flowering of one's self, is to do away with it, to give it wholly to any and everybody, without division or reserve. And that is sovereign happiness. Thus, the law of*

*'me' is fused with the law of humanity; and the
'I' and 'all' (in appearance two opposite extremes) each suppressing itself for the sake of
the other, reach the highest peak of their individual development, each one separately.*

*This is exactly the paradise that Christ offers.
The whole history of humanity, and of each individual man and woman, is simply an evolution towards and an aspiration to, struggle for,
and achievement of, this end.*[29]

(iii) Heaven as the Vision of God

As we have mentioned above, the traditional formulation of the meaning of heaven has been in terms of the beatific vision. If, before, I highlighted the mediating role of the incarnate Word, I must now emphasise the character of the mystery he mediates. For the blessed see God 'face to face': 'My knowledge is imperfect now; then I shall know even as I am known' (I Cor. 13:12).[30] The Thomist tradition, with its strong intellectualist emphasis, made the beatific vision the essential feature of heaven, even though it allowed for an accompanying beatific love and joy. As a Church doctrine, the nature of this vision of God was, from the early fourteenth century, defined as 'intuitive or even face to face' knowledge of God, with the divine essence revealed 'plainly, clearly, openly'. Before such teachings were declared, the Council of Vienne (1312) stated, against the Beghards and Beguines, that such a vision, because it transcends any natural capacity, needs an ultimate divine gift, the light of glory, *lumen gloriae*.[31]

The notion of the beatific vision has served theology well, above all, in its classical Thomist tradition. For fulfilment as the immediate vision of God is a radical explanation of how the human spirit is radically and finally divinised. Even in the holiest life, though it was possible to have the perfection of charity in conformity to God's will, there remained a basic limitation in the believer's knowledge of God. Love reached toward an unknown mystery. The reality of that mystery was indeed mediated through all the variety of words and symbols and effects of God's saving action in the world. But the divine reality itself remained in the cloud of unknowing. The imperfection of faith's way of knowing God 'in a mirror dimly' is replaced, through the beatific vision, with an immediate, face to face, knowledge. In a final act of grace, the divine Word informs and actualises human intelligence, to overcome all limitation and to reveal the divine mystery in its essence. In this way, the knowledge of the blessed catches up, as it were, the real union with God that love had made possible. Thus, in the knowledge of vision, we possess the mystery that love had lived. In an ultimate illumination, we see God as he is.

Yet, this model of the beatific vision has had limitations connected with a rather abstract consideration of the soul with its different faculties of intellect and will. Theological traditions made different choices. The Thomist tradition came down in favour of the intellect: in the beatific vision, the radically new activity was the mind knowing the divine essence. The Franciscan school accented more the will: after all, there was as much scriptural warrant to conceive of heaven in terms of the will's perfection in loving union with the divine. Predictably, the good points of both traditions are being brought together in most modern thinking. Let me offer a few indications.

First, the knowledge concerned has too often been understood in a very visualist manner, as we mentioned before. Now, there are limitations in thinking of knowledge merely as vision, or more prosaically, just having a good look! Such limitations become clearer when one reflects on significant moments of knowing: for example, we might come to a special moment of insight or illumination—something far more intimate and mysterious than having a good look. Such moments are characterised by an experience of a sudden release and delight: 'Now I've got it!' and are not unlike the *eureka*! of the scientist, the 'Aha!' of the artist and the liberating breakthrough into self-consciousness achieved in successful therapy. In such instances, knowing is more like an ecstatic expansion of the self into the real world, a joyful self-transcendence into the universe of what truly is a moment of homecoming for the questioning existence that we are. The precious moment of truth happens when the knowing self and the reality known come together. The reality of the world comes to consciousness in the self, and the self expands ecstatically into the real world.

This is hardly a revolutionary insight given the Thomistic philosophical tradition and Bernard Lonergan's brilliant retrieval of it in recent times.[32] Still, a simplistic notion of knowledge, just 'having a good look', has distorted the rather more mysterious experience of our actual knowing as an ecstatic form of self-realisation within the universe of meaning. One consequence is that the theology of the beatific vision suffered: it became just looking at God from the outside, rather than an ecstatic immersion in the ocean of mystery.

Second, the older concentration on the different faculties of intellect and will have yielded to a more concrete, dynamic analysis of human consciousness. This is more holistically conceived as a continuing self-transcending movement, culminating typically in a state of 'being-in-love'.[33] In such a state, whether it manifests itself in the intensity of personal relationships, or dedication to a great cause, or in surrender to ultimate mystery, knowing and loving necessarily interpenetrate: the greater the love, the greater the capacity and the desire to know the beloved other; the greater the resultant knowledge, the more is love further inspired to wonder and dedication. This, in turn, leads to further enjoyment of the other, and to the desire to communicate the excellence, the beauty, the value of who or what has become so radiantly worthwhile. This more concrete analysis of human consciousness provides a more satisfactory analogy for the face-to-face encounter with God. The division of faculties into intellect and will yield to a more holistic sense of human consciousness awakened to the divine mystery as the supreme meaning, truth, value, beauty, and presence.

Thirdly, in line with what we mentioned earlier, the beatific vision must be understood in terms of God's trinitarian self-communication. In such a vision, the blessed do not see the Trinity, as it were, from the outside, as one object, however sublime, among many. Rather, they participate in God's own self-knowledge and joy. In heaven, we are enfolded into the communal life of the three divine persons. As the divine Spirit transforms our finite capacities, the human spirit becomes pure receptivity to the Word of God, in unrestricted, unconditional, surrender to the Father. Drawn into the trinitarian communion, the saints in glory now have 'inside' knowledge of God. They participate, transformed, in the very being of God, in what God is—self-giving, infinite life. In this connection, theology, in its fumbling efforts to express the meaning of the beatific vision, has often had recourse to the words of Psalm 36:9:

*They feast on the abundance of thy house,
and thou givest them delight from the river of
thy delights.
For with thee is the fountain of life;
in thy light do we see light.*

It is *within* the divine mystery, as drawn into union with the divine persons, that the blessed share in and yield to the reality of God. Thus, they see, taste, inhale the divine limitless mystery. In so doing, they see all things in God, the reality of the cosmos in its emergence as God's creation. The saints dwell in the world of God's creation as a *uni-verse*, a world wholly existing and made whole in God, a world appreciated precisely as the manifestation of God, a cosmos 'charged with the grandeur of God'. In short, the spatial image most suggestive of the meaning of the beatific vision is not one of looking at God 'from the outside', but one of being immersed in the great living ocean of divine communication.

Fourthly, we must avoid the impression that God ceases to be absolute and inexhaustible mystery in the beatific vision. Seeing God in the immediacy of face-to-face vision does not mean that the mind now masters what was once too difficult or too obscure. No doubt, many mysteries will be solved in the light of God, but God is not one of them. For God can never be placed in some larger context to be understood in some more manageable frame of reference. The infinite essentially surpasses all contexts, all reference points, the universe itself. So, to see God face to face is finally to see that God is the limitless, all-surpassing and all-giving mystery of true life, implied in, but always immeasurably more than the universe of his creation. But this divine incomprehensibility, to use the technical word, does not remain as a form of eternal frustration for the human mind. The light of glory is the luminous space in which everyone and everything will appear to manifest the divine radiance. To see God is to have the evidence that the divine mystery in neither contained nor fully comprehended by the created universe, in whole or in part. Caught up into such infinity, the human spirit finds its basic delight, in the joy that God, and God alone, is truly...'God'. For to see God means to see God as *really* infinite, immeasurable by any created mind, yet inexhaustibly attractive as the luminous realm of endless expansion. Such a notion of the beatific vision inspires hope to imagine definitive union with God, not only as the peace of a final homecoming, but also as the joy of an ever new beginning in a transformed life of unending, adoring exploration.

A dim analogy here is our intimate knowledge of other persons. The more intimate the knowledge, the more the beloved other is known in his or her incomprehensibility, in the sheer originality of his or her existence. To feel that we have fully summed up, or fully exhausted, the reality of such others is usually a tragic confirmation that we never really knew them or wanted to know them in the first place. That would have meant allowing them to be the uniqueness of who and what they were, thus respecting, and surrendering to, the originality of those we love. Such a perception grounds the theological distinction between the immediate vision of the essence of God and the radical incomprehensibility of the divine mystery which always remains. No doubt, because it did not want to take away with one hand what it was giving with the other, theology was not much inclined to stress that the vision of God was precisely our liberation into the 'excess of God', the space of limitless mystery.

To say anything further presents an enormous problem for theological expression. But the failure to address such a gracious problem as the abiding excess of God has tended to trivialise heaven. Too often, it has been presented as something less than a life of unending adventure into God—as though to see God meant being snap-frozen in endless inactivity. Even Karl Rahner admitted to a sense of defeat in this matter, though he, more than most, had emphasised the enduring incomprehensibility of God. The following long quotation is taken from one of his last talks. The great eighty-year-old theologian is pondering on how to speak of the mystery of the heaven of God:

> *But how? When the angel of death has gutted our spirit of all the useless rubbish we call our history...when all the stars of our ideals with which we have presumed to adorn the heaven of our existence fade and are extinguished; when in faith we have accepted the vast silent*

emptiness of death as the true essence of our being; when our life up to now, however long, simply appears to us as but one brief eruption of our freedom which took place in a moment of time extended as it were under a magnifying glass, an eruption in which question turned into answer, possibility into actuality, time into eternity, freedom offered into freedom attained; when, in a shattering shout of joy, it turns out that the vast silent emptiness which we experience as death is filled with the Mystery of mysteries which we call 'God', filled with his pure light and his all-embracing and bestowing love.

And when out of this fathomless Mystery the face of Jesus, the Blessed One, appears to us and looks at us, and this concrete individual is the divine surpassing *of all our correct surmises about the incomprehensibility of the fathomless Godhead—then, much as I would like to be able to describe more accurately what happens, I can only stammeringly point out how one can in anticipation await 'the One who is to come' by experiencing the descent of death itself as the very ascent of what is coming. Eighty years is a long time. However, for each one, the life span allotted to him is but a brief moment in which what should be becomes.*[34]

It appears that theology can never rest content with its expression of what hope might really hope for.

To conclude: heaven is an irreplaceable symbol in the language of Christian hope. It is irreplaceable since hope is always looking to its fulfilment in terms of its Christ, its God, its body, its loves, its questions. Yet to such a hope, heaven remains a symbol of what is not yet, and of what can never be fully known. Its meaning radiates within the chiaroscuro of our present, where the truly ultimate always surpasses human imagining, to be best known in expectant adoration.

1. C.S. Lewis, *The Weight of Glory*, Macmillan, New York, 1949, p.4. and Collins Publishers.
2. An earlier form of this chapter has appeared in Tony Kelly, *The Range of Faith: Basic Questions For A Living Theology*, St Paul Publications, Homebush, NSW, 1986 (Australian edition); and The Liturgical Press, Collegeville, MN, 1986 (US edition), pp.185–199.
3. For a beautiful treatment of this theme: *See* Peter Kreeft, *Heaven: The Heart's Deepest Longing*, Ignatius Press, San Francisco, 1989, pp.43–59.
4. Originally from an interview with *Excelsior* of Mexico City.
5. *Gaudium et Spes*, par. 39.
6. Dag Hammarskjöld, *Markings*, tr., W.H. Auden and Leif Sjöberg, Faber and Faber, London, 1964, p.169.
7. *See* Colleen McDannell and Bernhard Lang, *Heaven: A History*, Yale University Press, New Haven, 1988. The methodological confusion of this survey makes it a resource of very uneven quality.
8. Writers such as Rahner, Boros, Phan, Hayes, Martelet, and Ratzinger have done much to stress the christological character of heaven.
9. The classical reference is the Constitution, *Benedictus Deus*, issued by Pope Benedict XII in 1336. It states that the blessed:

    *...see the divine essence with an intuitive vision, and even face to face, without the mediation of any creature by way of object of vision; rather, the divine essence immediately manifests itself to them plainly, clearly, openly, and in this vision they enjoy the divine essence. (*Neuner and Dupuis, *The Christian Faith in the Doctrinal Documents of the Catholic Church, n. 2305)*

10. *See* P. Phan, *Eternity in Time...*, pp.138–142.
11. J.Ratzinger, *Eschatology...*, p.234.
12. 'Vita est enim esse cum Christo; ideo ubi Christus, ibi vita, ibi regnum.' (St Ambrose, *In Luc.X*, PL 15: 1834).
13. *See* Tony Kelly, *Trinity of Love...*, pp.103–107; 165–168.

14. St Augustine, *Ennar.in Psal.30*, PL 36,252.
15. For a profound and informed analysis of the history of this topic: *See* S. Tugwell, *Human Immortality...*, pp.125–156.
16. For an attractive presentation of this position: *See* L. Boros, *Pain and Providence*, Burns and Oates, London, 1966, pp.32–44; and for sound scriptural comment, Brendan Byrne, 'Life after Death—Some Scriptural Evidence Reconsidered', *Australian Catholic Record* 49/4 October, 1982, pp.399ff.
17. Theology is still groping for a good theology of the body. Three resources that appear most important to me are: (i) Thomistic hylomorphic theory; (ii) The phenomenological method of Merleau-Ponty; and (iii) The cosmic, processive context of Teilhard de Chardin.
18. Mark Doughty, 'This Impossible Universe', *The Tablet*, 26 September, 1981, p.929.
19. *ibid.*, p.929. For a more philosophical approach: *See* John Jefferson Davis, 'The design argument, cosmic "fine tuning", and the anthropic principle', *Philosophy of Religion* 22 (1987) pp.139–150.
20. Quoted by Donald Nicholl, in 'Symphony of the Universe', *The Tablet*, 16 April, 1988, p.432.
21. P. Kreeft, *Heaven...*, pp.99–117.
22. *De excessu fratris sui*, bk 1. PL16,1354.
23. *See* Karl Rahner, 'The Interpretation of the Dogma of the Assumption', *Theological Investigations I*, tr. C. Ernst, Darton, Longman and Todd, London, 1961, pp.215–227.
24. P. Kreeft, *Heaven...*, pp.100–108.
25. *See* Roland E. Murphy, 'The Song of Songs', *The New Jerome Biblical Commentary*, pp.462–465, for introduction and commentary.
26. Helen Luke, *Commentary on The Divine Comedy*, as quoted in R. Haughton, *The Passionate God*, Darton, Longman and Todd, London, 1981, p.50. Rosemary Haughton's book is, itself, a profound confirmation of the point we are making here.
27. B. Lonergan, *Method in Theology*, p.105.
28. *ibid.*, p.105.
29. Quoted by Yves Congar, *The Wide World My Parish*, Darton, Longman and Todd, London, 1961, pp.60f.

30. Mark S. Smith, '"Seeing God" in the Psalms: The Background to the Beatific Vision in the Hebrew Bible', *The Catholic Biblical Quarterly*, 50/2, April 1988, pp.171–183, presents a carefully nuanced position on the origins of 'beatific vision' doctrine in the tradition of Israel. He carefully qualifies M. Dahood's thesis that numerous passages in the psalter point to ancient Israelite belief in the 'beatific vision' (*See* M. Dahood, *Psalms I. 1–50, Anchor Bible 16*, Doubleday, New York, 1966). I cite Smith's conclusion:

    The beatific vision in the Bible, strictly speaking, is found only in NT passages, such as Matt. 5:8 and I John 1:5,7. Other NT sections, like I Cor. 13:11–12 and II Cor. 3:18, describe the incipience of seeing God in this life, with the fullness and clarity of this experience to be realised in heaven. The NT language of seeing God in the afterlife was modelled on the eschatological language of seeing God in the OT, as found in Second Isaiah. Isa. 40:5 (cf. 35:2 and 52:10) announces that all humanity will see the glory of God when God comes to deliver Israel. Like Ezek. 43:1–5, this description of God projects into the future the present, paradisiacal experience of the divine conveyed by the psalms that speak of seeing God. This language in the psalms belongs to a larger semantic field of the light of the divine face that overlapped with the solar language applied to God in Israelite tradition. (Art. Cit., p.183.)

31. See Neuner and Dupuis, *The Christian Faith in the Doctrinal Documents of the Catholic Church*, pp.684–686; Z. Hayes, *Visions of a Future...*, pp.196–198; and P. Phan, *Eternity in Time...*, pp.142–145.

32. For a treatment of knowledge: *See* B. Lonergan, *Method in Theology*, pp.6–10.

33. *The transcendental notions, that is, our questions for intelligence, for reflection, for deliberation, constitute our capacity for self-transcendence. That capacity becomes an actuality when one falls in love. Then one's being becomes being-in-love...Once it has blossomed forth, and as long as it lasts, it takes over. It is the first principle. From it flow one's desires and fears, one's joys and sorrows, one's discernment of values,*

one's decisions and one's deeds. (B. Lonergan, Method in Theology..., p.105).

34. 'Karl Rahner's Last Words on the Last Things', *America* June 16, 1984, p.452. Reprinted with permission of America Press, Inc. 106 West Street New York, NY 10019
© 1984 All Rights Reserved.

11 Conclusion: Hope in Action

This prolonged reflection on Christian hope can be fittingly concluded only by a return to the concrete: the imperative to live such hope, and to express it in a life of radical hopefulness. It should be stressed that everything that has been expressed in terms of the foundation of hope and its various contexts is really nothing but the objectification of a continuing process of conversion, as many-sided as it is demanding.

All such expressions are provisional because the conversion they objectify is on-going, never fully achieved. As one's standpoint is more and more firmly based in a solidarity with the hope-filled and hopeless of the world, or moves to ever higher ground through a greater love and a greater hope, so too one's outlook is extended, and one's horizon made more luminous. Old themes can suddenly come together in new forms, and traditional questions begin to receive more illuminating answers. Yet the possibilities of conversion are endless, and every account of hope consequently provisional.

While we will always be waiting for a more complete eschatology, there is no reason for such patience in the actual living out of the hope we have. By this I mean that owning of oneself in the concrete drama of a given life-story, with all its particularities of time and place, in the context of a particular community, in the experience of specific sufferings, in the grace of a given vocation. It is as though each of us must express his or her life in a particular 'apocalyptic form'.[1] If our hope is going to be more than a theological theory, we need to embody, in the dramatic pattern each of us of calls 'my life', an expectation of God's absolute future. The form and movement of our life must communicate that something is really happening in the here and now, something decisive for the future of the world. As we step beyond the securities of the present, we give expression to what is hopeful within us by staking all, in some realistic sense, on what is coming to be. It means not being defeated by the apparent dead ends and failures that always tend to enclose one's world in despair. Paul seems to combine a sense of joyous hopeful mysticism with a challenging tough-mindedness when he wrote:

> *We rejoice in our hope of sharing the glory of God. More that, we rejoice in our sufferings, knowing that suffering produces endurance, endurance produces character and character produces hope* (Rom. 5:1–5).

It is not only a question of each of us rehearsing, as it were, the last breath of our own particular death as an ultimate surrender to the transforming Spirit of Christ. Hope must be affirmed as a clear, strong word in the daily conversation of our lives.

For the actual life of hope does not stop in an inspiring theology or even in a concerned ethical stance. If it is not going to wilt, it must enter into the character of our personal existence with a kind of defiant toughness and creativity. Above all, it has to show the endurance that comes from occupying the most hopeless point in our particular worlds, in solidarity with all those who are furthest from hope—those in one's world who are unloved, valueless, who no longer count, who have been left behind as failures, catastrophes in the prevailing success story. Just as I can exclude no one from my future, I can leave no one behind.

The defiance of such living hope is manifested above

all in longing for God's judgment, and in a passionate anger contesting the banal, self-serving, elite scenarios of the 'rulers of this world'—those well served by the way things are. In inspiring a risking of all for the sake of the one thing necessary, hope begins to imagine the world 'otherwise'. Such an imagination, to use Wallace Stevens' expression, 'is the irrepressible revolutionist'.[2] The ecclesial form of such imagination comes to historic expression in Vatican II's Pastoral Constitution, *Gaudium et Spes*:

The joy and the hope, the griefs and the anguish of the people of our time, especially those who are poor or afflicted in any way, are the joy and the hope, the grief and the anguish of the followers of Christ as well. Nothing that is genuinely human fails to find an echo in their hearts. For theirs is a community composed of human beings, who united in Christ and guided by the Holy Spirit, press onward to the Kingdom of the Father, and are bearers of a message of salvation intended for all.[3]

Such a passage signals the entry of a new kind of hopeful imagination into the life of the Church. If, increasingly, we live in a world of images and a society of masks, radical hope, intent, on a face-to-face vision of God, practises its future intimacy with eye-to-eye contact with the suffering others of our present world: 'Behind and beyond the image a face resides: the face of the other who will never let the imagination be.'[4]

Classically, this apocalyptic imagination of hope is expressed through the three vows of religious profession. In such a tradition of Christian life, some Christian communities embark on a life of radical self-offering 'for the sake of the Kingdom of God'.[5] In a way that goes beyond the structures of the routine human fulfilments of career, possessions and family, religious life is a form of exposure to the originality of what is to come. Today, it is not difficult to discern this apocalyptic character of hope in many other styles of life. Given the drastic erosion of personal value in technocratic culture, there are often dreaded fidelities associated with the experience of marriage and parenthood today. To give oneself in unconditional, exclusive love as the affirmation of the unique value of one's spouse, and in a self-commitment to the nurture and support of one's children, have become the activities of an often unacknowledged, but uniquely subversive hope. For the human and Christian values involved demand nothing less than a continuing, intimate self-sacrifice in the present social and cultural context of human relationships.

It is precisely when and where a culture tends to make its peace with hopelessness that Christian hope must exhibit what has been imaginatively called 'an apocalyptic sting'.[6] This is the point at which hope demands a defiant creativity. Here it stands against what is degrading and dehumanising, but also stands with and for any movement of liberation from the systems of thought or the structures of institution which would prevent the occurrence of a more human future. In the name of the God 'who will be what he will be', hope must remain resolutely and critically open to 'what has not yet appeared' in terms of the fullness of our humanity.

Various intensities of this apocalyptic sting are present in the witness of those dedicated to work for 'hopeless cases' who are beyond the power of medical or social rehabilitation. The same quality can be discerned in those who care for the dying; or who, themselves patiently accept a life or a death of terrible suffering; as also with those involved in the risks of peace-making through disarmament, or who commit the social folly of renouncing class, position and privilege in the interests of solidarity with the oppressed and suffering. It is also foreshadowed in the emergence of new life-styles responsive to the current ecological crisis precipitated by the addictive consumerism of our day.

To my mind, these are all evangelical instances of losing one's life in order to save it. The apocalyptic sting common to them consists in experiencing the grief of a world ending—even if the world in question is limited to the particular world of one's own comfort, security, and autonomous disposition of one's life. Comparing our age to the previous century, Christopher Dawson makes an apposite remark:

The eschatological aspect of Christianity...has once more become relevant and significant. For even though we may not believe in the imminent end of the world, it is hardly possible to doubt that a world is ending. We are once more in the presence of cosmic forces that are destroying or transforming human life, and therefore we have a new opportunity to see life in religious terms and not merely in terms of humanism and social welfare and political reform....For that (the preceding) *age, the Four Last Things...had become remote and unreal. But today they are real enough even for the unbeliever, who knows nothing of the Christian hope of eternal life. The Christian way of life has indeed become the only way that is capable of surmounting the tremendous dangers and evils that have become part of the modern experience of modern man. No doubt as the Gospel says, men will go on eating and drinking and buying and selling and planting and building, until the heavens rain fire and brimstone and destroy them all. But they do this with only one part of their minds; there is another part of their minds that remains uneasily conscious of the threat which hangs over them; and in proportion as they realise this, they feel that something should be done and they seek a way of salvation, however vaguely and uncertainly.*[7]

As Christian believers we have no choice but to face what is unfinished in themselves and hopeless in their world. But that is where our hope comes into its own, as an energy and imagination longing for completely transfigured humanity. To the degree that we grow in solidarity with the hopeless, we learn from such suffering and oppression the form of the Kingdom by the shape of its absence. Still, at the same point, we come to appreciate a presence inspiring a revolutionary surrender to the God of our only future.

So we end. All that has gone before has been simply a hopeful attempt to increase our appreciation of the hope to which we are called:

> *...that you may know the hope to which he called you, what are the riches of his glorious inheritance in the saints and what is the immeasurable greatness of his power in us who believe, according to the working of his great might which he accomplished in Christ when he raised him from the dead...*(Eph. 1:18–20).

1. 'Apocalyptic' is a notoriously slippery word in modern biblical and theological thought. In general, it stands for a tendency to imagine the future out of an intense dissatisfaction with the present, in the conviction that the judgment of God will be revealed in a precise historical form, as justifying the suffering elect and as bringing destruction on their persecutors. This, of course, can lead to all kinds of destructive fantasies. But the basic usefulness of this word today, it seems to me, lies in indicating the power of eschatological hope to inspire a new imagining of one's way of being in the world, critical of the prevailing culture. The person of hope thus becomes conscious of his or her life as a unique vocation, the dramatic expression of hopeful solidarity with the suffering and 'hopeless' other. *See* P. Phan, *Eternity in Time...*, pp.72–75.

2. Quoted by Richard Kearney, *The Wake of the Imagination*, Hutchinson, London, 1988, p.359. This whole book

is a most valuable exploration of the meaning of imagination, and, indeed, of its most hopeful forms.
3. *Gaudium et Spes*, par.1.
4. R. Kearney, *The Wake of the Imagination*, p.365.
5. *See Lumen Gentium*, par.44.
6. Johann Baptist Metz, *Faith in History and Society*, tr. D. Smith, Burns and Oates, London, 1980, pp.74; 169–177.
7. Christopher Dawson, *The Historic Reality of Christian Culture*, Harper and Row, New York, 1960, pp.23f. Reprinted with permission of Christina Scott, Literary Executrix for Christopher Dawson.

SELECT BIBLIOGRAPHY

Becker, E. *The Denial of Death*, The Free Press, New York, 1973.

Bernier, P. *Bread Broken and Shared: Broadening Our Vision of Eucharist*, Ave Maria Press: Notre Dame, Ind., 1981.

Berry, T. 'The New Story: Comments on the Origins, Identification and Transmission of Values', *Cross Currents* Summer/Fall, 1987, pp.187–199.

Bloch, E. *The Principle of Hope*, tr. N. Plaice, S. Plaice, P. Knight, MIT Press, Cambridge, Mass., 1986.

Boros, L. *The Moment of Truth: Mysterium Mortis*, tr. G. Bainbridge, Burns and Oates, 1962.

Collopy, B. J. 'Theology and the Darkness of Death', *Theological Studies* 39/1 (1978) pp.22–54.

Congar, Y. *The Wide World My Parish*, Darton, Longman and Todd, London, 1961.

Conn, W. *Christian Conversion: A Developmental Interpretation of Autonomy and Surrender*, Paulist Press, New York, 1986.

Couture, A. 'Réincarnation ou résurrection? Revue d'un débat et amorce d'une recherche', *Science et Esprit* XXXVI/3, 1984, pp.351–374; and XXXVII/3, pp.75–96.

de Chardin, T. *The Divine Milieu*, Harper and Row, New York, 1960.
Science and Christ, tr. René Hague, Collins, London, 1965.

de la Potterie, I. *The Hour of Jesus*, tr. G. Murray, St Paul Publications, Middlegreen, Slough, 1989.

Delooz, P. 'Death and the Herafter', *Pro Mundi Vita: Dossiers*, 4/1985, pp.1–20.

Donovan, V. *The Church in the Midst of Creation*, Orbis, Maryknoll, 1989.

Durrwell, F. X. *L'Eucharistie, sacrement pascal*, Cerf, Paris, 1981.

Fingarette, H. *The Self in Transformation: Psychoanalysis, Philosophy and the Life of the Spirit*, Harper Torchbooks, New York, 1963.

Greshake, G. and Lohfink, G. *Naherwartung-Auferstehung-Unsterblichkeit. Untersuchungen zur christlichen Eschatologie, Quaestiones Disputatae 71*, Herder, Freiburg, 1982.

Gutierrez, G. *The Truth Shall Make You Free: Confrontations*, Orbis, New York 1990.

Haughton, R. *The Passionate God*, Darton, Longman and Todd, London, 1981.

Hayes, Z. *Visions of a Future: A Study of Christian Eschatology*, Michael Glazier, Wilmington, Del. 1989.

Heidegger, M. *Being and Time*, tr. J. Macquarrie and E. Robinson, Harper and Row, New York, 1962.

Johnstone, B. 'Eschatology and Social Ethics: A critical survey of the development of social ethical theory in ecumenical discussion 1925–1968', *Bijdragen* 37 (1976) pp.47–85.

Joós, E. 'What If We Have a Soul?', *Science et Esprit* XXXVI/2 (1984), pp.211–232.

Kasper, W. *Faith and the Future*, Crossroad, New York, 1982.

Kearney, R. *The Wake of the Imagination*, Hutchinson, London, 1988.

Kehl, M. and Löser, W. (eds.) *The von Balthasar Reader*, tr. R. J. Daly and F. Lawrence, T.& T. Clarke, Edinburgh, 1985.

Kelly, A. J. *The Range of Faith: Basic Questions For A Living Theology*, St Paul Publications, Homebush, NSW, 1986 (Australian edition); and The Liturgical Press, Collegeville, MN, 1986 (US edition), 1986. *Trinity of Love: A Theology of the Christian God*, Michael Glazier, Wilmington, Del., 1988.

Kreeft, P. *Heaven: The Heart's Deepest Longing*, Ignatius Press, San Francisco, 1989.

Küng, H. *Does God Exist? An Answer for Today*, Vintage Books, New York, 1981.

Eternal Life?: Life after Death as a Medical, Philosophical and Theological Problem, tr. E. Quinn, Doubleday and Co., New York, 1984.

Lash, N. *A Matter of Hope: A Theologian's Reflections on the Thought of Karl Marx*, Darton, Longman and Todd, London, 1981.

Le Goff, J. *The Birth of Purgatory*, tr. A. Goldhammer, The University of Chicago Press, Chicago, 1984.

Lonergan, B. *Method in Theology*, Darton, Longman and Todd, London, 1971.

Lovett, B. *Life Before Death: Inculturating Hope*, Claretian Publications, Quezon City, 1986.

Maas, W. *Gott und die Hölle. Studien zum Descensus Christi*, Johannes Verlag, Einsiedeln, 1979.

Macquarrie, J. *Christian Hope*, Mowbray, London, 1978.

Maloney, G. *The Everlasting Now*, Ave Maria Press, Notre Dame, Ind., 1980.

Marcel, G. *Homo Viator: Introduction to a Metaphysic of Hope*, tr. E. Crauford, Harper and Row, New York, 1962.

Martelet, G. *L'au-delà retrouvé: Christologie des fins dernières*, Desclée, Paris, 1975.
The Risen Christ and the Eucharistic World, tr. René Hague, Seabury Press, New York, 1976.

McDannell, C. and Lang, B. *Heaven: A History*, Yale University Press, New Haven, 1988.

Metz, J. B. *The Emergent Church: The Future of Christianity in a Postbourgeois World*, tr. p.Mann, Crossroad, New York, 1981.
Faith, History and Society: Toward a Practical Fundamental Theology, tr. D. Smith, Burns and Oates, London, 1980.

Miller, A. and Acri, M. *Death: A Bibliographical Guide*, The Scarecrow Press, Metuchen, NJ, 1978.

Moloney, F. J. *A Body Broken for a Broken People*, Collins Dove, Melbourne, 1990.

Moltmann, J. *God in Creation: An Ecological Doctrine of Creation*, tr. M. Kohl, SCM, London, 1985.
Theology of Hope, tr. J.W. Leitch, SCM, London, 1967.

Moore, S. *The Fire and the Rose are One*, Darton, Longman and Todd, London, 1980.
Jesus the Liberator of Desire, Crossroad, New York, 1989.

Murphy, M. *New Images of the Last Things*, Paulist Press, New York 1988.

Neuner, J. and Dupuis, J. (eds.), *The Christian Faith in the Doctrinal Documents of the Catholic Church*, Collins, London, 1982.

O'Collins, G. *Jesus Risen*, Darton, Longman and Todd, London, 1987.

Ó Murchú, D. *The God Who Becomes Redundant*, Mercier Press, Dublin, 1986.

Pelikan, J. *The Melody of Theology: A Philosophical Dictionary*, Harvard University Press, Cambridge Mass, 1988.

Percy, W. *Lost in the Cosmos: The Last Self-Help Book*, Farrar, Straus and Giroux, New York, 1983.

Perkins, P. *Resurrection: New Testament Witness and Contemporary Reflection*, Doubleday, New York, 1984.

Phan, P. *Eternity in Time: A Study of Karl Rahner's Eschatology*, Susquehanna University Press, Selinsgrove, 1988.

Pieper, J. *Hope and History*, Burns and Oates, London, 1969.

Rahner, K. *Foundations of Christian Faith*, tr. William V. Dych, Crossroad, New York, 1978.

Ratzinger, J. *Eschatology: Death and Eternal Life*, tr. M. Walstein, The Catholic University of America Press, Washington, D.C., 1988.

Ratzinger, J. *Introduction to Christianity*, tr. J. R. Foster, Burns and Oates, London, 1969.

Rossé, G. *The Cry of Jesus on the Cross: A Biblical and Theological Study*, Paulist Press, New York, 1987.

Scanlon, M. 'Anthropology, Christian', in *The New Dictionary of Theology*, Joseph A. Komonchak, *et al.* (eds.) Michael Glazier, Wilmington, Del., 1988, pp.27–41.

Scheffczyk, L. 'Apocatastasis: Fascination and Paradox', *Communio* 12, Winter 1985, pp.385–397.

Schillebeeckx, E. *Christ: The Christian Experience in the Modern World*, tr. J. Bowden, SCM Press, London, 1980.

Sonnemmans, H. 'Soul, Afterlife, Salvation', *Communio* 14, Fall 1987, pp.248–261.

Stanley, D. *Jesus in Gethsemane*, Paulist Publications, New York, 1980.

Steiner, G. *Real Presence*, University of Chicago Press, Chicago, 1989.

Swimme, B. *The Universe is a Green Dragon: A Cosmic Creation Story*. Bear and Co., Santa Fe, 1984.

The New Jerome Biblical Commentary, Geoffrey Chapman, London, 1989.

Toffler, A. *Future Shock*, Bantam Books, New York, 1970.

Tugwell, S. *Human Immortality and the Redemption of Death*, Darton, Longman and Todd, London, 1990.

Van de Walle, A. R. *From Darkness to Dawn: How Belief in the Afterlife Affects Living*, tr. John Bowden, Twenty-Third Publications, Mystic, Conn. 1985.

Voegelin, E. 'Immortality: Experience and Symbol', *Harvard Theological Review* 60/3, July 1967, pp.235–279.

Von Balthasar, H. U. *Mysterium Paschale, Mysterium Salutis. Grundriss heilsgeshichtlicher Dogmatik: Das Christusereignis*, Band III/2, eds., Johannes Feiner and Magnus Löhrer, Benziger Verlag, Einsiedeln, 1969.

Von Balthasar, H. U. *The Glory of the Lord: A Theological Aesthetics. I: Seeing the Form*, tr. E. Leiva-Merikakis, eds. J. Fessio and J. Riches, T. & T. Clark, Edinburgh, 1988.

Wainwright, G. *Eucharist and Eschatology*, Epworth, London, 1971.

Wildiers, N. *The Theologian and His Universe: Theology and Cosmology from the Middle Ages to the Present*, Seabury, New York, 1982.

Wink, W. *Unmasking the Powers: The Invisible Forces That Determine Human Existence*, Fortress Press, Philadelphia, 1986.